Teaching Young Language Learners

Second edition

Published in this series
Oxford Handbooks for Language Teachers

Teaching Young Language Learners

Second edition

Annamaria Pinter

OXFORD
UNIVERSITY PRESS

OXFORD
UNIVERSITY PRESS

Great Clarendon Street, Oxford, OX2 6DP, United Kingdom

Oxford University Press is a department of the University of Oxford.
It furthers the University's objective of excellence in research, scholarship,
and education by publishing worldwide. Oxford is a registered trade
mark of Oxford University Press in the UK and in certain other countries

ISBN: 978 0 19 440318 4

Printed in China

This book is printed on paper from certified and well-managed sources

ACKNOWLEDGEMENTS

*The authors and publisher are grateful to those who have given permission
to reproduce the following extracts and adaptations of copyright material:*
p.58 Extract from: Bebop Level 1 Student's Book © Lorena Peimbert
and Myriam Monterubbio 2014, Published by Macmillan Publishers
Limited. Used by Permission. All Rights Reserved. p.60 Extracts from
Family and Friends Starter Class Book by Naomi Simmons © Oxford
University Press, 2014. Reproduced by permission. pp.61–62 Oxford
Classic Tales: *The Magpie and the Milk* retold by Rachel Bladon © Oxford
University Press, 2015. Reproduced by permission. p.64 Extracts from
Stories and Storyline (Teaching English to Young Learners) Kindle Edition by
Sharon Ahlquist and Réka Lugossy © Sharon Ahlquist and Réka Lugossy,
2015. Reproduced by permission of Candlin & Mynard ePublishing.
p.66 Extracts from *Incredible English Class Book 5 (2nd edition)* by Sarah
Philips, Peter Redpath and Kirstie Grainger © Oxford University Press,
2012. Reproduced by permission. p.67 Extracts from *New Treetops Class
Book 2a* by Sarah Howell and Lisa Kester-Dodgson © Oxford University
Press, 2012. Reproduced by permission. p.82 Extracts from *Oxford
Phonics World 5 Letter Combinations* by Kaj Schwermer, Julia Chang
and Craig Wright © Oxford University Press, 2013. Reproduced by
permission. p.83 Story by Babita Sharma Chapagain, reproduced
by permission of Babita Sharma Chapagain. p.85 Oxford Read and
Imagine, Level 2 *The Big Storm* by Paul Shipton © Oxford University
Press, 2014. Reproduced by permission of Oxford University Press. p.89
Extracts from *New Treetops Class Book 3a* by Sarah Howell and Lisa Kester-
Dodgson © Oxford University Press, 2012. Reproduced by permission.
p.93 Extracts from *Oxford Discover Student's Book 3* by Kathleen Kampa
and Charles Vilina © Oxford University Press, 2014. Reproduced by
permission. p.104 Extracts from *Oxford Discover Student Book 5* by Kenna
Bourke © Oxford University Press, 2014. Reproduced by permission.
p.105 Extract from Oxford Classic Tales: *The Heron and the Hummingbird*
retold by Rachel Bladon © Oxford University Press, 2013. Reproduced
by permission. pp.106–7 Extracts from *Young Learners (Resource Books
for Teachers)* by Sarah Philips. (Series Editor: Alan Maley) © Oxford
University Press, 1993. Reproduced by permission. p.117 Extract from
Cross-Curricular Resources for Young Learners by Immacolata Calabrese
and Silvana Rampone © Oxford University Press, 2015. Reproduced
by permission. p.121 Extract from *Teaching Young Learners to Think: ELT
Activities for Young Learners Aged 6–12* by Herbert Puchta and Marion
Williams, Copyright © Helbling Languages. Reproduced by permission
of Helbling Languages. p.124 Fotobabble data by Jihu. Reproduced by
permission of Heeyang Park. p.128 Extract from *Oxford Discover Student
Book 1* by Susan Rivers and Lesley Koustaff © Oxford University Press,
2013. Reproduced by permission. p.130 Data extract from study by
Jennifer Joshua, reproduced by permission of Jennifer Joshua. p.131
Learners' opinions by Madhuri Modugala, reproduced by permission
of Madhuri Modugala. p.133 Adapted version of 'The Grasshopper
and the Ants' from *The Best Of Aesop's Fables* by Margaret Clark, Text
© 1990 Margaret Clark. Illustrated by Charlotte Voake. Reproduced
by permission of Walker Books Ltd, London SE11 5HJ. p.143 Extracts
from *Cambridge Young Learners English Tests – Flyers* by Petrina Cliff,
Oxford University Press, 2010. Reproduced by permission. p.157
Translated diary entry by Mrs Zhao, from *Young Children as Intercultural
Mediators: Mandarin-Speaking Chinese Families in Britain (Languages for
Intercultural Communication and Education)* by Zhiyan Guo © 2014, Guo
Zhiyan. Reproduced by permission of Multilingual Matters. p.161
Extracts from *Teen2teen Plus Student Book 3* by Joan Saslow & Allen Ascher
© Oxford University Press, 2015. Reproduced by permission. p.165
Extracts by Ying (a pseudonym). Reproduced by permission of Déirdre
Kirwan. p.167 PARSNIP Acronym by David Valente. Reproduced by
permission of David Valente. p.174 Extracts by Samaneh Zandian.
Reproduced by permission of Samaneh Zandian. p.178 Questionnaire
by Dinadi Nadhewna Wickramanayake. Reproduced by permission
of Iresha Udayangani Attanayake. p.190 Poem 'Cats Sleep Anywhere'
by Eleanor Farjeon taken from Blackbird Has Spoken (Macmillan's
Children's Book, 2000), copyright © Eleanor Farjeon 2000. Reproduced
by permission of David Higham Associates. p.191 Poem 'Mice' by
Rose Fyleman, taken from I like This Poem (Penguin, 1979), copyright
© Reproduced by permission of The Society of Authors as the Literary
Representative of the Estate of Rose Fyleman. p.195 Extracts from MA
dissertation by by Maria Vasilopoulou. Reproduced by permission of
Maria Vasilopoulou.

Sources: p.65 *Our World 5: Student's Book* by Ronald Scro. Series Editors:
Dr. JoAnn Crandall and Dr. Joan Kang Shin (Heinle-Cengage, 2014). p.91
Our World 6:Student's Book by Kate Cory-Wright. Series Editors: Dr. JoAnn
Crandall and Dr. Joan Kang Shin (Heinle-Cengage, 2014)

Illustrations by: Oxford Designers and Illustrators pp.13, 17, 105, 106, 123

Although every effort has been made to trace and contact copyright
holders before publication, this has not been possible in some cases.
We apologize for any apparent infringement of copyright and if
notified, the publisher will be pleased to rectify any errors or omissions
at the earliest opportunity.

CONTENTS

ACKNOWLEDGEMENTS

I would like to express my gratitude to the colleagues, friends, students, and children I have worked with over the last ten years. You have inspired me to continue to develop my ideas about teaching languages to children. I would also like to thank the EFL teachers and trainers from all over the world who have used and enjoyed the first edition of this book. Your feedback has been invaluable and I have tried to incorporate much of it into this second edition. Finally, my thanks also go to Sophie Rogers and Julia Bell at Oxford University Press for their unfailing help and support during the process of writing this new edition.

PREFACE TO THE SECOND EDITION

In this second edition of the original 2006 publication of *Teaching Languages to Young Learners*, I am building on the invaluable feedback I have received over the years from teachers, teacher trainers, MA and DELTA students, and other colleagues and friends who have used the first edition. What this new edition offers is updates on teaching practice and on research, as well as a fresh angle on new, emerging priorities in teaching young language learners.

What has changed in the world of teaching languages to young learners?

Young language learners worldwide

Today more and more children around the world are learning English either as a foreign language or as a second language. The contexts in which children are learning English are perhaps even more varied than before. In some parts of the world, children are learning English in well equipped classrooms, in small groups, with innovative materials, and with the help of two teachers collaborating or team-teaching. In other parts of the world, children are learning English in large, under-resourced classrooms without up-to-date resources and with teachers who may not have appropriate qualifications. While different languages may have been available in many contexts ten years ago, now it is almost exclusively English which is offered in the primary sector, and in many parts of the world the gap between those who can afford so-called 'elite' English programmes—such as bilingual or content-based programmes, Content and Language Integrated Learning (CLIL) programmes, or private classes—and those who cannot has further widened. Teachers working in primary classes also increasingly face the challenges of working with students from a variety of cultural backgrounds, with mixed-ability classes, and with learners with special educational needs.

Diversity and technological advances

Growing diversity in the primary school sector is evident. Global travel and migration have been on the increase, and many primary classrooms where children are learning English are becoming much more heterogeneous and multicultural. For example, in UK primary schools more than 200 languages are spoken as a first language. Diversity and intercultural understanding, therefore, have become ever more important concepts for primary-level English teachers.

Technological innovations are also advancing fast, although there is a great deal of difference between regions and countries with regard to what technology is available in schools. A recent British Council survey by Garton, Copland and Burns (2011), for example, suggests that computers and the internet remain a luxury in many schools across the world.

In contexts where new technologies are available, however, even one occasionally-used computer in the classroom can open up new, authentic opportunities for children to engage with others and learn English in an exciting and motivating way. Where computers, phones, and tablets are readily available both at school and at home, there are multiple new possibilities for teachers to consider when it comes to innovating their practice. The internet itself is offering ever more sophisticated opportunities for learning, and young children in many contexts become socialized into using information and communications technology (ICT) tools at an early age. Teachers face great challenges in terms of how best to keep up with these technological advancements, how to make use of them, and how to keep their learners safe on the internet, but at the same time these developments present great foundations to build on.

New curricula and new educational goals

In our fast-changing, globally connected world, more and more governments realize that their traditional educational goals, systems of delivery, and assessment practices are becoming inadequate. In many countries, educational authorities recommend competency-based curricula. For example, according to the Council of Europe, all citizens must develop the so-called 'key competences' for lifelong learning. These competences include: communication in the mother tongue, communication in foreign languages, mathematical competence, and basic competences in science and technology. Further important competences are digital competence, learning to learn, social and civic competences, a sense of initiative and entrepreneurship, and, finally, cultural awareness and expression. Even though this is a lifelong learning process, the foundations are to be built in elementary and primary schools.

In particular, due to the fast rate of change, there is a realization that—even at basic levels of education—there is a need to focus more on learning to learn and on equipping children to become more autonomous, more flexible, and more proactive as learners. Educational leaders, policymakers, and business leaders originally came up with this in the USA, but variations of this framework are now in use in Europe as well as elsewhere in the world. The framework describes the skills learners need to succeed in life and work effectively in the 21st century. The relevance of this cannot be ignored for even the youngest of school learners. The most often quoted components of the framework relevant to primary learners are the so-called '4Cs', sometimes referred to collectively as 21st century skills (P21, 2009). The 4Cs stand for Critical thinking, Communication, Collaboration, and Creativity. These are thinking and learning skills essential at every level of education. In addition to the 4Cs, literacy skills are also mentioned—in particular

ICT literacy—and also cultural competence, social responsibility, and life skills. Pedagogical approaches need to embrace question-based, inquiry-based teaching where learners have a chance to work collaboratively, using multiple sources flexibly and effectively. In these learning environments, the teacher's role is changing from that of a knowledge transmitter to that of a facilitator or guide.

With regard to assessment practices, there is more and more pressure on even the youngest learners because of the widespread implementation of standardized tests for accountability reasons in all core school subjects.

In view of all these emerging priorities that impact on both the teaching of languages to children and their learning, and considering the recent research in the area, many changes have been made to the content of the book (see updated summaries of chapters on pages 2–4).

INTRODUCTION

Who is the book for and what kind of book is it?

This book is for teachers with some experience and an interest in teaching English to children. It is for those teachers especially who wish to reflect on and explore their teaching in view of the discussion of the links between practice, research, and theory. It is also intended for teacher trainers working with teachers on professional development courses. This book is not a resource manual that offers a list of ideas ready to be implemented in the classroom. Rather, it is a book that attempts to discuss and bring together research relevant to the area of child language learning and principles in classroom practice. Although it is my personal account, my hope is that individual teachers will engage with some ideas and questions discussed in this book and will develop them further in their own practice.

Focus on teachers

In this book, it is argued that teachers play a key role in the success of any Teaching English to Young Learners (TEYL) programme. Their willingness and readiness to monitor the opportunities and limitations of their own contexts is the basis of success. It is also argued that teachers need time for reflection and experimentation so as to explore issues and questions in collaboration with children and colleagues. Teachers may also want to foster positive and active relationships with parents/carers, who are the most important source of information about the children in their classes. It is to be hoped that this book will provide the inspiration for such explorations by offering a starting point with discussion of both the theory underlying practice and the principles that apply in the classroom.

What age groups are covered in the term 'young learners'?

Primary education is very different in various parts of the world. In some countries, children attend primary school from five to 11 years of age, while in other contexts children start school later, at the age of six or seven. State primary school can carry on until children are 14 years of age, although primary school in these cases is often divided into lower and upper primary sections. Children may start learning English at different stages of their primary education, or even before they are at school. In some contexts, children start learning English in preschool or kindergarten at the age of five, or even earlier. In other contexts, they may start at eight or ten. In order to embrace most situations where English is taught to children, the ideas in this book can be applied to all these age groups, from five to 14 years of age. When discussing teaching principles and ideas for children, rigid age brackets such as four- to six-year-olds, seven- to nine-year-olds, 10- to 11-year-olds, or 12- to 14-year-olds would not work.

Characteristics of younger and older learners

Teachers and parents/carers know that every child is unique, and even in the same context there are often significant differences between children within the same age range. This is because children learn at their own speed; they change quickly and develop new skills and abilities in spurts. There are also substantial differences between, for example, eight-year-old children in different cultures and educational contexts. However, it would be equally problematic to leave 'young learners' entirely open as an umbrella term, as it covers such a range of ages. In order to compromise and be more helpful to teachers, this book will tackle age groups on a continuum of younger to older learners, and it will offer in most chapters some principles and ideas for both ends of the continuum. Table i.1 attempts to summarize features of the two ends of the continuum. This is a very basic starting point which will be elaborated on in later chapters.

These general descriptors for the two ends of the continuum can only serve as initial guidance for teachers. It is ultimately the teacher's responsibility to place their own learners on the appropriate part of this continuum, based on their knowledge of their learners and their context. Teachers are in the best position to exercise their judgement about the suitability of the specific ideas suggested in this book.

Variety of contexts

Teaching English to children has become a worldwide phenomenon due to the international expansion of English teaching combined with the general commitment of governments worldwide to reduce the starting age of learning English and include it in the curriculum in the primary school.

In some chapters an attempt has been made to include examples from different parts of the world, describing, for example, the variety of contexts where children may be learning English in different countries: at home or at school, in an English or a non-English environment. Many of the practical suggestions can be adapted to all kinds of contexts in either private or state schools in second and foreign language contexts. However, the main emphasis in the book remains on learning **English as a foreign language (EFL)**.

What do the chapters offer?

The first four chapters provide background. Chapter 1 covers issues of general development and learning as a background to language learning, while Chapter 2

YOUNGER LEARNERS TO OLDER LEARNERS	
Learners are at preschool or in the first couple of years of schooling.	These learners are well established at school and are comfortable with school routines.
They have a holistic approach to learning language which means that they understand messages but cannot yet analyze language.	They show a growing interest in analytical approaches, which means that they may take an interest in language as an abstract system.
They have lower levels of awareness about themselves as language learners as well as about the process of learning.	They show a growing level of awareness about themselves as language learners and the process of learning.
They have no, or limited, ability to read and write, even in their first language.	They may have well developed skills as readers and writers in their first language and will be interested to learn to read and write in their second language.
Generally they are more concerned about themselves than others; they have limited knowledge about the world.	They have a growing awareness about others and the world around them.
They enjoy fantasy, imagination, and movement.	They begin to show interest in real-life issues.
They may be familiar with smartphones and tablets, and may have used the internet.	They are likely to have access to computers and the internet, they may own a smartphone, and they may be regular users of social media and/or regular online game players.

Table i.1 Some differences between the characteristics of younger and older learners

addresses first language learning so that teachers can familiarize themselves with where children are in their first language development. Building on this background, Chapter 3 moves on to issues of second language learning, covering a range of contexts where English is taught, including contexts where English is used outside the classroom and where it is not. This review aims to highlight the variations and circumstances that make a difference in learning and thus encourage teachers to begin to analyze carefully their own contexts. Chapter 4 discusses issues of policy and summarizes the factors that contribute to the overall success of TEYL programmes. The hope is that, armed with this information, teachers can make the most of their circumstances but can also, in some cases, influence policy decisions in their own contexts.

Following these background chapters, the second half of the book is devoted to the discussion of teaching the four language skills and the language system. Chapter 5 covers the teaching of listening and speaking, the two most important skills in TEYL programmes. Chapter 6 addresses issues of teaching reading and writing, highlighting the circumstances where it can be argued that the introduction of these two skills is beneficial. Chapter 7 discusses the teaching of the language system, both vocabulary and grammar. Chapter 8 turns to issues of **learning to learn**, underlining the importance of involving children in decisions concerning the learning process, and linking with the discussion in previous parts of the book. Chapter 9 is about materials evaluation and offers some basic principles of lesson planning and materials design. Chapter 10 deals with assessment, offering a variety of tools and useful principles for any context. Chapter 11 focuses on issues of diversity and developing intercultural competence—a growing concern of language teachers worldwide. Finally, Chapter 12 concludes the book with issues of researching TEYL classrooms; it covers issues related to research relevant to child subjects, but it also offers some ideas to teachers who wish to initiate small-scale explorations into their own practice. The opportunities of working with children as co-researchers in these classrooms are also discussed.

In addition, each chapter offers a list of Suggestions for further reading to follow up. Most chapters also contain examples of activities from a variety of internationally published children's coursebooks, resource books, and actual materials from teachers and children I have worked with. At the end of the book there are suggested Tasks for teachers to explore their own classrooms. Some of these tasks include classroom materials, activities, and some classroom data. Many of these tasks can be easily adapted to suit the needs of groups in either pre-service or in-service training. At the end of each chapter the reader will be recommended to look up particular tasks which relate to the content of that chapter.

The book also offers a Glossary, which lists alphabetically all the terms and concepts that are highlighted in bold the first time they are used in the text, and, finally, concludes with a full list of References.

1 LEARNING AND DEVELOPMENT

Introduction

This first chapter is devoted to questions about how children develop and learn at home and at school. There are many different learning theories that teachers may find useful to study. For example, it would be possible to take a historical view and go back to the influential forefathers from many centuries ago—such as John Locke in the 17th century or Jean-Jacques Rousseau in the 18th century—who initiated an interest in children and suggested child-focused approaches to learning and teaching. Here, due to space constraints, I will first of all focus on Piaget and Vygotsky, two scholars representing the two best known 20th-century theories of learning. Other ideas will only be touched upon very briefly, but teachers should be encouraged to engage with learning theories more broadly and to explore the personal and practical significance of these theories in their classrooms.

This chapter will discuss how children learn new concepts and develop new ideas about the world, how adults (parents/carers, and teachers) can help them to make the process of learning as successful as possible, and how they learn to interact with their peers. The aim is to make meaningful links between what we know about children's development and learning in general, and language learning in particular. It is important for language teachers to explore these links and to think about children's learning and their cognitive, social, and emotional development in a **holistic** way. Many of the principles discussed in this chapter will be referred to and built on in subsequent chapters.

Active learning: 'constructivism'

Learning is an active process. All parents/carers and teachers who have observed children in learning situations can testify just how actively they are involved when they are interested. For example, they can be completely absorbed in the story that they are listening to or in the pretend game that they are playing. When they are motivated, children are happy to try new things and to experiment with ideas and thoughts in conversations with adults and teachers. Children learn through their explorations and play, and through opportunities to talk things through with others, usually adults. Exploring can refer to things in concrete terms (for example, playing with sand and water or building with toy bricks) or in abstract terms in conversations with others. Often the two happen simultaneously; for example, children and adults can play together with sand and water and talk about what they are doing.

Jean Piaget, who began to develop his ideas in the first half of the 20th century, was one of the most famous child psychologists of all time. He referred to active learning as **constructivism**. He suggested that children construct knowledge for themselves by actively making sense of their environment. For example, a young child might know that baby birds such as chicks and ducklings are hatched from eggs. When this child comes across other animals during a visit to a farm, they assume that the pigs are hatched from eggs, too. According to Piaget, this is the process of **assimilation**. The child assimilates information to fit their own interpretation of the world and existing ways of thinking (i.e. all animals are hatched from eggs). At a later stage, perhaps, in a conversation about animals, a parent might explain that piglets are not hatched from eggs. At this point the child will have to adapt or change their way of thinking to accommodate this new idea. Piaget refers to this process as **accommodation**. Without this adaptation— something that children have to do for themselves—learning would not take place. Assimilation and accommodation thus describe two sides of the same process, i.e. learning. Such interaction between the environment and children's existing knowledge is ongoing, and throughout the years further and further refinements are added to the growing knowledge base. In this way, children are active constructors of their knowledge of the world.

Piaget's stages of development

Teachers and parents/carers can often judge very well what students can or cannot yet do or understand. Even though children are all unique learners, they also share some characteristics in common with their peers. When parents/carers who have children of a similar age talk together they often realize that their children act similarly in a range of situations. For example, parents/carers of five-year-olds find that their children use much the same arguments in conversations or enjoy very similar games, activities, and jokes.

Such similarities within age bands were observed by Piaget, too, and he developed his famous framework which suggests that there are four universal stages of development that all children go through. Piaget and his colleagues constructed tasks and conducted experiments based on this theory and produced a detailed description of the four stages. In 1923, Piaget published *The Language and Thought of the Child,* in which he argued that development was a process of acquiring the principles of formal logic. He referred to basic logical abilities as **operations**, hence the naming of the stages. Each child follows these stages in exactly the same order, and development unfolds as a result of the biological processes of growth and the development of the child's brain.

Table 1.1 summarizes the main characteristics of children's development within each 'Piagetian' stage.

Sensori-motor stage (from birth to two years of age)	The young child learns to interact with the environment by manipulating objects around him.
Pre-operational stage (from two to seven years of age)	The child's thinking is largely reliant on perception but he or she gradually becomes more and more capable of logical thinking. On the whole this stage is characterized by egocentrism (a kind of self-centredness) and a lack of logical thinking.
Concrete operational stage (from seven to 11 years of age)	Year seven is the 'turning point' in cognitive development because children's thinking begins to resemble 'logical' adult-like thinking. They develop the ability to apply logical reasoning in several areas of knowledge at the same time (such as maths, science, or map reading) but this ability is restricted to the immediate context. This means that children at this stage cannot yet generalize their understanding.
Formal operational stage (from 11 years onwards)	Children are able to think beyond the immediate context in more abstract terms. They are able to carry out logical operations such as deductive reasoning in a systematic way. They achieve 'formal logic'.

Table 1.1 Piagetian stages of development

It is useful for teachers to be familiar with the Piagetian framework because teaching English to children can mean working with very different age groups with varying interests and needs. Teaching a class of 12-year-olds requires very different materials, methods, and teaching styles from those for a class of six-year-olds. As it seems that the starting age for language learning is being lowered in most contexts (see Chapter 4 on policy), the majority of teachers will probably have to be able to respond to the needs and interests of various age groups, including those in the Piagetian pre-operational stage.

Piaget's 'thinking' revolution: from pre-operational to operational stage

It is worth exploring Piaget's 'thinking' revolution in a bit more detail. Piaget's assessment of children under seven years of age was that they were lacking logical thinking. Instead, young children are characterized by **egocentrism**, which means that they typically look at the world around them from their own point of view and they find it difficult, if not impossible, to appreciate someone else's point of view. One of Piaget's famous experiments was the so-called 'three mountain experiment' (see Figure 1.1). In this exercise, Piaget and his colleagues asked young children to walk around a three-dimensional display of three mountains where each mountain was distinguished by a different colour and a distinctive summit. Once the children had had a chance to look at the mountains, the experimenters placed a doll at the opposite side of the display facing the children from the other end. At this point they asked the children to choose a photo which showed the doll's perspective. Typically, children under the age of seven in this experiment were unable to choose the correct photo. Instead, they chose the photo which was identical to their own perspective. This was considered as proof of these children's egocentrism.

Figure 1.1 The three mountain experiment

Many tasks similar to the one above were given to children of seven years of age and younger. Some of these tasks tested **conservation**, i.e. the understanding that moving two sticks of the same length away from each other does not change their length, or that pouring water from one container into another does not add or take away anything from the original amount of water. Other tasks tested **class inclusion**, i.e. the relationship of subcategories and main categories and principles of hierarchy; for example, how the concepts of animals, types of animals like dogs, and types of dogs like terriers relate to each other. Typically, the great majority of children under the age of seven gave incorrect answers to all the questions. Piaget concluded that their development had not reached the stage where they could have applied the rules of logic.

Criticism of Piaget's stages

The pre-operational stage

Both parents/carers and teachers worldwide may feel that Piaget's assessment of children under the age of seven was a bit harsh. One of Piaget's main critics is Margaret Donaldson, the Scottish child psychologist. She suggests that Piaget underestimated young children. First of all, the language used by Piaget and his colleagues in the tasks was confusing for them. In particular, the questions Piaget and his colleagues asked were unnatural and ambiguous. For example, 'Are there more yellow flowers or flowers in this picture?' was a typical question that was put to the children in one of the class inclusion tasks. Donaldson argued that questions like this were uncommon in everyday language use and that the children could not make sense of them. Another source of criticism was the context of the Piagetian experiments. Many children failed because they misunderstood the context. For example, in the conservation tasks when the adult experimenter rearranged the sticks, the children expected a change as a result of the adult's manipulation of the objects. Many children thought that something must have changed, otherwise it would not make sense to ask the same question again. Donaldson decided to redesign some of the original experiments in a more child-friendly format. In *Children's Minds* (1978), Donaldson reported that once these tasks were presented in a familiar context, the majority of the results for children under the age of seven improved. In fact, it has repeatedly been demonstrated that when young children are presented with familiar tasks, in familiar circumstances, introduced by familiar adults using language that makes sense to them, they show signs of logical thinking much earlier than Piaget claimed. These findings and criticisms have important implications for teachers, in particular with regard to issues of testing and assessment in young learners' classrooms. Unfamiliar tasks, unfamiliar contexts, and unfamiliar adults can cause children anxiety, and as a result they may perform well below their true ability or not respond at all to the questions or tasks.

The operational stages

Even though the most important criticisms concerned Piaget's pre-operational stage, the description of operational stages turned out to be problematic, too. Children between the ages of seven and 11 all develop formal thinking to some extent, but this is usually due to their schooling, which promotes such thinking. However, their contexts and cultural practices vary hugely and this leads to a great deal of variety across this age group worldwide. With regard to the final stage, Piaget's descriptions were simply overconfident. The ultimate intellectual challenge of being able to think according to the rules of formal logic is actually not fully and automatically achieved by all teenagers, or even adults. Indeed, people do not need to think in a logical fashion in most everyday contexts. Analytical development leading to formal logic is also the result of formal schooling rather than natural maturation, and different educational systems contribute to maintaining differences between children or teenagers of the same age in different parts of the world. In addition, it is also reasonable to propose that development does not actually stop at the age of 11 or 12 but continues well beyond this age—after Piaget's last stage.

While it is true that Piaget's original ideas have been challenged, most developmental psychologists would still support the existence of some stage-like development in children, even though the stages are believed to be less rigid and perhaps less deterministic than he originally suggested. What is important for teachers to learn from Piaget's theory? It is important for teachers to be sensitive and open to the needs and interests of various age groups and to continually monitor their changing needs. Careful monitoring and regular feedback from children will help teachers to select suitable materials that are developmentally appropriate for the given age group in a given context. As stated in the Introduction of this book, particular attention will be paid to differentiating between the needs of younger and older children. In the following chapters, where appropriate, principles underlying the use of tasks, activities, and other materials with both younger and older learners will be offered.

The role of interaction: 'social constructivism'

Vygotsky's theory of learning

With the stage theory, Piaget emphasized the biological basis of development and the universal progression from stage to stage in every child. However, there is an important social side to children's development, too. The social environment, the cultural context, and, in particular, the influence of peers, teachers, and parents/carers engaged in interactions with children are also major sources of learning and development.

Social constructivism is associated with the ideas of the Russian psychologist Lev Vygotsky. Vygotsky was a contemporary of Piaget and shared some of his basic beliefs about child development. He agreed with Piaget that children construct knowledge for themselves and that they actively participate in the learning process. However, he pointed out that the social environment also has an important role to play. In his book, *Mind in Society: The Development of Higher Psychological Processes* (translated into English in 1978), he explored the role of culture and social context. He turned teachers' and parents'/carers' attention to the powerful effect of the social context: hence 'social' is added to constructivism. Quite apart from which Piagetian stage a child belonged to, Vygotsky was interested in the learning potential of the individual, recognizing the fact that all children are unique learners. He was interested to explore what individual children were capable of achieving with the help and support of a more knowledgeable partner. Accordingly, the most famous Vygotskian concept was born: the **Zone of Proximal Development (ZPD)**. This concept describes the difference, or zone, between the current knowledge of the child and the potential knowledge achievable with some help from a more expert peer or adult. Vygotsky argues that working within the ZPD is a fertile ground for learning because it starts with what children already know and carefully builds on it according to their immediate needs for progression. Figure 1.2 gives a visual representation of the ZPD.

For example, think of a four-year-old boy who is sitting down to share a storybook with a parent when he notices that the cover page of the storybook is full of colourful stars. He is eager to start counting the stars and he is able to count up to about 15 or 16, but beyond that he gets confused with the counting. He will say things like 'twenty ten' instead of 'thirty', leave out some numbers altogether, or just stop, not knowing how to carry on. Left to his own devices, he will probably abandon the task of counting. However, a parent or teacher, or even an older brother or sister, can help him to continue. They can prompt him by inserting the next correct number or by giving a visual clue (for example, showing the number on their fingers) or by pronouncing the first sound of the word (*twenty-f-f-f*) that follows.

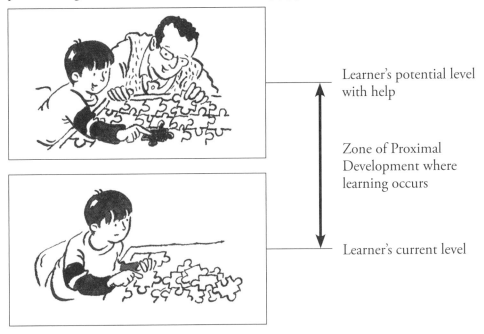

Learner's potential level with help

Zone of Proximal Development where learning occurs

Learner's current level

Figure 1.2 The Zone of Proximal Development

Helping children to learn by offering systematic support

Given this kind of help, the child may be able to count up to 50 or even 100. When such help is provided in a systematic manner, it is often referred to as **scaffolding**. Building on both Piaget's and Vygotsky's theories and work, Jerome Bruner, an American psychologist, and his colleagues introduced this term in 1976 (see Wood, Bruner & Ross, 1976). Scaffolding is essentially an instructional strategy which ensures that the child can gain confidence and take control of the task (for example, counting the stars), or parts of it, as soon as they are willing and able to. At the same time, they are offered immediate, meaningful support whenever stuck. During the interaction that takes place in the ZPD, the adult encourages the child with praise, points out possible difficulties, and makes sure distractions are avoided. The adult also ensures that the learner stays on track and is motivated to finish the task. The support is carefully adjusted to the needs of the individual child.

The importance of language for learning

The language used in interactions with parents/carers and teachers is important because it is the vehicle through which understanding and learning take place. It is language that allows us to make messages accessible to our listeners. It is language that allows us to ask questions and clarify what is not clear, and it is language that allows us to express our ideas with great precision. According to Vygotsky, all learning happens in social interactions with others. Learning occurs in conversations, as a result of understanding and interpreting for ourselves what others are saying. At the beginning, when children are very young, parents/carers support them by explaining new ideas carefully and by repeating information in different contexts until they are satisfied that the messages have got through. In other words, early on, adults take responsibility for, or **regulate**, children's learning. One of the most important tools parents/carers use to regulate their children's learning is language: in particular, dialogues. Using language, they remind children what they already know, explain how to go about solving problems, and in general support their learning. Later on, children learn to signal when something is not clear or ask questions to clarify a point. As children mature, they learn to regulate more and more aspects of their learning. Chapter 2 will discuss the crucial role of carers' language to children in more detail, Chapter 8 will explore children's development in taking more responsibility for their learning, and Chapter 12 will suggest that some children can even act as research partners alongside their teachers, taking responsibility for important decisions in classroom investigations.

The significance of language has important implications for teacher talk in all classrooms, including, of course, the foreign or second language classroom. For example, **English for Young Learners** (**EYL**) teachers need to be aware that their language use is often the main source of language input. Children learn new language forms in meaningful contexts, so listening to the teacher is essential both for modelling pronunciation and for providing opportunities for understanding new input from context. Children also need opportunities to join in and interact with the teacher and with each other. Teachers will need to think about how they can best scaffold children's early language production in their English classes, what questioning techniques they will use to elicit language from their learners, and how they can encourage children to use language meaningfully with each other.

Social learning

In addition to Piaget and Vygotsky, two other influential theorists are worth introducing here because of the relevance of their work to educators working with children. Both these theorists advocate social learning principles. While Albert Bandura focuses on individuals, Urie Bronfenbrenner focused on global influences in the social world. It is important for teachers to think about these influences because we live in a fast-changing environment and we need to be acutely aware of the implications of change in our contexts.

Bandura, a Canadian psychologist, emphasizes the role of imitation and identification. Children imitate the behaviours of others and they copy adult patterns of behaviour they see around them. In new situations, they may behave in a way in which the adult that they have identified with would. This means that children behaving in an aggressive manner, for example, may have identified with someone who is actually aggressive in their immediate environment. Children observe adults intensely and this observation extends to both verbal and physical behaviours, and they imitate and identify with fictional characters as well. For teachers these ideas are important in that they may notice both positive and negative patterns of imitation and identification in their learners. Teachers can have a unique chance to influence these processes by putting themselves forward as role models or by simply bringing favourable behaviours to children's attention. Bandura also greatly emphasizes the importance of **self-efficacy**, the child's belief in their abilities to do well and succeed in certain situations. Children with poor self-efficacy may want to avoid tasks altogether, and they will convince themselves that they are not good at language learning. Again, teachers have an important role to persuade their students that they are all equally able to learn a new language and they are all equally appreciated for their different strengths as language learners.

Bronfenbrenner's ideas are also related to social learning. He places a significant emphasis on the influence of the wider environment. He describes the layers of these social emphases as Russian dolls, where smaller dolls are placed inside larger ones, as depicted in Figure 1.3. First of all, there is the immediate environment of the family, school, peer group, and local communities. This is called the *micro-system*. Then the next is a larger layer called the *meso-system*, which comprises the connections between the immediate environment, such as the school, and the home. The next layer is the *exo-system,* which comprises settings that indirectly affect the child, such as the parent's workplace. Outside this layer is the *macro-system,* which is the larger cultural system, such as national economy or political culture, and finally there is the *chrono-system*, which represents the pattern of environmental events and transitions across one's lifetime.

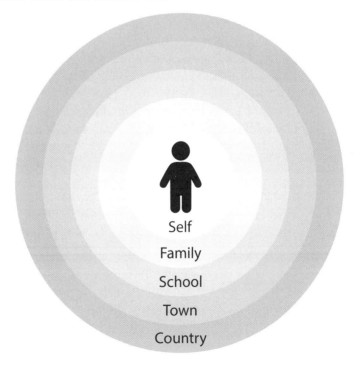

Figure 1.3 Social learning contexts from micro- to chrono-systems

Socio-economic status (**SES**), which can be understood as a feature of one's micro-system, is an important variable when it comes to children's success at school in general. Socio-economic background and, in particular, parents'/carers' knowledge of and attitude to foreign language learning, was shown to play an important role in children's eventual achievement and attitudes, according to the *Early Language Learning in Europe (ELLiE)* study which was carried out in seven countries in Europe (Enever, 2011). Typically, children who come from middle-class families, where they receive a lot of encouragement and support at home, and where parents/carers themselves might be fluent speakers of English, achieve better results with English at school.

In the case of any one child in any teacher's class, all these influences discussed by Bronfenbenner play out all the time. A child who is a new arrival from another country will have to deal with changes in all layers, from micro to macro. A child whose family life breaks down is likely to experience major changes in several of the layers, too. These are influences that will have substantial effects on the learning progress of the individual child and, therefore, teachers need to be mindful, patient, and empathetic.

Children are all unique learners

Gardner's framework for multiple intelligences

Teachers and parents/carers often notice that individual children enjoy different activities. For example, if we take working with stories, children who are musical often enjoy singing and dancing and expressing themselves through drama and ballet. At the same time, they may show very little interest in writing, drawing, or colouring. Other children might get embarrassed if asked to join in with singing and dancing but enjoy writing or drawing based on the story. When assessing children's intelligence, many psychologists have argued for the need to take such differences in individuals into account. Howard Gardner, an American psychologist, suggested that intelligence had no unitary character; rather, it manifested itself in many different ways in different children (Gardner, 1983). In his original framework, Gardner suggested seven intelligences: linguistic, logico-mathematical, musical, spatial, bodily-kinaesthetic, interpersonal, and intrapersonal. Later on, after exhaustive debates and discussions, he updated the list and added a new intelligence: the naturalist (Gardner, 2006). Critics and other scholars have proposed adding others, such as humorous intelligence or moral intelligence, but so far Gardner has not agreed to extend the list further.

New ideas and new practical interpretations with regard to the types of basic intelligences are constantly developing, and educators all over the world have welcomed this framework to help them to support learning in their context by inviting learners to explore their various different intelligences. Table 1.2 summarizes the main features of each type of intelligence.

Linguistic:	sensitivity to the sound, rhythm, and meaning of words and the different functions of language
Logico-mathematical:	sensitivity to and capacity to detect logical and numerical patterns, ability to handle long chains of logical reasoning
Musical:	ability to produce or appreciate pitch, rhythm, or melody and aesthetic-sounding tones, understanding of the forms of musical expressiveness
Spatial:	ability to perceive the visual/spatial world accurately, to perform transformations on those perceptions, and to recreate aspects of visual experience in the absence of relevant stimuli
Bodily-kinaesthetic:	ability to use the body skilfully for expressive as well as goal-oriented purposes, ability to handle objects skilfully
Interpersonal:	ability to detect and respond appropriately to the moods, temperaments, motivations, and intentions of others
Intrapersonal:	ability to discriminate complex inner feelings and to use them to guide one's own behaviour, knowledge of one's own strengths, weaknesses, desires, and intelligences
Naturalist:	ability to recognize and classify varieties of animals, minerals, and plants

Table 1.2 Gardner's Multiple Intelligences (Adapted from Berk, 2012)

According to Gardner's framework, in the example about working with stories, the first group of children would be described as showing particular strengths in the areas of musical and bodily-kinaesthetic intelligences while the second group exhibit linguistic and spatial intelligences. Teachers who are aware of this framework can use tasks that combine as many of these intelligences as possible.

Learning styles

These descriptions of intelligences can be related to another term commonly used in educational literature, i.e. **learning styles**. Styles can describe personality types, such as more careful and reflective children as opposed to impulsive and more interactive children. Other styles, related to personality features, describe cognitive categories such as analytic or global learners. **Analytical learners** are those with an attention to detail, and **global learners** are those who are more holistic in their approach. Finally, some styles describe perceptual differences. Some children prefer listening to new input while others need lots of visual stimuli. Yet others are **kinaesthetic**, which means that they like to feel and touch things and move their body in expressive ways to aid their learning and communication.

It is important for teachers to take into account that all children have stronger and weaker aspects of their **multiple intelligences** and preferred learning styles. Some early preferences and styles might change with time, but there will always be a variety of learners in every class. Therefore, teachers need to incorporate a mix of activities into second and foreign language classrooms to ensure that everybody's preferences are catered for, at least some of the time. For example, when new rhymes or songs are introduced in an English class, it is a good idea to present them using a variety of techniques. Children can listen to the teacher or the audio material saying or singing the rhyme or song. This will cater for learners with an auditory preference. Children can also look at the text of the song or rhyme, or look at the illustrations. This activity will appeal to visual learners. Finally, children can watch the teacher miming the actions and join in with the words and actions, too, which caters for kinaesthetic learners. Incorporating various 'senses' also makes learning memorable and fun. Once aware of having to accommodate different intelligences, teachers can make their lessons more accessible to all children.

Learning environments

Balance between collaborative and competitive tasks

Learning environments and, in particular, what types of activities and tasks are used in a lesson, also influence children's learning processes. One important principle is for teachers to balance collaborative and competitive tasks. Competition is instinctive in young children and they will readily engage in competitive tasks, while collaboration is less natural to them. Collaboration requires that children take note of other people's views and ideas, and this ability develops gradually. (See Chapter 8 on **learning to learn**.)

Competitive learning activities encourage children to push themselves to do better than their peers, either individually or in groups. Well-known competitive activities include games such as 'Who can finish the puzzle first?' or 'Who can collect the most words within three minutes?'. Comparing yourself to others in competition is motivating for high achievers, but not for those who rarely win. Competitive learning is associated with traditional classrooms where children put their hands up to answer the teacher's questions and where it is important to be the first to speak or answer, either in class or online. Some competition is necessary for children's balanced learning and development, but it is important for teachers to vary the tasks and introduce an element of luck into the competition sometimes, just to avoid the situation where some children never win and therefore lose interest in learning.

In order to provide a balanced learning environment, teachers can also introduce collaborative tasks in their classes. Collaboration, which is one of the key 21st century skills, is based on the idea that a group or a pair is more likely to do better than an individual. Collaborative tasks promote **interdependence**, i.e. a need to communicate effectively, learn from one another, and organize the learning processes within the group. Another benefit is that collaboration can lower anxiety levels because it is often more comfortable to speak up or perform in front of a group of peers rather than in front of the whole class. From the teacher's point of view, when children are working collaboratively in groups there is simultaneously more English speaking and more practice happening. One very popular collaborative activity is jigsaw reading. Children work in groups of four. For each group, a text is cut up into four pieces and each child is given a piece of the text. Each child reads their piece of the text and they then work together to put the pieces in the correct order. When the 'jigsaw pieces' are in the correct order, they can answer questions together about the whole text. (See Figure 1.4.)

Figure 1.4 Jigsaw reading

Group games can combine a bit of competition as well as collaboration. Children need to collaborate within the group by listening to one another attentively, speaking in a quiet voice, and helping one another with any misunderstandings. At the same time, groups are competing against each other and eventually one group will win, overtaking everyone else in the class. Such games create a great deal of excitement and they can be very motivating for children who are instinctively competitive.

Often, the same activity can be presented either as a competitive task or as a collaborative task. For example, imagine that children are to brainstorm words about a poster or picture. One approach may be to encourage children to shout out ideas individually, while another approach may be to let them work in groups and then compare word lists between groups after five minutes. The second approach encourages children to notice that they can achieve more in a group than individually.

Learning a second language and a sense of self and identity

Children's understanding of themselves is also very important in language learning. What they think about themselves, their perceived abilities in language learning, and their self-esteem are all important influencing factors of success. Children also develop second language identities over the years, and teachers can influence this process in a positive way.

An interesting study by Sharon Besser and Alice Chik (2014) explored the identities of young second language learners in Hong Kong, where speaking English is a desired skill but the population is predominantly Chinese speaking and opportunities to use English are limited for most children. Identity development is a dynamic process and for a child it is a constant back-and-forth pull between what parents/carers want, what they themselves desire, and what the opportunities and physical resources allow. In Hong Kong, there is a strong expectation in the community to become proficient in English because the language carries a great deal of status. Twenty-four children—12 boys and 12 girls between ten- and 12-years-old—were invited to participate in this study. These children were followed for three years using a variety of data collection tools to gain some insights into their English-learning experiences. For example, the children were given cameras and were asked to take photos of English-learning opportunities, and then discussions were organized around these photos. Two types of identities emerged: 'cosmopolitans' and 'pragmatists'. The cosmopolitan is characterized by a cultural openness drawing on popular culture and **English medium instruction (EMI)** in some schools. EMI schools are seen as a pathway to a secure future and economic success. These children also saw their own teachers as cosmopolitan role models. They used tablets, computers, and English books and engaged with popular culture, social networking, and games online. The pragmatists, on the other hand, are children with limited proficiency and little or no identity in English. While cosmopolitans moved comfortably between Chinese and English, actively seeking out English resources, pragmatists emphasized parental pressure and uncertainty about whether they would be accepted into EMI schools. Such uncertainty and anxiety was linked to limited identity development in English. Overall this study indicates that young language learners at this age are already divided into more or less favourable groups in terms of identity development. The authors argue that teachers need to understand the link between social class and identity development and, if possible, they should develop children's agency and identity in positive ways, building on what they bring from home. Encouraging informal engagement with English for pleasure and promoting motivation and real language use through authentic activities may help.

The role of friendships

Children need to be able to feel comfortable in terms of working together with their peers. They often clearly express a preference for working with a friend and they achieve better outcomes in friendship groups. Even though it might not be realistic for teachers to put friends together all the time, their preferences are worth keeping in mind.

The nature of friendships changes across different phases of childhood and friendships become more complex with age. Preschool children at the ages of three and four make friends easily and they refer to all other children they know and play with as 'friends'. When they are together young children often play in 'parallel' rather than together, each one focusing on slightly different activities or aspects of the same game. In primary school, certainly by the age of six or seven, children develop more complex friendships and become more selective about friends. Many children may have a best friend. Boys and girls typically develop different friendship patterns; boys have more competitive, game-based friendships whereas girls have more intimate friendships based on sharing and talking. By adolescence friendship becomes more sophisticated and is based on trust, reciprocity, and mutual interest. However, whatever the age of the child, friends have a positive influence on children's success and well-being at school and, therefore, teachers may want to exploit friendship groups as fertile grounds for learning, talking, and sharing ideas in second language classrooms as well.

Exceptional children and mixed-ability classes

In almost all contexts, teachers will have to deal with exceptional children: learners with very high ability or slower learners with emotional and/or learning difficulties of various types. Many teachers work with large, mixed-ability classes and they face a similar sort of problem when they have to cater for different needs within the same class. It is essential that all children of all abilities find learning a new language a motivating and rewarding exercise and that they can progress at their own pace. It is the teacher's challenge to provide them with suitable tasks and rewards according to their individual needs. Exceptionally gifted children will need to learn early on to work independently so that they can carry on with motivating tasks while the rest of the class are engaged in something else. Similarly, slower learners need suitably challenging tasks and special support that will keep them motivated and ensure small successes.

Learners with special educational needs should also be encouraged to take part in foreign language learning classes. There are growing levels of awareness of these learners—for example, primary school learners with dyslexia—as well as more support and materials available for them. DysTEFL (www.dystefl.eu) is a website where materials are freely available to teachers who work in foreign language classrooms with young learners who have been diagnosed as dyslexic.

In one way or another, all teachers have mixed-ability classes, and all their learners are unique personalities with their own needs and interests. Therefore, all teachers will find strategies of differentiation helpful in their classes. You can differentiate simply by putting children in groups to work on different tasks. New technologies can help a great deal with providing opportunities for differentiation. Faster learners can access additional online games and activities both in class and at home.

Summary

Children within the same age group may show similar characteristics, but at the same time they are also individuals with differing strengths and preferences as learners. While teachers can benefit from familiarizing themselves with the universal aspects of children's development, it is also important that this is balanced out with focus on the individual child. Teachers will have to use their best judgement in deciding about the most suitable materials and techniques to fit learners of different ages in different contexts. Learning about the children by talking to them, observing them, and talking to their parents/carers can help teachers to understand the children they are working with. By incorporating variety into everyday practice, teachers of children can make their lessons full of stimulation for all learner types and intelligences.

Suggestions for further reading

Berk, L. (2012). *Child development.* Boston, MA: Allyn and Bacon.
This is a comprehensive book on child psychology which covers cognitive, emotional, and social development from birth to adolescence. It is of interest to those teachers who want to refresh their knowledge about child development in general.

Cohen, D. (2002). *How the child's mind develops.* Hove: Routledge.
This is a thought-provoking and entertaining account of child development for both interested parents/carers and teachers. The main theories are summarized in a highly accessible manner. The book contains many interesting topics such as the effect of television and computers on children.

Gray, C., & **MacBlain, S.** (2012). *Learning theories in childhood.* London: Sage.
This is an excellent book providing a comprehensive overview of children's learning. The authors guide the reader through the most influential philosophies of learning from a historical/chronological perspective and consider both the strengths and weaknesses of each approach. The reader is encouraged to reflect on how each approach can have an effect on their own practice.

Tasks

If you would like to explore your own practice related to the content of this chapter, you can try the following tasks:

Task 1: Exploring different age groups (page 183)

Task 3: Observing children outside English classes (page 185)

Task 9: Planning lessons (page 188)

Task 14: Collaborative writing and reflection (page 191)

Task 19: Exploring group presentations (page 195)

2 LEARNING THE FIRST LANGUAGE AT HOME AND AT SCHOOL

Introduction

In Chapter 1, development in childhood in very general terms was considered, and although some examples have already been introduced to show the relevance of these ideas to language learning, it has not yet been explored in detail. In this chapter, the focus will be on learning the **first language** as well as drawing parallels between learning both the first and **second language** in childhood. Looking at first language learning can offer important insights to teachers about the rate and nature of development and the continuity between learning the first language and other languages.

Why is first language development of interest to EYL teachers?

The comparison between first and second language learning is relevant and important because children in second or foreign language classes are still in the process of learning their **mother tongue**. First language acquisition is a long process that continues well beyond childhood so, by definition, it cannot be complete for any child learner. Depending on the starting age, these two processes can be more or less closely intertwined. The younger the child is, the more similar the two processes will be, because very young children lack the ability to manipulate and think about language in a conscious way. This is especially true for children in **naturalistic learning environments** such as in **immersion environments**.

How are child learners different from adult learners?

Adult learners can rely on a number of useful resources when they learn a new language. They can analyze language in an abstract way. This ability will allow them to compare patterns and linguistic forms that are similar or different in their mother tongue and in the other language. Knowing at least one language very well, adult learners can hypothesize quite deliberately about features of another language. For example, an English native speaker may hypothesize that past tense verb forms in German (a closely related language) can be either regular or irregular, just as in English. Such a conscious attitude might lead the adult learner to notice verb features in German earlier. Adults can also use their knowledge of the world and different contexts to make guesses about unknown words or phrases. They also have a good understanding of the rules of communication. For example, for something as simple and straightforward as everyday conversation, they know that they have to use set phrases to open and close the conversation, and they need to judge the level of politeness depending on who they are talking to. Mature language learners also use a variety of strategies that help them to memorize and rehearse patterns and words, and they regularly reflect on how well they are doing.

By contrast, children cannot make use of these advantages yet, or at least there are significant differences between various age groups in the extent to which they can do so. For example, a class of six-year-olds will be largely unable to reflect on how their first language works, and will show no interest or inclination to notice language forms in either their first or second language. They will pick up and learn the second or foreign language if they are having fun and if they can work out messages from meaningful contexts. This means learning holistically without attention to abstract language forms. As we progress to older children, accomplishments in the process of acquiring their first language will allow them more and more opportunities for useful comparisons between the languages they know. Their growing abilities in their mother tongue—for example to construct phrases, sentences, or questions, to create and retell stories, or to hold a conversation—will all be important direct or indirect sources of support in the process of learning another language.

Universal processes in language learning

Another reason why it is important to consider first language development is that research shows that there are many universal aspects of language development whatever language (first or second language) and whatever type of learner (adult or child) we consider. For example, in both first and second language learning in English there is a stage of development where speakers omit auxiliaries (for example, 'is' or 'are') such as in the sentence '*Where you going?', or the third person singular marker -*s*, such as in the sentence '*He like singing' (an asterisk * denotes an incorrect form). There is also a universal order of acquisition with regard to many aspects of English morphology (word structure). For example, in verb forms, morphemes include the -*ing* ending or -*s* for third person singular. Particularly striking is the similarity between the order of acquisition by English mother tongue learners and naturalistic **English as a second language** learners, i.e. those who learn the language immersed in an English environment. In the case of children who are learning a second language in regular timetabled classrooms, the relative lack of input and the type of instruction can of course alter this order. However, the natural order is still relevant for teachers. For example, many teachers I have worked with mentioned that they noticed mistakes in their learners' speech and writing to do with the third person -*s* even though this grammatical feature is often covered right at the beginning of children's courses. For example, in the sentence 'She sleeps late on Sundays', they omit the *-s* in the verb. The fact that learners still make this mistake later in the course indicates that the third person *-s* may be naturally acquired much later than originally thought. Spending too much time and effort in the classroom to eradicate this error may well be a fruitless exercise.

How is the first language acquired?

The role of input and interaction

Provided that the necessary input and opportunities for interaction are available, most children learn to use their mother tongue to communicate in familiar contexts by the time they are four or five years old. All babies and young children need to be talked to so that they can receive input and begin to learn to participate in interactions. All humans have the inborn capacity to produce baby talk—special simplified talk directed to babies. Even children do this with their younger siblings. Research in the 1970s, such as the study by Catherine Snow in 1972 (in Fletcher & Garman, 1986), showed that mothers' speech to their babies was slower and more repetitive than their normal speech to adults. They used various simplifications and modifications in their speech and these were shown to be very helpful in making the input comprehensible to children. Such simplified talk contains a lot of repetition, a slower rate of speech, exaggerated intonation patterns, and the use of higher pitch. With regard to content, carers typically talk about topic areas immediately relevant to the child such as the family, home environment, toys, animals, body parts, and food.

The role of Universal Grammar

While children are learning from input and interactions with their parents/carers, their inborn capacities are also at work. The famous linguist Noam Chomsky argued that children often produced language that they could not have heard in natural interactions with others. For example, all children learning English as their mother tongue produce past tense constructions such as *flyed, *writed, and *buyed. They are attaching the regular past tense marker to irregular verbs. Chomsky argued that these constructions show evidence that children make constant efforts to hypothesize about the structure of the language. Based on these, Chomsky proposed the theory of Universal Grammar (UG), which can be imagined as a kind of device in one's head containing representations of abstract facts about human language. While this kind of evidence (*flyed and *writed) from children continues to interest and puzzle language acquisition experts, most recently the number of UG supporters has declined and more attention has been given to usage-based models.

Usage-based models

This approach is often referred to as 'emergentism' and is associated with the work of Nick Ellis (2013) and his colleagues. Emergentism suggests that language use and language knowledge are inseparable and we come to know more and more about language by using it. Ellis and his colleagues propose that language learning happens in a communicatively rich social environment where the human brain is eager to exploit the functionality of language. Human learning is 'associative', i.e. it happens as we form memories of experiences. In language learning, this happens by paying attention to the frequency of forms and to the co-occurrence of these forms with others. Learning is also 'probabilistic', which means that it is gradual and to some extent based on guesswork, and as such always involves some ambiguity and uncertainty. Finally, the third characteristic of emergentism is 'rational contingency', which means that the mind is paying attention to the best possible evidence in the output based on the contextual clues.

One of the usage-based approaches to how languages are acquired is offered by Michael Tomasello (2003), who claims that human language learning is located in intention reading, i.e. a joint effort between the young child and the adult. This is accomplished by using a mixture of cognitive or thinking skills and social skills. Communicative intentions are read and interpreted at sentence/utterance level. For example, as Caroline Rowland (2014) explains in her summary of usage-based models, we can imagine a scenario where a young child sees a rabbit hopping along. Then the child's mother says something such as 'glorp the gavagai'. If the child believes that the mother's intention is to simply direct his attention to the rabbit, he will interpret the utterance as something like 'look at that rabbit'. However, if the intention is read differently, such as the mother might want him to catch the rabbit before it escapes, he might interpret it as 'stop the rabbit'. It is the context that will help enormously to decide what the intention was. The correct reading of the intention is key to interpretation and, ultimately, to understanding meaning and language learning.

The achievements of the first five years

Language development starts well before children are able to say anything. In the beginning, babies exercise their receptive skills, and only with considerable delay do they start producing language. It takes several years to move slowly from fragmented language use to a fully productive command of the language. In English, children progress from one-word utterances (such as mummy, daddy) to two-word ('mummy go') and three word ('where mummy gone') utterances. Different children have so-called 'language bursts' at different times, but typically between the ages of two and three they acquire a huge amount of vocabulary and begin to tackle the grammar of English. Word learning takes place at an astonishing speed. A great deal of guesswork goes on in both listening and speaking—for example, words are often used before they are understood fully. The developments in understanding and production are interrelated and gradual. Learning English grammar requires tackling patterns that often have a multifunctional purpose. This means that the same form is used for different functions. For example, 'get' is used in different ways, such as 'get up', 'get someone an ice cream', and 'get someone to go to sleep'. Children will acquire an item for a single purpose first and gradually add other functions.

During these early years, children are immensely creative with language and enjoy playing with words. They make up their own words, create jokes, and experiment with language even when they have to rely on limited resources. The following examples come from children I have worked with. One child called a cactus a 'hedgehog flower' because he had learned the word 'hedgehog' and was looking for a way to name a plant that looked like a hedgehog. Another child who had chicken pox and was covered in spots saw a Dalmatian and referred to it as 'a dog with chicken pox' because the spots on the dog reminded him of his own spots. The implication here for teachers is that, given appropriate opportunities, creativity and willingness to play with the language could carry over to the learning of second and foreign languages as well. Teachers can encourage children to experiment with language and enjoy language for its own sake. Drama activities or simple poetry writing, for example, which allow children's imagination and fantasy to flourish, can be regular activities in TEYL classrooms. Language play can take many other forms such as playing with forms, sounds, rhyme, and rhythm, and creating imaginary or nonsense words.

By the time they are four or five, most children have acquired their first language more or less fully in terms of the basic grammatical control and lexis needed for normal conversations. However, while five-year-olds are effective communicators in the home environment, they still have a long way to go in terms of continuing to learn their mother tongue for communicating with people outside that environment, in particular in more formal contexts and unfamiliar settings.

While it is true that the processes of first language acquisition in early childhood (before age five in one's mother tongue) are quite different from learning a new language in primary school contexts, this review of early development is interesting to teachers of English as a second or foreign language for a number of reasons. For example, it is important for teachers to appreciate just how long it takes for children to learn even their mother tongue. In some contexts, children as young as five years old (and sometimes even younger) start a new language. Having some awareness about what a five-year-old child can say and do in his or her first language can help teachers to appreciate what is realistic for that age group in a second language. It is generally a good idea to monitor children's abilities in their mother tongue in order to inform second or foreign language teaching and learning.

This brief review is based on learning English rather than any other languages. Although many principles may hold true for other languages as well, teachers of English to children of various mother tongues will always find it useful to understand more about the children's first language development, whatever that language may be.

The influence of school on first language development

Language use at home

At home with parents/carers and siblings, children are already confident communicators. Their parents/carers share most of their experiences, which makes it easier to talk about things. Parents/Carers also tend to take the lead in conversations and are eager to work out their children's half-formed ideas. There is no need to be explicit and precise with language use at home. Parents/Carers naturally scaffold their children's language in dialogues. (See Chapter 1.) While at home most communication is embedded in the shared immediate context, school language use is more independent of immediate contexts. Teachers do not know children as well as parents/carers, and their understanding of the children's experiences is limited, which makes it harder to work out what children mean. It is often difficult for young children to make the jump from home to school language use, i.e. from implicit to more explicit ways of using their first language. Studies show that rich linguistic interactions between parents/carers and their children at home can be important in preparing children to be successful communicators at school. Gordon Wells (1981, 1985) and his colleagues conducted some classic studies which showed that 'good' interactions offer corrections, valuable feedback, and supportive encouragement. Children who are talked to and read to on a regular basis, and who have the chance to initiate ideas for joint exploration in dialogues with parents/carers, start with a great advantage at school.

Language use at school

At school, children are often required to talk about past experiences, future plans, or other people's perspectives, i.e. things that are not related to the immediate context. They will continue learning about their first language at school, and they may come across a standard version of their first language which might be quite different from a dialect used at home. With regard to more complex grammar, they will learn to handle clause types, complex sentences, and the rules of connecting ideas in speaking as well as writing. They will also acquire formal, literary, historic, and archaic phrases and come in contact with varieties of their mother tongue, such as other regional accents. Throughout the school years, the rate of vocabulary learning will continue to be very high. Susan Foster-Cohen (1999), a researcher interested in first language development, reports that an average eight- or nine-year-old knows between 4,000 and 10,000 words, and it is estimated that about 800 to 1,200 words are learned at school every year from this age onwards. This is a staggering amount of new vocabulary to learn. Children will also learn about various spoken and written genres such as stories, plays, letters, descriptions, or science reports. The process of becoming confident readers and writers in their first language will continue into the years of secondary education.

At school, learning happens through talk. (See Vygotsky in Chapter 1.) Research has explored what makes for effective talk in classrooms. Both the quality of the teachers' talk and the learners' talk matter. The 'Thinking Together' approach described by Neil Mercer and Karen Littleton (2007) is a pedagogical approach of using talk in the classroom whereby the teacher guides the learners through modelling language use in an inclusive climate for discussion. In these classrooms, opportunities with peers for dialogue are frequent, and children can explore ideas together both by building on each other's input and by working through disagreements or alternative ideas in a systematic way. Children need careful input and training in using such **exploratory talk** effectively in their first language and this has clear implications for second language teachers. Young learners working together in their second language in groups may need some training and help with how to respond to each other and use talk effectively when working with a given task. It may be that they need help to talk effectively even in their first language.

Organizing school knowledge and experiences

Monitoring own learning

In addition to learning subject content such as geography, history, maths, science, or English at school, children also need to learn to begin to monitor their own learning. This is often referred to as children's growing **metacognitive ability**. Development in their ability to plan, monitor, and evaluate their performance and their learning will increase as children progress through the school years and, as mentioned in the Introduction, these 21st century skills have become increasingly important in new curricula. These ideas will be explored further in Chapter 8, on learning to learn. In both first and second languages, they will gradually learn to stand back from and think about language in an abstract way, and reflect on what they can do or would like to be able to do. For example, during primary school children learn to define words and appreciate multiple meanings or puns, riddles, and metaphors in their mother tongue. All these learning experiences require that they analyze language as an abstract system. The emerging ability to think about language as a system has important implications for second and foreign language learning and opens up possibilities of analyzing, comparing, and discussing language forms in the second or foreign language classroom.

Memory development

The ability to remember facts, figures, and labels, such as the capital city of France, sums in mathematics, names of famous people, important dates, or words in a foreign language are tasks that require effective memory strategies. These strategies also generally improve with age. Research shows that expertise has an important influence on children's memory performance. Children who know a particular area or topic well show increasingly superior memory capacities for retrieval as compared to those who do not. Two out of many interesting studies that report on findings in this area were carried out by Michelene Chi in 1978 and Wolfgang

Schneider and David Bjorklund in 1992. Both of these studies looked at the ability of children to recall items with and without some background knowledge of the topic. Chi gave pictures of chessboard arrangements to expert child chess players and adults who knew how to play chess but were not experts. Chi found that the expert children recalled the chessboard combinations much better than the adults because of their knowledge of chess and their ability to remember chess patterns rather than individual items. Wolfgang Schneider and David Bjorklund gave a list of soccer-related words to learn and remember to a group of children who were experts in soccer and to another group who were not experts. The findings showed that the experts remembered far more items from the soccer list than the non-experts did. The implication of these findings for teachers of English as a second language to children is that it is important to find out what their children are good at and what they know about. Whether it is dinosaurs, butterflies, spaceships, or sports that the children are interested in, remembering and retrieving new vocabulary will be a lot easier for them if they know about the topic and are enthusiastic about it.

Summary

There are important parallels between children's first language and second language development, and TEYL teachers can benefit from being familiar with first language processes. It is important to know what children can do and like doing in their mother tongue because teachers can usefully build on this knowledge in their second or foreign language classes. In some contexts, the English teacher may not be familiar with the children's first language, and this is a distinct disadvantage, but even here teachers may be able to take steps to familiarize themselves with the children's linguistic profile.

Suggestions for further reading

Foster-Cohen, S. (Ed.). (2009). *Language acquisition.* Basingstoke: Palgrave Macmillan.
This is an edited collection that brings together different papers in the area of child language acquisition. The volume represents the variety of approaches taken to study this field and it touches on topics such as bilingualism versus first language acquisition, language disorders, and cultural patterns in language acquisition.

Lightbown, P. M. & **Spada, N.** (2013). *How languages are learned, fourth edition.* Oxford: Oxford University Press.
This is a classic book for both language teachers and students specializing in language studies. It is a highly accessible account of theories of both first and second language learning. The book contains practical activities to bring the theory alive. Online resources and free sample material can be found at: www.oup.com/ elt/teacher/hlal

Mercer, N. & **Littleton, K.** (2007). *Dialogue and the development of children's thinking.* London: Routledge.
This book discusses classroom research with a focus on talk. The data presented in the book provides compelling evidence that the quality of talk in any classroom is linked to the quality of learning and thinking. The book is accessible in style and it discusses the importance of spoken dialogue for children's educational development.

Rowland, C. (2014). *Understanding child language acquisition.* London: Routledge.
This is a comprehensive book that introduces the reader to every aspect of child language acquisition from learning sounds to conversational strategies. The author focuses on key similarities across languages to make the discussion useful to an international audience. The book describes underlying research and debate in the field and also gives insights into what children of different ages are able to accomplish in their first language.

Tasks

If you would like to explore your own practice related to the content of this chapter, you can try the following tasks:

Task 2: Exploring children's first language performances (page 185)

Task 3: Observing children outside English classes (page 185)

3 LEARNING SECOND LANGUAGES AT HOME AND AT SCHOOL

Introduction

There is an enormous variety in the world with regard to at what age, how, and why children learn second languages. This chapter will outline some of these circumstances, starting with natural acquisition of two languages at birth and moving on to different types of bilingualism. Important differences between the demands of learning a language in informal situations such as everyday conversations, and more formal learning such as at school, will be discussed. Both younger learners' and older learners' advantages as language learners will be considered. This brief overview of second language contexts will compare English as a second language (ESL) contexts, where English is taught in an English environment, and English as a foreign language (EFL) contexts, where English is taught as a timetabled subject in a non-English environment. At the same time, it is true to say that ESL and EFL are not as distinct as they used to be because of global travel, global communication opportunities through the internet, and the recent spread of bilingual and immersion programmes such as **Content and Language Integrated Learning** (**CLIL**) programmes all over the world.

Bilingualism

Early bilingualism

The earliest possible chance to learn two languages is at birth. This early process is often referred to as the 'simultaneous acquisition' of two or sometimes more languages. In a mixed-nationality marriage, for example, one parent may use only French with the children while the other parent uses only English. Suzanne Romaine (1995), a well-known researcher in the area of bilingual studies, refers to this as the 'one person one language' scenario. When this strategy is systematically followed by both parents/carers, children can acquire two languages at the same time. Studies indicate that bilingual babies as young as just a few months old are already tuned to two languages and they are able to, for example, discriminate between the sounds of both languages. Ultimately, differences between the levels of competence in the two languages will, of course, almost always be inevitable due to factors such as: which language is dominant in the society, whether or not the parents/carers speak or understand each other's languages, how consistently they use the 'one parent one language' strategy, and what language will be focused on when the child goes to school.

There is a large body of research that shows that bilingual children achieve the same milestones in their linguistic development as monolingual children, although at the beginning stages bilingual children may appear to develop more slowly, i.e. they may say their first words a little later and learn fewer words and grammatical structures in each language. However, if lexical items and grammatical structures are accounted for in both languages, bilingual children do not lag behind their monolingual peers. Some children who have more extroverted personalities and like taking risks might start talking just as early as monolingual children.

Bilingual children go through a phase of mixing the languages in the first two years. Then, at around three years of age, they start to separate the two languages and will begin to address people in different languages depending on their relevant language background. However, when and to what extent this happens also depend on social factors, such as the extent to which parents/carers attract the child's attention to the existence of two languages and the attitude children acquire to the two languages. Even in the case of early bilingual children, the development of both languages will continue in a balanced way only if opportunities are regularly available to practise and develop competence in both languages.

Other types of bilingualism

Victoria Murphy is a researcher who specializes in child bilingualism. Her comprehensive overview of this research field (Murphy, 2014) suggests that children can become bilingual in different ways: from birth (as discussed above) or sometime later in childhood. In terms of the function of their bilingualism, children can be heritage language learners, minority language learners, or majority language learners.

Heritage language users are children who learn a heritage (culturally significant) language alongside a more widely used official language. For example, children in Wales are bilingual Welsh and English speakers. Similarly, children in one region of Spain use both Catalan and Spanish, with Catalan being the heritage language. Heritage language learners in many contexts often begin life as balanced bilingual children but typically shift towards the majority language used in society.

Minority language learners are immigrant children who arrive in a new country where their own first language is considered lower status than the majority language of the society. For example, Turkish-speaking children are considered minority speakers in Germany. Research suggests that there are often academic achievement gaps between the local native-speaking children and their minority language learning peers. This gap manifests itself in lower vocabulary and reading scores. Many factors play a role in this, such as parental education, cultural factors, and socio-economic background. One crucial finding from this research is that these children ideally need equal opportunities to develop their first language and second language at school to maximize their educational potential.

Finally, majority language learners are children who enter CLIL and immersion programmes where they learn two high-status languages. Such bilingual programmes are inspired by the original success of North American immersion programmes. Most recently, two-way immersion programmes have become most popular, where some children are native speakers of one language while the others are native speakers of the other language. For example, in the USA, in a two-way immersion programme, some of the children are native Spanish speakers and some of them are native English speakers. Their curriculum would be delivered partly in English and partly in Spanish, benefiting both groups of learners.

Some benefits of being bilingual

For a long time it was believed that learning two languages at the same time was detrimental to children's development. However, research in the last 40 years, especially in Canada, has now convincingly demonstrated that this is not the case. Merrill Swain (2000) and her colleagues in Canada have shown that in fact quite the opposite is true. Bilingualism is advantageous for children, especially with regard to their early metalinguistic awareness, i.e. their ability to manipulate and label language. As they are exposed to two languages, bilingual children are more aware of language systems. For example, they realize earlier than monolingual children that words are arbitrary symbols and the same object can be referred to by using different labels. In general, they are more conscious of language structures and patterns and learn to reflect on these earlier.

An interesting recent study conducted by Raluca Barac, Ellen Bialystok, Dina Castro, and Marta Sanchez (2014) discusses bilingual children's cognitive benefits. One of the cognitive advantages of bilingualism is related to children's **executive control** function. The executive control helps children to switch between conflicting rules by suppressing one of the rules. For example, imagine a task or a game where images are presented to children that vary in two dimensions such as colour and shape (i.e. blue, yellow, red, and green triangles, circles, and squares). In the first task, the child needs to sort them according to shape but in the second task according to colour. When two rules are in conflict, children need to switch to a new rule and suppress the old rule. For this they use their executive control skills. According to a body of research that evaluated the executive functions of bilingual and monolingual children, children who are dual language users can do these tasks significantly faster than monolingual children. Interestingly, these advantages apply no matter what languages the child speaks and even after just a short period of being exposed to two languages. These findings suggest that even after a brief period of exposing children to two languages through CLIL instruction, for example, important cognitive benefits may be gained in addition to the purely linguistic ones.

The effect of age

Critical Period Hypothesis

Folk wisdom holds that children are very successful second language learners. It has been observed repeatedly that children who move to another country pick up the new language seemingly effortlessly and quickly as opposed to their parents/carers, who often find language learning more of a challenge. This observation led to assumptions about the advantages of starting learning a second language at a young age and also to a great deal of enthusiasm around the world for introducing English in primary school, or even earlier. One reason why early language learning has become so popular is that many psycholinguists have explained the advantages by proposing a so-called 'sensitive period' in childhood for language learning. Originally, Eric Lenneberg proposed the Critical Period Hypothesis (CPH) (1967), which suggested that brain plasticity was only conducive to language learning until puberty. While the original claims of the CPH have been called into question, it seems that young children do have some advantages when learning a second language.

Younger learners

A comprehensive summary by Robert DeKeyser (2012) suggests that young children's advantages apply in so-called 'natural learning environments'. For example, studies that looked at the relationship between the **age of arrival** (**AOA**) of young children in the new country and their language competence found an effect for age in implicit language learning ability. This means that young children can acquire grammatical structures without explicitly thinking about them, i.e. they just naturally soak these up from the rich input around them. Also, studies which examined the relationship between AOA and phonological ratings indicate that younger learners do consistently better with pronunciation. DeKeyser (2012) reminds us, though, that not all aspects of language are affected in the same way.

Leaving behind naturalistic environments, research into the advantages of younger learners in formal school environments is not so conclusively positive. If we compare those who started learning a second language younger, in primary schools, with those who started a bit later, in secondary schools, most studies show that the advantages of the early starters tend to disappear by the time children are 16.

Carmen Muñoz (2014) also attests that the long-term advantage conferred to young learners by an early start in a naturalistic context does not seem to work in an EFL context because of the input limitations. EFL studies all show a rate of advantage of late starters when learners' performances are compared after the same number of instructions. When exploring the second language performance of learners after 15 years of learning English, looking at whether starting age would play an important role or not, Muñoz found that the length of instruction and starting age were not important factors. Instead, the key factors were varied and frequent contact with native speakers (good-quality input) and opportunities for immersion, i.e. for intensive **exposure**.

While children learning English in formal classrooms can't ever be surrounded by similar levels of input as naturalistic learners, they can still enjoy some advantages as young learners. For example, young children have an intuitive grasp of language and they have an ability to be more attuned to the phonological system of the new language compared to adults. Children are sensitive to the sounds and the rhythm of new languages, and they enjoy copying new sounds and patterns of intonation. In addition, younger learners are less anxious and less inhibited, and they worry less than older learners about mistakes or how they come across as non-native speakers.

Older learners

Older learners and adults are often labelled as less successful as language learners but, of course, the truth is somewhat more complex. Older learners use more efficient strategies, have a more mature conceptual world to rely on, have a clearer sense of discourse, and, more importantly, have a clearer sense of why they are learning a new language. Adults and older learners are more analytical and give attention to detail, which helps with language learning. The only area that is difficult to compensate for seems to be pronunciation but, even here, cultural and identity issues may play a role. Adults and older children might not want to sound English because they want to preserve their own identity. There is another argument which challenges the supposed advantages of an early start. There are some rare but exceptionally successful cases of adults who start learning a second language quite late in life and succeed nonetheless in achieving native, or near-native, levels of competence.

A very interesting study by Ciara Kinsella and David Singleton (2014) explored the complex factors that contribute to exceptional adult learners' second language success. The participants in this study were all native speakers of English, and spoke French as a second language. Their first significant exposure to French occurred after the age of 20, thus excluding those with any possible CPH advantage. The study showed that age is indeed not the critical factor. Instead, the participants all shared some key characteristics: they all made long-term investments into French learning; they had all lived in France for a long time—in some cases for more than 25 years; they were firmly integrated into their local communities; and they all married French natives and had bilingual or French-speaking children. In their homes, French was the language spoken and they conducted nearly all their social interactions outside the home in French, too. It was important for them to speak a high standard of French and they all took pride in their ability.

Learning a second language in the playground and at school

From informal to formal contexts

Children tend to pick up language in everyday situations from other children in their environment relatively quickly because they want to play and make friends. Familiar routines and games offer great opportunities for hearing the same language again and again and for learning to take part in simple conversations. When children move to another country (for example, a Mexican child to the USA, a Turkish child to Germany, or an Iranian child to the UK), after a short silent period, when they are absorbed in listening to input, they can acquire the so-called conversational genre or playground talk fairly quickly. This means that they can communicate, make friends, and function well in everyday conversations as quickly as within the first one or two years of arrival in the new country.

To master the language that is needed for school is quite a different matter. Differences between home language environments and school language environments have already been discussed. (See Chapter 2.) In the case of children who are learning English as a second language, such differences remain relevant. Canadian researcher Jim Cummins published *Language, Power and Pedagogy: Bilingual Children in the Crossfire* (2000), in which he reviewed research evidence about school second language learning and offered advice to teachers working in contexts where there is a cultural diversity of learners in the same class. He also makes a basic distinction between home language use and school language use. The research summarized by Cummins shows that it takes much longer to catch up with the academic language skills necessary for successful participation in school discourse than with those necessary for informal conversations. It may take as long as five to seven years before children reach academic levels comparable to those of native speakers of the language. Cummins' findings also suggest that bilingual education can be very beneficial for children with regard to their general development, cognitive, metacognitive, and other skills. One factor which seems important in this process is to develop children's mother tongue and second language literacy skills in parallel, rather than neglecting the first language to make way for the second. Respect for their mother tongue and support with their second language are essential. Cummins suggests that educational programmes need to invest a considerable amount of effort into making this process of catching up as rewarding, supportive, and motivating as possible. He refers to these practices as 'transformative multi literacies', where children are encouraged to work across their languages and at the same time develop a multilingual identity (Cummins, 2009).

To help these children, teachers will have to think hard about providing a rich language environment where formal and scientific terms and concepts are carefully introduced and explored, starting with informal concepts, words, and phrases that the children are already familiar with. The work of Pauline Gibbons (2002, 2006, 2009) offers a range of practical ideas to teachers interested in managing multicultural classrooms. Gibbons emphasizes the importance of integrating language with content so that language and curriculum knowledge can be developed hand in hand. This means that teachers need to plan their language use in class explicitly and carefully. For example, when teaching children about magnets it is a good idea to start with language they already have for describing magnetic phenomena, such as 'pull together' or 'pull apart', and then introduce formal terms such as 'attract' and 'repel'. New terms and concepts are introduced with careful attention to both content and language. This is the very basis on which CLIL is built, as will be discussed in Chapter 4.

Virtual learning spaces: the internet

Whether a child is learning a second language in an ESL or EFL context, in formal or informal environments, sustained access to the internet can offer additional learning opportunities and, in some cases, can link formal and informal learning.

For many children one popular use of the internet is to play games, and many play them in English. From a language input perspective, games are very rich because they combine different contextual clues via animation, audio, video, and other multimedia. They also attract and hold children's attention because of the content. In one study, Yuko Butler, Yuumi Someya, and Eiji Fukuhara (2014) investigated the game-playing behaviours of nearly 4,000 children in four age groups (between four and 12 years of age) in Japan. They found that the children who played regularly improved their English proficiency, although this was not specifically visible in the school English tests. Games which included appropriate levels of challenge, some mystery in content, an opportunity to take control of the game, and a multiplayer option were most popular. Children learn new words and proactively look up phrases they do not know so that they can continue with the games. They may also speak to other players and read important messages to help them to progress with the game. Playing the same game means encountering the same sort of language repeatedly, which is very beneficial for practising and learning. This study showed that the game-playing characteristics of children under the age of ten are very different from older children's characteristics, but all the age groups enjoy playing. The authors argue that teachers of English may want to investigate what games the children in their classes are playing online so that they can better understand and possibly build on these out-of-class learning opportunities.

Summary

In this chapter, a variety of circumstances in which children may be learning second languages have been reviewed. These included the advantages of early bilinguals, and the differences between informal and formal immersion contexts. It has been pointed out that younger learners do have some advantages, especially in naturalistic contexts, but older learners can also do well given favourable circumstances. Children often learn English in both formal and informal contexts thanks to the expansion of new ICT tools. The next chapter will be devoted to the discussion of factors which ensure that in non-English environments learning English can still be a motivating and worthwhile experience, and that children can make good progress in learning to communicate in English.

Suggestions for further reading

Enever, J. (Ed.). (2011). *ELLiE: Early language learning in Europe*. London: British Council.
This book provides the summary of a large-scale study which was focused on teaching foreign languages in primary schools in seven European countries with varying linguistic, cultural, and demographic characteristics. Data was collected from over 14,000 learners over several years. The book discusses findings and implications relevant for most primary language teaching contexts.

Llinares, A., Morton, T., & **Whittaker, R.** (2012). *The roles of language in CLIL*. Cambridge: Cambridge University Press.
This book is based on the extensive research of the authors into aspects of CLIL classrooms. The corpus of classroom data is analyzed with a focus on the role of language in bilingual CLIL students' development. This is an excellent resource for teachers who work in CLIL contexts and are interested in understanding their own students' language development.

Murphy, V. (2014). *Second language learning in the early school years: Trends and contexts.* Oxford: Oxford University Press.
This is a comprehensive book that brings together current research and debate in the area of second language learning for children in different contexts internationally. Some children learn two languages from birth, others learn their first language as a heritage language in addition to the official language in the given country. Yet others learn an additional language at school and, depending on how the new language is introduced and its status compared to the children's first language, their achievements will vary. The great strength of this book is the way the author compares and contrasts the different contexts and helps the reader to make sense of the emerging patterns. The first chapter is free to download at: www.oup.com/elt/teacher/sllearly

Singleton, D., & **Ryan, L.** (2004). *Language acquisition: The age factor, second edition*. Clevedon, UK: Multilingual Matters.
This book considers evidence for the age factor in language learning, discussing relevant research in both first and second language acquisition. It contains studies of clinical speech therapy as well as language teaching.

Pinter, A. (2011). *Children learning second languages.* Basingstoke: Palgrave Macmillan.
This volume covers different aspects of children's second language learning. It offers insights into foreign language learning contexts, immersion education, and bilingual education. The book also gives an overview of current research into child Second Language Acquisition (SLA) and pedagogy, highlighting the strengths and

weaknesses of different traditions. A central chapter discusses eight case studies researching different aspects of child second language learning. The final chapter of the book offers a resource bank of both theoretical and practical materials related to the title.

Philp, J., Oliver, R., & Mackey, A. (Eds.). (2008). *Second language acquisition and the young learner: Child's play?* Amsterdam: John Benjamins Publishing Company. This is a collection of papers in the area of child SLA. All papers emphasize the distinctiveness of child SLA as compared to adult. The chapters describe the learning paths of different children, from preschoolers to young adolescents, in both formal and informal contexts.

Tasks

If you would like to explore your own practice related to the content of this chapter, you can try the following tasks:

Task 2: Exploring children's first language performances (page 185)

Task 3: Observing children outside English classes (page 185)

4

POLICY: PRIMARY ELT PROGRAMMES

Introduction

While ever more young learners in formal primary education learn English as a second or foreign language as part of their compulsory curriculum, the circumstances of learning and teaching vary a great deal. This chapter will consider how local opportunities and resources can be exploited in order to implement primary foreign language learning programmes with the best possible potential for success. Individual teachers play a key role because their understanding of the benefits and limitations of their own contexts, and thus their informed decisions, can make a real difference with regard to the success of a particular programme. Understanding variables that influence success is also important to teachers who may be in a position to influence policy decisions.

Contextual factors in language teaching

Language settings

The introduction of any language course or programme, whether for adults or children, will be affected by a large number of contextual variables. Behind the language setting of any context, there are strong political influences. At the highest level, these influences are associated with the education ministry's views on languages in general in any given country. This has a knock-on effect on the allocation of funds for training, research programmes, and materials development projects. Governments promote English for political and economic reasons. In a global survey for the British Council, published in 2013, Shelagh Rixon reported that English was being taught at ever younger ages, putting pressure on educational resources across the world. Many countries also introduce English to children in pre-primary settings, such as in kindergartens and preschools.

Educational frameworks

What type of language programme is introduced will be dependent on the educational framework of the given country. Educational frameworks vary enormously between countries. In some contexts, there is a major divide between primary and secondary schools around the age of ten to 11, while in others primary schooling runs for eight years (from six to 14), divided into lower primary and upper primary sectors. In some countries, children start formal schooling at the age of four, but in others not until they are six or seven years old. There are also differences in the way the curriculum is structured and delivered, and these effects may carry over to the introduction of a new language. Even if English is introduced in a given country at a particular age across the board, there might still be large differences between English provision in rural and urban areas, and there are still many contexts where rural schools struggle to employ qualified English language teachers.

Many countries now promote competence-based curricula and lifelong learning, with 21st century skills and learning to learn as their core principles (see Preface and Chapter 8); and in terms of second/foreign language education, more and more contexts opt for integration between the second/foreign language and the rest of the curriculum. For example, in Spain and in other European and Asian countries many different types of bilingual programmes exist, even in primary school contexts. This is beginning to blur the distinction between EFL and ESL.

Status of English and attitude to English

One very important variable is the status of English in a given country. In some countries, English is not used widely in society, while in others it enjoys an equal status to the local language. In some contexts, very high stakes will be attached to English because children have to shift to English from their mother tongue in order to access secondary and tertiary education. This happens in many African countries, for example. In other contexts, such as Japan, the stakes are not quite so high; English is desirable, but without it children can still progress to good schools and successful careers.

Whatever its status, it is also important to consider learners', teachers', and parents'/carers' attitudes to English. In the case of children, these beliefs and attitudes are still malleable. Children of primary school age may not have strong opinions about other cultures or language learning in general, even though parental and teacher influences might already have made an impact. In addition, children with more favourable socio-economic backgrounds will be progressing with their schoolwork and with English more smoothly. (See Chapter 1.) Children whose parents/carers speak two or more languages and move comfortably between cultures will certainly be more likely to develop positive attitudes and accept different cultures more easily. Children who are brought up in a monolingual environment may meet a new culture and come across a new language through the experience of a primary foreign language programme. For these children this experience will be of crucial importance in establishing positive attitudes about other cultures and language learning in general.

The role of motivation

In comparison with the first language, motivation is key in learning other languages. When we learn our first language, it is all a natural part of growing up. When children move to another country and have to learn a new language, their motivation to learn is related to wanting to fit in with children in their new community. In formal foreign language learning contexts, however, the main source of motivation for children is usually their teacher and the enjoyable activities they experience in the English classes. The ELLiE Study (Enever, 2011), which was conducted in seven European countries, suggested that young learners were generally well motivated to learn English and showed positive attitudes. When asked about the sources of motivation, they pointed out vocabulary learning as motivating and they also frequently mentioned the teacher as the most important source of motivation. Over time, however, initial high levels of motivation tend to decrease, and by the time children become teenagers many of them are much less enthusiastic about learning English. As children get older they also compare themselves to their peers and become more aware of and realistic about their own strengths and weaknesses, and some of them lose their initial positive motivation.

In 2015, Jelena Mihaljević Djigunović, a Croatian researcher, reported on a study in which she had examined and monitored young learners' motivation over four years, from Grade 4 to Grade 8 (ages 9–13). At the end of each academic year, the participating children were asked to fill in a questionnaire about how much they enjoyed learning English, and they were also interviewed by Djigunović. The children's motivation varied over the four years, showing a downward trend from Grade 5 to Grade 7, with a particularly noticeable drop after Grade 6. However, motivation levels started to increase again in Grade 8. Djigunović suggests that children first lost their initial high levels of motivation perhaps because the novelty of the experience wore off; but by Grade 8 they became more aware of the practical usefulness of English for their future, and this gave them a new boost of motivation.

It is, of course, very important for teachers to motivate their learners in their English classes. One of the main experts on language learning motivation, Zoltán Dörnyei, wrote a practical book for teachers entitled *Motivational Strategies in the Language Classroom* (2001) to help them to sustain motivation in their classrooms. This book is not directed at primary teachers specifically, but the general principles suggested very much apply to all learners and all learning situations. Dörnyei suggests that there are four main components or stages of motivational teaching:

- The first stage is to create motivating conditions for learning. This means creating a pleasant and supportive environment in the classroom.
- The next stage is to introduce initial motivational techniques such as talking about values, showing positive attitudes to learning, creating materials that are relevant for the learners, and establishing expectations of success.

- After this initial stage, teachers need to take care to maintain and protect their learners' motivation by offering stimulating activities and fostering self-esteem, self-confidence, and cooperation among learners.
- Finally, motivating teachers take care to turn evaluation and feedback into positive experiences.

With older children, as part of an ongoing process of protecting motivation, it may be possible to work on self-motivating strategies. Ema Ushioda (1996, 2012), another expert on language learning motivation, has written a great deal about self-motivation. He describes learning and practising techniques to help learners think positively about their learning. For example, when children are disappointed by lower test results than expected, it is important for them to evaluate this experience in a constructive way so they can learn from it, move on, and try harder next time.

Aims and expectations

There are many good reasons why primary school children can benefit from foreign language learning. The aims and objectives of primary English programmes usually include the following:

- develop children's basic communication abilities in English
- encourage enjoyment and motivation
- promote learning about other cultures
- develop children's cognitive skills
- develop children's metalinguistic awareness
- encourage learning to learn
- develop intercultural awareness and global citizenship
- develop values related to diversity.

Most countries tend to emphasize one or both of the first two aims above. The first typically involves teaching children to talk about themselves and their immediate environments, to understand and respond to basic English instructions, and to communicate about topics of interest. The second aim is related to the need to make English an attractive school subject to children so as to foster their motivation and encourage them to want to learn languages in the future. At this initial familiarization stage, it seems crucial to introduce a foreign language in an enjoyable way. Some contexts may add another dimension, such as an intercultural or cross-cultural aspect, and raise learners' awareness about 'otherness' through a different language and thus a different culture. This could include objectives such as learning to take different perspectives, modifying stereotypes, unlearning prejudices, preventing discrimination, and acquiring tolerance. (See Chapter 11.) These are often referred to as values related to diversity and intercultural understanding. Some contexts may list aims related to cognitive development and/or metalinguistic awareness. It is crucial for teachers to familiarize themselves with the aims and objectives of the programme so that they can set their expectations accordingly.

For example, in many contexts linguistic gains in the first few years of primary school will be limited, but there may be substantial gains in increasing language learning motivation and cultural awareness. Parents/Carers may have unrealistic expectations of children's progress, so it is a good idea for teachers to make the expectations very clear and transparent.

Exposure to English

How much English children hear and how often they have opportunities to interact in English are also important variables. It is, of course, not possible to achieve in the EFL classroom the levels of exposure found in acquisition-rich environments (such as the immersion classrooms in Canada), but the success of naturalistic learning can be built on. The British Council survey, mentioned on page 43 (Rixon, 2013), compared contact hours for English across different countries and found that the average exposure was about 100 hours a year, totalling about 400–500 hours in four years of primary learning. Of course, exposure alone is not entirely meaningful; it needs to be combined with optimal methodology. Classroom discourse patterns that involve teacher–learner as well as learner–learner interaction are desirable, as children need to be able to use, experiment with, and enjoy learning the language in a variety of ways.

Little is known about what actually happens in primary English classrooms around the world in terms of the quality of classroom discourse, although another global survey, conducted with thousands of primary English teachers, gives us some insights. In this survey, published in 2011, Sue Garton, Fiona Copland, and Anne Burns discuss the most frequently used activities in primary English classrooms worldwide. These are:

1 repeating after the teacher
2 listening to a tape recorder or CD
3 reading aloud
4 playing games
5 singing songs.

While it would not be possible to make definite claims based on this data, the responses from the participating teachers suggest that most activities used in the primary English classroom do not encourage learner–learner interaction in a way that would be ideal for language learning to take place. These are useful insights for language teacher education programmes to take on board.

Teacher skills and knowledge

It is important that opportunities are created in the classroom for children to be exposed to natural language and to interact with each other. In order to create these ideal conditions for learning, teachers need to be equipped with methodological skills and knowledge and to be competent in English. Teachers' confidence and willingness to use the language naturally in the classroom is a key component of success.

The primary class teacher who delivers the rest of the curriculum and who has a good knowledge of the children as well as the language is in the best position to succeed. Knowledge of the curriculum means that class teachers can integrate English easily and naturally into the day. Class teachers know the children and their specific needs, such as a safe and encouraging environment, stimulation, fun, and variety, as well as plenty of recycling. Finally, primary English teachers need to have adequate proficiency in the language to provide comprehensible input and natural exposure to the target language. An interesting survey by Yuko Butler (2004), explored primary English teachers' own perceptions of their proficiency. She compared the opinions of primary English teachers from three Asian contexts: South Korea, Japan, and Taiwan. To the question of whether they saw their own proficiency level as adequate to teach the curriculum effectively, all answered that they felt they fell below the necessary level of competence. They identified spoken competence as the area of most concern. Butler suggests that it is important to explore further just what proficiency levels are needed in primary schools and how teachers could be supported. Many teachers may lack confidence in their own proficiency, but with constant practice and good supplementary materials (including audio) they will both manage and improve.

For the successful introduction of English into primary schools in any country, the government needs to invest in recruiting and training teachers. This applies to both pre-service and in-service teacher training and professional development opportunities for teachers. Many countries run well-established primary English teacher training courses. However, many countries also face a difficult situation with a critical shortage of qualified teachers.

Integrating English into the curriculum

How does English fit into the rest of the primary curriculum? The school might follow a programme where English is treated as a separate subject, or it might integrate English as naturally as possible into the existing primary programme. Some countries follow quite rigid subject-based teaching in the primary school and so English as a separate subject might fit better. In these contexts, English is timetabled for about two hours a week, and a specialist teacher delivers the English lessons, as opposed to the children's class teacher. Other countries have already opted for an **integrated** approach where English is carefully embedded into the primary curriculum. In these contexts, English is taught by the class teacher. This means that the children have the opportunity to link their knowledge in other school subjects with English. Some sort of integration between the rest of the curriculum and the foreign language seems sensible for a great many reasons. For example, if we believe that younger children learn holistically, then it would make sense to integrate English into other subjects. Revisiting various concepts and words in a foreign language can reinforce previously taught information.

Integration also carries the underlying idea that everything can be talked about in both the first and the foreign language. Some contexts advocate only a small degree of integration—for example, at the level of using basic mathematical operations in the foreign language, or giving instructions in a PE lesson in English. At a different level, teachers may decide to spend a series of lessons on a topic associated with a particular area of the curriculum. If children are learning about construction materials and types of houses in their geography lessons, there may be opportunities for the English teacher to plan a series of English lessons around the same theme. There are a great many schools in many contexts where English is used across the curriculum in a systematic way throughout the primary years. In these schools, the term **Content and Language Integrated Learning** (**CLIL**) is often used.

Content and Language Integrated Learning (CLIL)

CLIL is a predominantly European approach. According to Do Coyle (1999), the essence of CLIL is described as the 4C framework, bringing together Content, Communication, Cognition, and Culture. This means that the foreign language becomes the vehicle to teach specific content in the curriculum.

In 2015, Kay Bentley reported that primary CLIL is now widely used in various parts of Europe, with specific examples referred to in Spain, Finland, Belgium, Italy, Slovakia, and Poland. CLIL can cover a range of language options, but in practical terms most programmes are in English. At primary level, CLIL can take different forms, such as: teaching a portion, typically up to 40 percent, of the curriculum in English; teaching only three subjects in English, such as maths, music, and PE; or teaching only about 10–12 percent of the curriculum in English. According to CLIL researchers Christiane Dalton-Puffer and Ute Smit (2007), the primacy of meaning in language learning and its purposefulness have the potential to reduce anxiety and increase interest and motivation. Using the second language meaningfully and purposefully to learn about history, geography, maths, or music means learning new language items as well as developing cognitive skills in a holistic way, which is very different from the typically drier and less integrated way of learning in ordinary EFL classes.

In the primary years, children typically do less reading and writing and rely more on speaking and listening. Therefore, typical activities might include recounting instructions for a PE exercise, being able to describe a hands-on experiment in science, or naming the parts of a plant or animal. The constant use of both first language and second language, i.e. early 'code-switching', is very much a part of effective CLIL teaching, especially at the early stages. At the beginning, teachers need to allow learners to respond in a variety of ways. The challenge facing teachers is to move the learners from **lower-order thinking skills** (**LOTS**), such as naming/labelling and the use of the present tense, to **higher-order thinking skills** (**HOTS**) such as evaluating, analyzing the consequences of certain choices, and describing the cause-and-effect relationship of two events. HOTS will require more complex language such as the use of modal auxiliaries.

CLIL teachers need to be keenly aware of learners' language needs and content needs and of how these two types of knowledge are inseparable. It is important to be able to detect where the cause of the problem is in a CLIL lesson, i.e. whether it relates to content or language. There are many challenges in CLIL programmes, such as finding teachers who are equally competent as content and language specialists, and creating locally suitable materials for the different CLIL contexts.

Even in contexts where English is not integrated into other areas of the curriculum, it is important to note that, with their increasing access to the internet, authentic English input for learners is just 'a click away', as long as they know how to find these learning opportunities. For example, they can listen to stories on YouTube and/or read authentic articles, play online games, or watch films in their original language. This means that the EFL/ESL divide is less pronounced, and for those children with regular access to internet materials outside their classrooms such extra learning can make a big difference.

Continuity and the private sector

Here continuity means the opportunity students have at secondary level to build on the knowledge brought over from primary school. This is a major challenge for the implementation of successful primary programmes. In many contexts, there is no agreed outcome associated with primary programmes, and children from different primary schools may have been taught very different things from very different teaching materials. This is why many secondary programmes decide to start again from the beginning, which can have a negative effect on learners' motivation levels and will present additional challenges for teachers in secondary schools.

Many countries refer to the Common European Framework of Reference for Languages (CEFR) when it comes to goal setting for English achievements in the primary years. However, this is rather problematic because the CEFR was not intended for young learners, and it is not a convenient framework for them in terms of topic areas and content coverage. As most primary students would not achieve levels beyond A1, it would perhaps make sense to break band A down into further sub-levels and/or revise it to make it more suitable for younger learners. (See Chapter 10.)

In some countries there is also a thriving private sector of language schools for young learners. These private language schools often run parallel to state primary English programmes, and many children attend them to learn English in addition to their regular classes at school. There is also a culture of encouraging children to prepare for internationally recognized language tests such as the Cambridge English: Young Learners tests, the KET for Schools, the Trinity Graded Exams in Spoken English, or the TOEFL Junior tests. Parents/Carers believe that attending additional courses will be more effective in the long run. Both parents/carers and children are attracted by intensive summer courses and the English-only policy in these private schools, where children are often taught by native speakers. These programmes could be even more effective if they built on children's English learning in state schools.

Summary

David Hayes (2014), whose research has looked at what counts as success in primary language teaching programmes, summarizes the key messages as follows. English is best taught by the generalist teacher or class teacher who ideally has a level of English at CEFR B2 or C1. It is also desirable that the English teachers have access to focused continuous development, and that they are trusted and respected, enjoying at least some degree of freedom. It is also important that these teachers bring positive attitudes to English to motivate learners, and follow a curriculum which allows for meaningful language use. A realistic target needs to be set for the children's learning, with instructional time concentrated towards the end of primary education, and where some materials are prepared by teachers to tap into children's interests and needs. In such a system, private classes would not be regarded as necessary and English could be made available to all in an equitable way. Finally, standardized tests that have the potential to determine children's progress in a second language in a negative way early on are to be avoided at primary level.

Different teachers face varying challenges in their own contexts, and some of these obstacles or restrictions will be beyond their control. However, every teacher can make the best of their own circumstances by continuing to update their methodological skills and their English language competence, and by acting as the best source of motivation for the children.

Suggestions for further reading

Ball, P., Kelly, K., & **Clegg, J.** (2015). *Putting CLIL into practice*. Oxford: Oxford University Press.
This is a handbook for teachers interested in practical solutions to the challenges in CLIL classrooms. It provides practical support for both novice and experienced teachers. It offers real-life examples and suggestions for teaching, teacher training, and materials design, as well as assessment. Online resources and free sample material can be found at: www.oup.com/elt/teacher/clil

Enever, J., Moon, J., & **Raman, U.** (Eds.). (2009). *Young learners English language policy and implementation: International perspectives*. Reading: Garnet.
This book contains 28 papers exploring the debates about the policy and implementation of language teaching programmes for children. The papers all contribute to current thinking about the sustainable implementation of language programmes nationally and internationally, taking local restrictions and global factors into account.

Hayes, D. (2014). *Factors influencing success in teaching English in state primary schools*. London: British Council.
Against the backdrop of an international comparison of education systems, the author explores the role of teaching/learning a foreign language for children. Different countries and their policy decisions are presented for close analysis and,

based on comparisons and some discussion of background literature, the author then draws up a list of factors that are most likely to influence the success of foreign language learning for children in any given context.

Lightbown, P. (2014). *Focus on content-based language teaching.* Oxford: Oxford University Press.
This is a research-led handbook that examines the challenges and solutions to teaching language alongside an academic subject. The book contains classroom extracts where students and teachers interact in different types of content-based classrooms. Practical activities are included which help to bring together theory and teachers' own classroom practice. Online resources and free sample material can be found at: www.oup.com/elt/teacher/cblt

Mourão, S., & **Lourenço, M.** (Eds.). (2015). *Early years second language education: International perspectives on theories and practice.* Abingdon: Routledge.
This is a book that discusses research and practice with regard to the suitability of language programmes for very young children: those under the age of six. The authors bring together a range of international case studies where children are learning a new language either at home or in preschool.

Rixon, S. (2013). *British Council survey of policy and practice in primary English language teaching worldwide.* London: British Council.
This survey contains a large amount of data on global practices in primary-level language teaching worldwide, covering issues such as: age of starting a language in a given country, teacher supply, curriculum, assessment, and transition from primary to secondary level. Sixty-four countries and regions are represented in the study, based on questionnaire data.

Thorner, N. (2017). *Motivational teaching.* Oxford: Oxford University Press.
This is a short, practical book which gives strategies and teaching ideas for motivating older primary school and secondary school children in the language classroom. Online resources and free sample material can be found at: www.oup.com/elt/teacher/itc

Williams, M., Mercer, S., & **Ryan, S.** (2015). *Exploring psychology in language learning and teaching.* Oxford: Oxford University Press.
This is a handbook that looks at how concepts from educational and social psychology apply to language teaching and learning. The authors explore the importance of teachers' and learners' beliefs about how languages should be learned and taught and address the role of motivation, emotions, and group processes such as collaborative learning and relationships in groups. The authors include hands-on activities throughout for reflection. Online resources and free sample material can be found at: www.oup.com/elt/teacher/exploringpsychology

Tasks

If you would like to explore your own practice related to the content of this chapter, you can try the following task:

Task 4: Exploring teaching and learning contexts (page 185)

5 TEACHING LISTENING AND SPEAKING

Introduction

Just as in mother-tongue learning, English should start with an emphasis on listening and then speaking. These are the two main skills to teach first because children often cannot read and write at all yet, or not with much confidence. Young learners need to start with plenty of listening practice, and opportunities to listen to rich input will naturally lead to speaking tasks. In this way, listening and speaking can be truly integrated in the primary English classroom.

With the growing availability of the internet, children in many contexts have access to a range of listening materials through dedicated EFL sites and have the opportunity to enjoy YouTube stories, cartoons, and games on their tablets or computers at school or at home. In some contexts, though not all, technology also provides children with immediate opportunities for listening and speaking practice in English. Many coursebooks not only come with CD and DVD materials, but also have accompanying websites offering extra online practice materials and downloadable apps.

Teaching listening

Children in an EFL class will listen to a great variety of texts and, above all, to their teacher talking, singing, chanting, dramatizing dialogues, giving instructions, and telling stories. Teachers can be supported with good-quality audio and video materials to accompany their teaching if they are not yet confident about their own language proficiency.

Listening—aspects of difficulty

Listening is an active skill, and there are many factors that contribute to its difficulty. It is important in the early stages to avoid these sources of difficulty and introduce them only gradually. One source of difficulty is the type and length of the text the children listen to. Another factor is the familiarity of the person they are listening to. It is easier to listen to the teacher than to recordings because teachers can adjust the speed of their speech and modify their language. The teacher can also repeat messages and use gestures and facial expressions to help children to work out the meaning. What also makes a difference is the response the children need to make before, while, or after they listen.

There are two basic sub-skills that competent and mature listeners use all the time. One set of sub-skills is referred to as **bottom-up processing skills**. These help learners to build up the language from constituent parts. Relying on their knowledge of the linguistic system, listeners use bottom-up processing skills to segment the speech they hear and make sense of it. Knowing the language system helps learners to work out, for example, what the unstressed grammar words are in a particular sentence, even without hearing or listening out for every word. Speakers of all ages find this processing difficult, but children will have particular difficulties. Depending on their age and the type of teaching they have been exposed to, they may not know much about the abstract rule system of English and therefore they may lack the ability to manipulate the system from the bottom up. In parallel with bottom-up processing skills, successful listeners also do simultaneous **top-down processing skills**. They rely on their **schematic knowledge**, i.e. their mental frameworks for various topics and their world knowledge, to fill in gaps in their understanding, and make guesses and interpretations as they follow the listening text. In comparison with adults, children have less developed schematic knowledge about many topics; they know less about the world in general and therefore guess and infer meaning with more difficulty. The younger the child, the more this applies.

Support with listening

In order to support children with both bottom-up and top-down work, teachers may want to focus on giving them listening tasks that are meaning-driven and help them to develop these strategies slowly. In order to support top-down processing, teachers can make sure that listening is carefully embedded in the here-and-now context of familiar games and routines, such as stories and action rhymes, so that children do not need to infer the context or topic for themselves. Gestures and visuals will help, too. With regard to bottom-up processing, it is important that children are given tasks that do not require them to manipulate linguistic features that they do not know yet and are not interested in, such as translating, analyzing constituent parts of phrases and sentences, and substituting patterns. Instead, children should start with easier 'listen and do' activities. Many coursebook activities ask children to 'listen and read', meaning they can follow the text in the book or on screen as they listen, which helps with bottom-up processing. This, of course, is only helpful if they can read.

Teacher talk in the primary English lesson

In young learners' classrooms, especially at the beginning stages of learning a language, teachers talk a lot in the target language because they provide the language input. This helps children to get used to the intonation patterns and sounds of the language. Teachers talk and comment on what is going on as they point to pictures in the course materials or as they mime something. (See Figure 5.1.)

Figure 5.1 Examples of teacher talk

As children listen, they are engaged in working out what is going on, and for some of the time they may choose to remain silent and just absorb the language. This is similar to the first couple of years in learning the first language. Of course, they do not necessarily understand every word the teacher says, but most children will be able to work out the meaning from the context, the gestures, and the visual aids. When teachers use English (the target language) to give instructions, tell a story, or introduce a song or a rhyme, children who have just started learning may comment in their first language on what they think is happening because they cannot yet contribute in the second language. The teacher may want to accept children's comments in their first language and also encourage them by confirming their guesses and contributions, and incorporating their utterances into the target language. There is also an important social, affective function of teacher talk. Teachers will use a lot of praise and encouragement and will model social conventions such as saying 'hello' at the beginning of the lesson.

Interactional modifications of language

During interactions of any kind, in any language, there will inevitably be communication breakdowns. This simply means that the partners do not always understand what the other has just said. When a breakdown or misunderstanding is judged by the speakers to be unimportant, they might simply ignore it and just carry on talking. However, if the breakdown is serious the conversational partners will decide to repair and rephrase what has been said by modifying their original language use. This is often referred to as 'language modification'. Modifying language to avoid and solve misunderstandings can include using repetition, comprehension checks ('Do you understand what I am trying to say?'), clarification requests ('What did you say?'), and confirmation checks ('Did you say you got five?'). A linguist in the USA, Michael Long, and many of his colleagues conducted research studies in the 1980s with adult EFL learners to explore **interactional modifications**, and found that the processes of negotiating meaning (modifying language and asking for modifications from a partner) facilitated second language acquisition (Long, 1983).

The majority of empirical research in this area has, however, been conducted with adults. One study that stands out because it was conducted with children—and in an EFL setting—has interesting supportive evidence. This study was carried out in Spain with ten-year-old children. In 2001, Marcos Peñate Cabrera and Plácido Bazo Martínez investigated the effects of two types of story input in their English classes. One story was told to the children using simplified sentence structures and vocabulary, but without repetitions, comprehension checks, or supporting gestures (interactional modifications). The other story was told using the original story text with interactional modifications. The children's understanding was measured afterwards using a comprehension test. The results showed that the groups of children who heard the story with interactional modifications understood and recalled the story significantly better. The children were also asked in an interview for their opinion about which type of storytelling was easier to understand. All the children considered listening with interactional modifications to be easier. In addition to the linguistic features, the authors of this study also stressed the importance of using gestures as 'tools' to assist input.

To illustrate how teachers can modify their language and make messages more accessible to children, Figure 5.2 gives an example of a teacher's modifications to the story of 'The Three Billy-Goats Gruff'. This story is widely available as a folk tale for children and Materials extract 5.A gives a flavour of the original language.

We can see how the teacher in Figure 5.2 elicits information from the children, builds on what they already know, comments on the story, makes links with the children's experiences, and keeps them engaged by asking them to predict what will happen next. She also makes use of any illustrations and uses gestures which help learners to follow the storyline. She repeats language for emphasis and uses examples to highlight concepts, and she modifies language by offering alternatives and synonyms. Such input can be a very rich source of language learning and also serves as meaningful practice in listening.

The Three Billy-Goats Gruff

Once upon a time there were three billy-goats, who were to go up to the hillside to make themselves fat, and the name of all three was 'Gruff.'

On the way up was a bridge, over a burn they had to cross, and under the bridge lived a great ugly Troll with eyes as big as saucers, and a nose as long as a poker.

So first of all came the youngest billy-goat Gruff to cross the bridge.

'Trip, trap! trip, trap!' went the bridge.

'Who's that tripping over my bridge?' roared the Troll.

…

Materials extract 5.A Extract from 'The Three Billy-Goats Gruff' (www.gutenberg.org)

OK, children, have a look at this book. What is this story about? Look at the cover. It is about goats. Have you ever seen real goats? Can you count the goats? … OK, let's read the story. One upon a time there were three billy-goats. Which goat is the biggest? … Can you point? … Great! The three goats were going up the hill (gesture 'up') to find green grass. Goats like to eat grass, and grass makes them grow bigger. What do you like to eat? … The family name of these goats was 'Gruff'. What is your family name? … OK, so the goats were going onto a bridge, up on a bridge, this is the bridge, can you see the bridge? Can you point to the bridge? … What is under the bridge? … Yes, water or a river is under the bridge, and the green grass is on the other side of the river. The goats need to cross the … bridge, yes, bridge… (gesture 'to cross'). But look at this!! Who is this under the bridge? There is a great ugly troll under the bridge! An ugly troll is like a …? Yes, a monster. Troll or monster. Is he friendly? … Is he hungry? … He has got big eyes and a long nose. And his favourite lunch is … yes, goats! Who is going to cross the bridge first? … Let's see. Oh, it is the smallest billy-goat. Trip trap, trip trap, you can also make the noise with your feet, like this, trip trap, trip trap … Oh, no!!! Look here! Suddenly, the troll saw the smallest billy-goat and shouted: 'Who is that walking over my bridge?'

Figure 5.2 Teacher modifying language while telling the story

Listening activities for younger learners

Where do we start with younger learners? In order to give them plenty of listening practice and help them to tune into English, many young learners' coursebooks and resource books initially recommend activities which mainly require nonverbal responses. One such task is to listen to rhymes, action stories, or songs and enjoy them by miming the actions rather than immediately producing the language. The nonverbal contributions help to make sense of the content. The important principle is that young learners have the opportunity to absorb the language before they have to say anything. Such responses to listening are associated with **Total Physical Response** (**TPR**), an approach to language learning originally developed in the 1960s in the USA. TPR links learning to physical actions and ensures that learners hear a great deal of natural English in meaningful contexts without having to respond verbally.

Materials extract 5.B is taken from *Bebop Band 1* (Macmillan). The children listen to the audio material and point to the pictures.

Materials extract 5.B (Peimbert & Monterrubio, 2014, pp. 38–9)

In this activity new language is introduced through a song and pictures, and at the beginning the children can just look and absorb the language and mime or sing along as and when they are ready. This activity can be repeated several times until all children are confident and ready to join in with the singing. At a later stage, the children can use the animal cut-outs from the back of the book and act out the song using animal face masks. Teachers and parents/carers can download a free app that comes with the coursebook, which contains all the songs included in the book.

Most children's coursebooks contain rhymes, songs, and action stories which can be used in this way. There are also resource books in which teachers can find additional materials, and some confident and creative teachers may feel inspired to write their own. (See Chapter 9.)

A great deal of listening practice in the early years can grow out of TPR. For example, there are the so-called 'listen and respond' games such as 'Listen and clap your hands', or 'Simon says'. In these activities, children have to listen and understand messages, decide whether they are right or wrong, and act accordingly. Other activities such as 'Listen and draw the picture' or 'Listen and colour in the clown's clothes' include drawing or colouring. Yet others include simple ticking or circling or require some writing, such as true and false exercises. Many of these are focused 'Listen and do' exercises with an end product such as a drawing, a colourful clown picture, or an animal mask to take home to show parents/carers. Because of the focused nature of these tasks, it is easy for the teacher to monitor what children have understood from the listening text. These activities not only give excellent listening practice but also offer opportunities for incorporating multiple intelligences into the English class through sticking, colouring, and making simple objects. (See Chapter 1.)

In Materials extract 5.C, taken from *Family and Friends Starter* (Oxford University Press), children first listen and point to different colours and say a chant. Then they practise with each other by pointing to different colours. They can ask for a coloured pencil ('Purple, please') and say 'Here you are', and then change roles. Making a rainbow is a meaningful task, as it allows the learners to produce a real outcome to take home. Further listening practice can be added here by the teacher before the children describe their rainbows. The teacher can say: 'Cut out a purple circle, then cut out a blue circle.' 'Start with the red circle and stick the orange circle on it, then stick the yellow circle on it.'

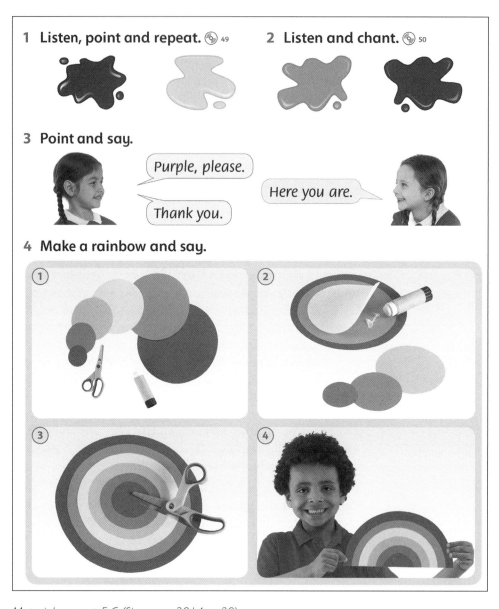

Materials extract 5.C (Simmons, 2014, p. 29)

Listening to stories is one of the most authentic and popular activities for all children, and primary English teachers can use storytelling as additional listening practice. Children will learn new language as well as having enjoyable listening practice. Language is picked up easily because stories contain repetition which makes linguistic input more noticeable. Songs, rhymes, and stories often use repetition to make the input salient in this way. Materials extract 5.D is a traditional tale, retold for young English language learners (Classic Tales, Oxford University Press). It features many types of repetitive pattern to make new language stand out.

The Magpie and the Milk

It's a beautiful day. The farmer looks in her bucket. 'Nice, warm milk! Thank you, Cow,' she says. 'I can make some cheese. But first I must make a fire.' A magpie sees the milk. 'Warm milk!' he says. 'Mmm.' He flies down and sits on the bucket. But the bucket falls over. 'Oh, no!' says the magpie.

'Bad magpie!' the farmer says, and she catches his tail. The magpie pulls and pulls. Oh! His tail comes off!

'Farmer, Farmer!' says the magpie. 'Please give me my tail.'

'Bring me some nice warm milk,' says the farmer. 'Then you can have your tail.'

The magpie talks to the cow. 'Cow, Cow,' the magpie says. 'Please give me some nice warm milk for the farmer. Then I can have my tail.'

'Bring me some long, green grass,' says the cow. 'Then you can have some milk.'

The magpie talks to the field. 'Field, Field,' the magpie says. 'Please give me some long, green grass for the cow. Then the farmer can have her milk. And I can have my tail.'

'Bring me some nice, cool water,' says the field. 'Then you can have some grass.'

The magpie talks to the river. 'River, River,' he says. 'Please give me some nice, cool water for the field. Then the cow can have her grass. The farmer can have her milk. And I can have my tail.'

'Fly up into the mountains and bring me some rain,' says the river. 'Then you can have some water.' So the magpie flies up into the mountains. He sees a big, white cloud.

'Cloud, Cloud,' he says. 'Please give me some rain for the river. Then the field can have its water. The cow can have her grass. The farmer can have her milk. And I can have my tail.'

I can help you, Magpie,' says the cloud.

And it rains. It rains on the mountains. Then the rain goes down the mountains and the river.

'Thank you, Cloud,' says the magpie. He flies down to the river.

'River, River, there's your rain,' he says. 'Now can I have some nice, cool water?'

'Yes, Magpie,' says the river. 'Here it is.'

'Thank you, River,' says the magpie. He takes the water to the field.

'Field, Field, here's your water,' he says. 'Now can I have some long, green grass?'

'Yes, Magpie,' says the field. 'Here it is.'

'Thank you, Field,' says the magpie. He takes the grass to the cow.

> 'Cow, Cow, here's your grass,' he says. 'Now, can I have some nice, warm milk?'
>
> 'Yes, Magpie,' says the cow. 'Here it is.'
>
> 'Thank you, Cow,' says the magpie. He takes the milk to the farmer.
>
> 'Farmer, Farmer, here's your milk,' he says. 'Now can I have my tail?'
>
> 'Yes, Magpie,' says the farmer.' Here it is.'
>
> She puts on the magpie's tail, and he flies away.
>
> 'There,' says the farmer. 'Now I can make my cheese.'

Materials extract 5.D (Bladon, 2015)

This is a **cumulative repetitive story**. Many simplified versions of classic tales are published as illustrated graded readers for young EFL learners. In this story (Materials extract 5.D), there is a pattern to what happens to the magpie when he asks for help from others. Each time the magpie asks for something, the same phrase is used: 'Please give me some …', and the characters always reply 'Bring me some …'. These are extremely useful phrases to practise and learn. In the second half of the story, the magpie can give everyone what they want. Here, a new set of phrases is repeated every time: 'Cow, Cow, here's your … Now can I have some …?' Because the key phrases and dialogues are repeated so many times, the story is like a meaningful drill. These patterns will be picked up by the children without much effort because they are so salient in the input. Predictability will enhance understanding, and the pictures in the book, gestures, and interactive modifications, will also help. Children will find they want to join in with parts of the story, and chanting together means that individual contributions are voluntary and safe. Those children who are not ready to can just listen. In addition to the listening practice, the recurring linguistic patterns in the dialogue between the magpie and the other characters can be developed as a model for follow-up speaking practice. Initially controlled dialogues and drill-like repetition can lead to freer dramatization or role-plays. Listening to stories, rhymes, and songs can also help children learn the words and phrases by heart, and this can be very useful because songs and rhymes contain reasonably fast connected speech in English, with shortened sounds and the use of schwa /ə/, such as in 'river' /rɪvə/.

Children of all ages like stories. Younger children enjoy stories even if they do not understand every word, and they tend to play with stories spontaneously. Heeyang Park, a South Korean teacher and parent, recorded how her five-year-old daughter played with stories in English (2014). She found that her daughter sometimes pretended to be the teacher and told a story to her teddy bears sitting on the carpet; and at other times she used objects in her bedroom, such as boxes and blankets, as props to create the scenes in the story and acted out the main roles. She also drew pictures, created story pages in writing, and enjoyed looking up her favourite stories on YouTube. She even used her mother's smartphone to record herself telling stories completely spontaneously. Park carefully recorded and documented her daughter's story-related play, talk, and writing/drawing to learn about how children enjoy stories for themselves. Such data can give teachers invaluable insights about children's spontaneous play and practice which can be used for planning future teaching materials.

Listening activities for older learners

The majority of the activities in the previous section can also be used with older learners. For example, 'Simon says' works with older learners as well, but perhaps the instructions themselves might become more challenging. Older learners also enjoy storytelling, but the teacher will have to make careful judgements about the types of story that are suitable. It is possible to look for longer stories or stories from other cultures. With older learners, it is a good idea to introduce a variety of speakers rather than just the teacher's input, because children will have to get used to faster speech, unfamiliar speakers, and different accents. Activities used with younger learners can be adapted for older ones by increasing the level of difficulty, for example by varying text length and activity types. For example, within the category of 'listen and do' it is possible to introduce activities which require quite a lot of processing, such as 'listen and identify one person', where the learners have to listen to a passage and work out which person is being described. The more people there are to choose from, the more difficult the task is. Task difficulty, therefore, is largely dependent on the kind of output required. Younger learners may be asked to join in with a story, while older learners can rewrite the story ending and act it out.

Sharon Ahlquist and Réka Lugossy, in their e-book entitled *Stories and Storyline* (2014), suggest a range of different techniques for teachers to incorporate stories for listening with older children. One of these techniques is getting learners to ask the teacher questions as they read a story (see Materials extract 5.E). This way, learners will be motivated to listen and focus on the story.

As children grow older, they get better at both bottom-up and top-down processing. They learn more about both the linguistic system and the world around them, which makes predictions and guesses more reliable. They can also alternate between these two processing skills depending on the task at hand.

Slightly older learners can also be asked to predict, describe, and explain what they hear and see. Another way to get them focused and active is to tell them the story and ask them to interrupt you with questions. This is a somewhat subversive technique, which learners of this age usually appreciate, as it is quite different from what students are traditionally expected to do (that is, listen and answer questions, rather than interrupting the teacher). Tell them that they can ask about anything and that the more interruptions, the better. Because this is an unusual task, it is important to explain the instructions carefully and, most importantly, to provide an example, so that they can clearly understand what they have to do. For example, if you start the story with: **Once upon a time there was a woman. She lived in the desert**, the spontaneous questions your students ask can include: **When? How old was she? Did she live alone? Why did she live in the desert? Which desert? What did she eat when she was hungry?** This task gives you feedback on whether learners follow the story, while it also creates opportunities for spontaneous interaction: students ask questions (which they otherwise rarely do in the classroom!) and the teacher provides more comprehensible input in the target language.

Materials extract 5.E (Ahlquist & Lugossy, 2014)

With older children, listening often goes together with speaking, reading, or even writing. For example, in Materials extract 5.F, taken from *Our World 5* (National Geographic Learning), children are asked to read an example of a description and then write their own descriptions of plants. Then the listening task comes in. They are asked to work in groups and listen carefully to each other's descriptions of plants. While they listen to each other, they take notes of their peers' descriptions. Listening to someone describing a plant and taking notes at the same time requires parallel top-down and bottom-up processing.

With smartphones and tablets more readily available, one very simple way to create authentic listening materials is to get children to record themselves. These recordings can range from short monologues that introduce a child's family, friends, house, or hobbies, to children recording dialogues, role-plays, or short presentations. These performances can be re-recorded as many times as children want to. Once the recordings are ready, they can be uploaded to a secure, shared website. Children are likely to be very motivated to listen to their own and others' recordings. Following feedback, they can further improve these recordings by using better intonation and longer sentences, or by avoiding certain grammatical mistakes. Such practice can be linked to developing metacognitive awareness and reflecting on one's own learning. (See Chapter 8.)

Descriptive Paragraphs

A descriptive paragraph describes what you see, feel, taste and hear. You can organise your description of a *person*, *place* or *thing* in different ways. You can describe the big parts first and then the small parts. You can go from big to small, from top to bottom, from the inside to the outside and so on.

18 **Read.** Read about the sensitive plant. How does the writer describe it? How does the writer organise the description?

The Sensitive Plant

Did you know that some plants can move? The sensitive plant moves when you touch it. The stem has tiny white hairs, and it stands straight up. It grows to about 50 centimetres. It has lots of thin green leaves. Each thin leaf is made of lots of tiny parts. The parts are like tiny leaves. These tiny leaves grow on both sides of each leaf stem.

When you touch a leaf, the tiny leaves fold up. Two by two, starting from where you touch, they close up. The leaf stem hangs down, too. It looks like it is hiding and does not want you to touch it. After half an hour, the plant stands up – until you touch it again!

19 **Write.** Write about the plant you invented. Describe it. Organise your description. Is your plant amazing? Why, or why not? Explain.

20 **Work in a group.** Share your writing. Listen and make notes.

Materials extract 5.F (Scro, 2014, p. 100)

Materials extract 5.G is a coursebook example promoting self-recordings from *Incredible English 5* (Oxford University Press). Teachers can, of course, adjust this by getting learners to record different individual or pair tasks, with or without a time limit.

Learning to learn - Recording yourself

Recording yourself is a good way to improve your speaking. You can record yourself on your computer or on your mobile phone.

1 Choose your topic and write notes – not sentences.

2 Start recording and speak.

3 Then listen to yourself.

Record yourself often. Start with 45 seconds and add 15 seconds every week.

Materials extract 5.G (Phillips, Grainger, & Redpath, 2012, p. 29)

Teaching speaking

Fluent speakers

Learning to speak fluently and accurately is one of the greatest challenges for all language learners. This is because, to be able to speak fluently, we have to speak and think at the same time. As we speak, we have to monitor our output and correct any mistakes, as well as plan for what we are going to say next. To be able to speak fluently in a foreign language requires a lot of practice. Speaking practice starts with practising and drilling set phrases and repeating models. A great deal of time in language classrooms is often spent on these repetitive exercises. Speaking practice, however, can also mean communicating with others in situations where spontaneous contributions are required. To be fluent, speakers will also have to learn a range of other things, such as what is appropriate to say in certain situations, how to manage conversations, and how to interrupt and offer their own contributions. It is a difficult and lengthy process to master all these sub-skills.

What is realistic for younger learners?

Children are not necessarily competent communicators even in their mother tongue with regard to some of the above sub-skills. For example, they may be unable to appreciate what other speakers already know (see Chapter 2), or may not know the rules of what is appropriate in which situation, or how to be polite when interrupting. It is important for teachers to familiarize themselves with what their students can do in their first language. At the beginning stages with children, it is a good idea to focus on simple but purposeful and meaningful pattern drilling and personalized dialogue building in order to prepare them to be able to talk about themselves and their world, and to begin to interact with their friends in class and other speakers of the language.

Speaking activities for younger learners

At the beginning in TEYL classrooms, teachers and children construct utterances together. Teachers can scaffold learners by building on and incorporating learners' utterances into their own talk. Children do not have to be able to produce complete sentences or questions to initiate an utterance. After children have been exposed to English through listening, they soon want and are able to participate in interactions with the teacher and each other.

Children also enjoy language play, and even the youngest children can enjoy simple poems, rhymes, and tongue twisters. Many coursebooks contain tongue twisters such as 'Rita rides round and round in red roller skates' (see Materials extract 5.H, taken from *New Treetops 3a*, Oxford University Press). Creative teachers and learners can collect these and even create their own examples. They are fun simply to practise with and enjoy, but learners will also remember vocabulary and structures from them.

Materials extract 5.H (Howell & Kester-Dodgson, 2012b, p. 75)

Many children will want to start saying simple phrases, join in with rhymes and songs, answer simple questions, introduce themselves, and memorize short dialogues. The first building blocks that allow children to move from listening to speaking and to begin to participate in interactions with others are so-called unanalyzed **chunks**. This means that children can remember phrases from previously heard input and use them without conscious analysis. Chunks will often be learned from the teacher's input or from other texts such as songs, rhymes, chants, stories, and dialogues. For example, if the teacher says 'See you tomorrow' at the end of every lesson, some learners will pick this up and learn it as an unanalyzed chunk. They may understand that it is like saying goodbye because the teacher always says it at the end of the lesson, but they will not be able to articulate, for example, that the phrase consists of three words, or what each word means in isolation.

All speakers of English use chunks. Some chunks are fixed while others can be complemented. Fully fixed chunks such as 'See you later', 'What a surprise', or 'What do you think' are complete and ready to use. Partially fixed chunks, such as 'Have you got', are those which require additional elements. Chunks help speakers to produce language faster because they do not have to think of the individual words. Chunks will be picked up effortlessly by the children but teachers can also explicitly choose to teach set phrases as chunks as in the following example:

A <What do you like>?

B <I like> pizza.

A <What do you like>?

C <I like> chicken.

This mini-dialogue, for example, contains a fixed chunk <What do you like> that teachers can present and practise as a whole. The other chunk <I like> is partially fixed, which the children can begin to complete by substituting the original dialogue with items that are personally relevant. These dialogues are quite limited and drill-like at the beginning, so it is essential that such practice is fun and as meaningful and purposeful as possible. One way to make drilling fun is through guessing games. For example, one child comes to the front of the classroom and mimes an animal. The rest of the class ask questions: 'Are you a monkey?' 'Are you a giraffe?' All their questions follow the same pattern. However, the purpose of the activity is meaningful to them, as whoever guesses the right answer gets to come up and mime another animal.

Many other language games which are enjoyed in foreign language classrooms also require such repetitive contributions. For example, 'I spy', 'What's the time, Mr Wolf?', 'I went to the market and got some apples, bananas, and pears …'. These activities give children a sense of security and confidence which in turn can increase their motivation levels.

Drama activities are also popular for practising speaking with young learners. Activities such as taking on new identities and talking to a finger puppet, acting out a character, or joining in a group performance all carry various benefits. Working through drama can help to develop linguistic skills, visual and spatial skills, and even emotional and affective skills. Janice Bland (2015) argues that too often young learners are presented with monodimensional texts rather than multidimensional texts involving sensory images. Drama is multidimensional, and it allows for emotional engagement and bonding with others. Drama might include work with patterned rhythmical texts, and it involves the whole person. Participating or watching drama activities can offer multiple clues for understanding. In scripted drama activities, learners can combine rote-learned lines and creativity. Performing in the second language in front of audiences brings accomplishment and pride.

Speaking activities for older learners

Many of the simple dialogues or drills can, of course, be used with older learners. Dialogues can also lead to interviews or role-play which may require some spontaneous, creative language use. Children will also have to learn how to manage more complex tasks. In order to use such tasks in classrooms, teachers may have to prepare learners. First of all, it is important to teach children phrases which allow them to check what they did not hear or cannot make sense of (for example, 'Sorry, I don't understand. What did you say?'). Teachers can equip learners with useful classroom language such as 'It's your turn', 'Please give me the dice', 'Which one is mine?', 'What have you got?' to manage interactive games and tasks. Such language can be displayed on posters. Some of the tasks might require that the learners pay attention to what their partner is saying, ask for and give clarification, repair a communication breakdown, or express themselves explicitly, with extra care. This is all part of learning to learn. (See Chapter 8.)

Collaborative activities are tasks that require children to work together—for example, acting out a scene or telling a story together, or recreating a text that was cut up. They need to be able to listen carefully to each other, suggest ways of doing things and discuss different alternatives, and finally make decisions as a group. All this means that they need to use their first language in most contexts, or a combination of first and second languages. If, however, teachers explicitly teach useful phrases in English, children may be able to switch to using their second language for these discussions for some of the time. (See Chapter 8.)

Need for meaning negotiation

Information-gap tasks, where participants A and B have different information, often require that children say things creatively on the spot and describe details of visuals to each other with some precision. They might have to initiate questions and volunteer information as well as respond to their partners' questions appropriately. These tasks also require that children learn to pay attention to what their partner is saying, check understanding, clarify meaning, and monitor the progression of the task carefully. Information-gap tasks, discussion tasks, and other complex speaking tasks can hide various demands. It is important for teachers to explore these difficulties with their students and provide plenty of practice of new task types. Table 5.1 summarizes the most common demands and provides simple examples.

Demands	Definition	Example
1 Linguistic	Aspects of difficulty such as what type of language is required for a particular task and to what extent the learners can select the linguistic forms they wish to use	In a picture description task, the learner is free to use 'I can see', 'I have got', 'In my picture there is', etc. without any restriction. Can the learners choose? Should the teacher model the language?
2 Referential	The need to establish unambiguously what the other person knows or has got	When learners reconstruct a picture from two incomplete versions, they first need to establish what parts they share. They need safe reference points to refer back to as they build the picture together. Can they establish these safe points? Have they got the English to do this?
3 Cognitive	Demands relate to attention, memory, and reasoning limitations. Logical or mathematical operations needed	The game called 'Complete a list of clock faces or numbers' (by discovering the rule) or playing 'noughts and crosses' in teams both require adhering to some rules of logic. Can the children play these games in their first language?
4 Metacognitive	Demands which refer to the need in a task or a game to monitor own performance closely while carrying out the task	Learners may need to change tactics midway in a noughts and crosses game depending on which squares the other team takes. Can they play this in their first language?
5 Interactional	Demands which refer to aspects of turn taking, i.e. whether it is obligatory or not in a particular task, conversational management skills, or meaning negotiation	The need to double-check confusing instructions on a map task by using meaning negotiation moves such as clarification requests

Table 5.1 Demands in interactive tasks

During games and interactive tasks, learners often have to negotiate meaning, i.e. make sure that they understand each other. Research shows that children's ability to negotiate meaning when they do not understand something grows gradually with age, and older learners can successfully repair conversation breakdowns. For example, in 2007 a study by Alison Mackey and her colleagues in Australia showed that ESL learners as young as seven or eight years of age were able to negotiate meaning and did especially well when they were working with familiar tasks as opposed to unfamiliar tasks. Various classic gap tasks were used in the study, where children had to place animals and objects on different parts of a picture by asking questions of their partners. The children willingly negotiated meaning in both types of tasks, but feedback that led to reformulations, i.e. the use of correct phrases following initial incorrect language, was more frequent in the familiar tasks. The authors of the study advise, however, that teachers may want to mix familiar and less familiar tasks and content in their classrooms to maintain high levels of motivation and avoid the boredom that comes from repeating the same familiar tasks over and over again.

It is important for teachers to exercise their best judgement when selecting tasks for older and more experienced learners, because tasks need to be motivating but not too difficult. Creating a positive learning environment can certainly help. Children will speak up and contribute to the lesson if they feel happy and secure. It is also crucial that children understand that they can speak up even when they are not sure about their contributions or have only a fragmented answer or idea to offer. Teachers can foster such understanding by providing careful error correction and plenty of encouragement. Children also need purposeful activities which create a communicative need and fuel their motivation to listen and speak. It is often a good idea to talk to children in their first language about the importance of practice in speaking. Teachers may want to encourage practising at home with parents/carers and siblings. Teachers may also want to advise parents/carers about how to help their children; for example, parents/carers can listen to songs, rhymes, and chants, practise dialogues, and encourage any discussion about English with their children.

Dynamic/emergent tasks

Learners creating listening and speaking tasks

New touchscreen technologies are changing the way listening and speaking tasks are designed and performed. Instead of tasks that are given to the children on paper or in coursebooks, more dynamic types of tasks are emerging. In a Canadian study published in 2014, Martine Pellerin reported on how young children in early French immersion programmes were taking charge of classroom tablets to create their own tasks. These six- and seven-year-old children were making their own finger puppets and then their own puppet shows. Working in pairs and small groups, the children then took turns to record their puppet shows on tablets. In this way, they created authentic listening activities for themselves and other children who wanted to see what their friends had created. All the children wanted to recreate their original shows and make them better. Pellerin describes this way of working as motivating for the children because it is multimodal, encourages genuine collaboration with peers, and requires high levels of engagement. Recordings of performances saved on a device can be further shared and uploaded to school websites for everyone to see.

Storyline: complex learner-driven projects

Sharon Ahlquist, in an *ELT Journal* article published in 2012, describes an inspiring variation of task-based learning in Sweden with learners of 11–13 years of age. In a **storyline**, learners assume roles in an unfolding narrative and work collaboratively on tasks that combine language work with practical jobs. In the example that Ahlquist describes, the learners develop their own characters as members of families that live on the same street somewhere in England. The learners work on their own identities and then on the design of their houses and gardens. In the course of the storyline, the learners worked on organizing a street party, interviewed the new residents, learned about environmentally friendly ways of living, created advertisements for selling things, and showed people around their houses. Ahlquist claims that learners found this way of working enjoyable because it seemed real to them, they could work collaboratively on meaningful tasks, and they felt they could use their imagination. The teacher also noticed that their language developed, they used their second language creatively and willingly, and they were eager to find out information and learn for themselves. Ahlquist argues that this is a great way of injecting motivation and excitement into a class and, even though she focuses more on storyline ideas for older children, she believes that storyline is an approach that is suitable for younger learners as well.

Summary

Listening and speaking are the two most important skills in most TEYL programmes. The development of listening can form the basis of initial speaking practice, and there should be many opportunities in the class to combine listening and speaking through meaningful activities. Both younger and older learners need plenty of practice with listening and speaking activities, and they need to be given the confidence to speak up. It is important for teachers to plan both their listening and speaking activities according to their learners' age, interests, and abilities.

Suggestions for further reading

Ahlquist, S., & **Lugossy, R.** (2015). *Stories and Storyline*. Hong Kong: Candlin & Mynard ePublishing.
This is an e-book about different kinds of stories used in a variety of ways, with a common purpose: to develop the communicative language skills of young learners. The book contains research-based support for the structured use of stories. Practical ways of working with stories are clearly explained, and there is a wealth of ideas about how teachers might explore the pedagogical benefits of stories or the storyline approach in their own classrooms.

Cameron, L. (2001). *Teaching languages to young learners*. Cambridge: Cambridge University Press.
This is a comprehensive book about classroom language learning for children, covering a large range of topics. It takes the view that teaching and learning the

spoken language through effective listening and speaking activities and tasks can provide an effective basis for developing later literacy skills.

Ellis, G., & **Brewster, J.** (2002). *Tell it again! The new storytelling handbook for primary teachers.* London: Penguin Longman.
This is an excellent resource for teachers and teacher trainers with some theory and plenty of practical ideas on storytelling. The book contains a collection of 12 popular stories used and told all over the world with suggestions on how to exploit them for learning English as a foreign language.

Mourão, S. (2015). The potential of picturebooks with young learners. In J. Bland (Ed.), *Teaching English to young learners: Critical issues in language teaching with 3–12 year olds.* (pp. 199–218). London: Bloomsbury.
Working with picture books is a rewarding experience for both teachers and learners, and the exploration of authentic content can involve a range of meaningful listening and speaking practice for children. This paper offers some excellent ideas about working with stories with interesting cultural content for all age groups, from preschoolers to young adolescents.

Oliver, R., & **Philp, J.** (2014). *Focus on oral interaction.* Oxford: Oxford University Press.
This is comprehensive book which explores the role of interaction in classroom language learning, making excellent links between research and practice via analyzing classroom extracts. Chapter 3 in particular looks at the role and nature of classroom interaction with children. Teacher–learner as well as learner–learner interactions are considered, highlighting features specific to children.Online resources and free sample material can be found at: www.oup.com/elt/teacher/foi

Tasks

If you would like to explore your own practice related to the content of this chapter, you can try the following tasks:

Task 6: Working creatively with materials (page 186)

Task 13: Recording your own lessons (page 191)

Task 17: Getting the children to record themselves regularly (page 195)

Task 19: Exploring group presentations (page 195)

Task 20: Cultural self-portraits (page 196)

Task 21: Exploring cultural content in books or other materials (page 196)

Task 22: Making class posters (page 196)

Task 23: Conversations with children based on drawings (page 197)

6 TEACHING READING AND WRITING

Introduction

Are there any good reasons why reading and writing should be introduced in the TEYL curriculum, despite the main emphasis in most programmes being on speaking and listening? In order to appreciate the demands of learning to read and write in other languages, this chapter will compare how first and second languages are taught and learned and suggest ways in which reading and writing in English as a second language can be introduced and gradually built up with children. Thanks to the ever-increasing availability of access to the internet, new reading and writing opportunities are also opening up online for younger learners of English.

Why teach reading and writing in TEYL classes?

Unfortunately, there is no formula to follow and no single most effective technique to use when it comes to teaching native-speaker children to read English. Needless to say, if there is no formula for teaching reading to children whose first language is English, then there is certainly no formula for teaching children to read in English as a second or foreign language, especially as second language contexts can be varied and complex. Whether reading and writing are introduced at all—and if yes, then when and how—will depend on many factors, such as the age of the children, the level of their exposure to English as a second language, their first language background, their ability to read in their first language, and their interest in learning to read in a second language.

In bilingual contexts, learning to read and write in two or more languages often happens at the same time. This means that certain reading skills, such as learning to guess the meaning from the context or using illustrations to help with the process of decoding, can be transferred between languages. In fact, for immigrant children in their new language environment, first language literacy can act as a useful scaffold. It makes sense to draw parallels between first and second language literacy practices. Jim Cummins' theory of a 'common underlying proficiency' (2000), for example, clearly suggests that academic skills in the first language promote the same skills in the second language, and that developing academic literacy skills in each language accelerates development in both languages. The problem is that in many contexts this is not feasible due to the lack of resources and trained teachers, and because many policymakers believe that focusing on one language alone—the second language—will ultimately bring more success.

In contexts where children are learning a foreign language, the general consensus is that children should learn to read in their mother tongue first, and when they are reasonably competent they can learn to read in a foreign language. It would be controversial to introduce reading and writing in another language to children who are not yet literate in their first language. However, once literacy in one language is established, children often expect to learn to read in the new language, too. In fact, the most convincing reason for teaching reading and writing in English is that many children show both interest and enthusiasm in doing so when they start learning English.

Many young learners are, in fact, active readers and writers in their first language and take second language reading for granted. One example is the case of those ESL/EFL learners who regularly play online games in English. In these games, children communicate with other game players by typing in messages, and they read instructions as well as authentic messages using their limited English. In a study published in 2014, a South Korean researcher, Sang Ah Sarah Jeon, found that, even though formal English instruction starts when children are nine years old in South Korea, a large majority of 10–14-year-olds participate regularly in online games, and many of them spend substantial amounts of time after school playing with children of different language backgrounds. Jeon found that the children who played regularly (six to ten hours a week) benefited greatly in terms of learning English, and also in terms of boosting self-esteem and developing a second language identity. In an environment where the game is the main focus, children feel less anxious about using their English, and they learn English without noticing it. Some of the children in this study also reported that playing with other children from various countries and using English for genuine communication is motivating, and they are now taking more interest in formal English learning by looking up phrases in dictionaries and other sources to be able to say more. Jeon conclusion is that it is very important for teachers in different contexts to find out what extra opportunities young learners may have for using English outside the classroom, as these experiences could be usefully built on in formal classroom teaching.

Early literacy in English as a first language

In order to make some principled decisions about EFL reading and writing for young learners' programmes, it is useful to explore how children learn to read in English as a first language. The process for EFL learners will be different, but this is still a useful starting point because, without some familiarity with the process in the first language, the process of learning to read and write in the second language cannot be understood.

Reading and writing during preschool years

During their preschool years, English-speaking children learn about literacy within their culture from a range of different experiences. Quite early on, often as early as at the age of three, they begin to recognize written words and signs in their environment, such as the name of their street, their local park, or their nursery school. Children who are regularly read to by their parents/carers will notice that storybooks contain letters and words in addition to pictures, and that adults actually look at the words to tell the story. Most children also have the chance to observe their parents/carers reading books or engaging in other relevant reading and writing activities at home, such as filling in forms, writing lists and cards, or reading and writing using tablets and computers. Children learn very early on to write their name and other significant words such as 'mummy', 'daddy', or a friend's or sibling's name. They will begin to understand that messages, stories, or anything we say can be represented on a page using symbols. All these experiences will prepare children to read and write themselves. They will begin to see reasons and purposes for reading: for enjoyment or simply to find out about something—for example, reading the television guide either in the paper or online to find out what time a cartoon is on. By the time children go to school in the UK, at the age of four or five, they have a fairly good understanding of many literacy practices and activities and are well on their way to being able to decode the system of symbols for reading and writing. Building on these initial experiences, the role of the primary school is to continue introducing ever more sophisticated literacy skills to children.

Reading and writing at school

English native-speaker children possess a great resource to build on when they begin to tackle reading formally at school. This resource is their oral competence in their first language, in particular their large bank of words and phrases. Oral language proficiency is directly related to the ability to learn to read, because the solid knowledge of oral language helps children to make intelligent guesses when attempting to read, simply by drawing on what they think would make sense. This is a great advantage in top-down processing. For example, let us imagine that an English native-speaker child is reading the beginning of a story and can work out that the first word is 'Once'. Then, without having to read the next word, they can make a reasonable guess that the rest of the phrase is 'upon a time'. This happens because the child knows this phrase is frequently used at the beginning of stories. This knowledge will make it unnecessary to decode the words on the page in isolation. Based on the context, the child can make good predictions about what would be a likely phrase or word.

For English native-speaker children, the process of learning to read and write takes rather a long time because in English the letter and sound correspondence is not at all direct and consistent. Esther Geva and Min Wang, researchers interested in cross-linguistic perspectives of learning to read, refer in their 2001 survey article to languages such as English as having **deep orthographies**. In English, the pronunciation does not always help with the writing! For example, think of words such as 'enough' and 'thought' or 'height' and 'weight'. The written similarities between these pairs of words do not lead to similar pronunciation. Many other languages that use the Roman alphabet, such as Spanish or German, for example, are described as having more **shallow orthographies** because there is more consistency between what a word sounds like and how it is written. In such languages, the process of learning to read and write takes less time and appears to be less complicated.

In order to teach aspects of the English language system that are regular, English primary schools teach letter–sound correspondence patterns (**phonics**) to all children. Songs and rhymes are great for teaching phonics because they contain rhyming words; for example, 'One, two, three, four, five, once I caught a fish alive', where 'five' and 'alive' both rhyme and follow the same written pattern. With this approach, learners are encouraged to recognize analogies below word level to help them to work out how to read and write words. They are taught to notice that each word has an onset (first consonant or consonants) and a rime (the rest of the word), and that it is useful to group together words which have a different onset but the same rime because they are pronounced the same way. For example, consider: c(at), b(at), m(at), s(at), p(at), h(at), fl(at). The initial consonant is salient, but the rime of all of these is the same. Recognizing patterns like this will be useful in reading. Traditional nursery rhymes are full of such rhyming pairs, so children find it quite easy to get a feel for rhymes. For example, consider: 'the cow jumped over the m(oon)' and 'the dish ran away with the sp(oon)'; or 'Humpty Dumpty sat on a w(all)' and 'Humpty Dumpty had a great f(all)'; or 'Jack and J(ill) went up the h(ill)'. Many native English children know these rhymes by heart, so it is easy for them to notice the patterns in a meaningful context.

With regard to words that are irregular, another strategy is used in teaching reading in schools. Often called the 'whole word method', it encourages the rote learning of some 'sight vocabulary' that children can immediately recognize when reading. This method helps children to see and remember words as visual images. The idea is that these words will be recognized immediately , making decoding unnecessary. Knowing a large pool of such vocabulary is helpful because it allows children to concentrate on processing longer, unfamiliar words, and therefore speeds up reading in general.

Teaching reading in TEYL classes

In most second language contexts, children do not have a strong background in oral English when they start learning to read and write in the language. Their oral proficiency is typically low, and they are not necessarily familiar with a wide range of songs, rhymes, and stories in English which feature everyday phrases useful for guessing words or for phonics work. Children can only benefit from phonics training if the meaning of the words makes sense to them. It is not good practice to get children to sound out words that they are not familiar with.

Children who are non-native speakers bring some advantages to the process of learning to read and write in English. The greatest of these is their experience of reading and writing in their first language. They usually come to English already able to read and write in their first language, and they bring with them some potentially useful strategies. Although the first language influences the process of learning to read in English, the point of similarity is that the children have some understanding of what reading involves. With regard to the strategies they bring, how they learned to read in their first language can influence how they read in the second language. Non-native speakers are likely to use reading strategies that worked in their first language, such as recognizing spelling patterns, trying to sound things out, and comparing sounds and letters. Of course, it is important to remember that the degree to which they have mastered one reading system can vary greatly.

The linguistic characteristics of their first language also make a difference. There are languages that use **morphographic** or **logographic** writing systems, where each symbol represents an idea (such as Chinese, and one writing system of Japanese); or syllabic signs (for example, Korean, where each word is made from alphabet letters which are combined to form compact syllabic blocks); and those that use **phonographic** writing systems (for example, English, Spanish, or Russian). Naturally, children whose first language uses a phonographic writing system—and, in particular, the Roman alphabet—will find beginning to read and write in English easier than those whose first language uses other types of writing system. For example, Russian children learn to read and write using the Cyrillic alphabet, and though this alphabet is closer to English than, for example, Korean or Chinese, it can still present some difficulties. So it will be important to discover the differences and overlaps between the Cyrillic and Roman alphabets. For example, Russian children will have to learn that the letter P in English is pronounced /p/ rather than /r/ as it is in their first language. In addition, children whose first language reads from right to left and/or top to bottom will have to start by learning to adapt to a different orientation when reading books in English.

Reading activities for younger learners

As was suggested in Chapter 5 on speaking and listening, reading and writing in the primary foreign language classroom do not need to involve the use of fully developed skills from the very beginning. Rather, it is advisable to start with working on sub-skills such as learning to decode familiar written language, match spoken and written forms, or complete short texts with personally relevant information.

The most basic sub-skills include learning to write the letters of the alphabet. Internationally available coursebooks for very young learners, who are just beginning to learn to read and write, include a great deal of basic letter-tracing types of exercise. Typically, these books go through the English alphabet and introduce each letter one by one and get the children to trace, circle, recognize, and write individual letters. There is an initial emphasis on the first letter of the words (A for apple, B for boy, C for cat, and D for duck). Materials extract 6.A is an example of these types of exercise, from *Family and Friends Starter* (Oxford University Press).

Materials extract 6.A (Simmons, 2014, p. 46)

Knowing the names of the letters will not help the children to read, but it will enable them to spell words in English. They can practise spelling their own or their friends' names, play word games such as Hangman, solve simple word puzzles such as guessing which letter has been removed from a sentence, match letters, or complete dot-to-dot exercises to find words hidden in 'letter boxes'. It is a good idea to display the alphabet in the classroom and practise singing the alphabet song on a regular basis.

At the beginning of a programme with younger learners, the teacher might introduce written words to familiarize children with the written language. For example, one could label objects such as tables, chairs, whiteboard, window, door, pictures, plants, books, and shelves by making word cards, laminating them, and hanging them up around the classroom. This would make the children curious about reading and writing and illustrate to them that words they are familiar with orally can be represented in writing. There are, of course, many other types of writing that can be displayed in any classroom. For example, one could make posters presenting commonly used phrases such as 'sit down', 'come here', and 'it is your turn', or a calendar with the names of the days and months, or a class birthday chart, or an English noticeboard. (See Figure 6.1.) Teachers can also introduce letter cards or magnetic letters to encourage children to play with letters and letter combinations to make words, and also make use of online games and apps.

Figure 6.1 A classroom full of written language display

In order to practise word-level reading, many different games and activities can be used. One well-known memory card game which involves matching pictures and words is often played. Children play in teams and pick up two cards each at their turn and see if they match. Similarly, games such as 'word snap' and 'dominoes' can be played in small groups or pairs. Teachers can make their own word cards and picture cards and play simple matching, categorizing, or 'spot the missing card' games. Many coursebooks for young learners have their own packs of cards, with a set of instructions for the teacher. Cards can be used during storytelling as well as other activities for vocabulary teaching. Doing a lot of work with word cards will help to build up children's sight vocabulary of commonly used words in English. These kinds of activities can also be done via digital platforms.

In order to reinforce patterns that are regular in English, it is advisable to include some phonics when teaching children to read and write in a second language. Activities can include categorizing words according to what sounds they begin with, and creating sound banks. The difficulty here is that the children's ability to create useful patterns is limited at the beginning by their relative lack of vocabulary. With phonics exercises, it is important to keep a balance between usefulness and pattern building. If the meanings are unknown, long lists of words exemplifying the same pattern are not useful to children. Familiar songs and rhymes can be exploited in this way to focus children's attention on patterns in a meaningful way.

Materials extract 6.B is an example of a short chant focusing on [ir] and [ur] from *Oxford Phonics World 5* (Oxford University Press). Creative teachers and children might like to write their own chants as well.

Materials extract 6.B (Schwermer, Chang, & Wright, 2013, p. 7)

Introducing reading beyond word level should happen gradually. Following on from practice with word cards, it is, of course, possible to play with sentences and phrases. The teacher can chop up sentences and get the children to put them back together in the correct order. Similarly, familiar songs, rhymes, and poems can also be chopped up and reconstructed. Depending on how familiar the language in these exercises is to the children, the activity can be of varying difficulty. Common sense suggests it is best to have plenty of encouraging practice with familiar language first. At a later stage, the teacher can introduce gap-fill activities which combine reading and some writing. Another supportive way to progress from reading individual words is to let children follow texts, dialogues, songs, or rhymes in the coursebook while listening to them. Teachers can get the children to read short texts and dialogues to provide them with oral practice.

In the case of younger children, it is important to progress slowly with reading in a foreign language. Reading is a holistic process which involves learning many skills, such as predicting, noticing patterns, and guessing. It is a good idea to make this process **multisensory** by including crafting, colouring, body movements, and sounds. (See Chapter 1.)

In some parts of the world, where books and other reading materials are in short supply, teachers can write reading materials themselves. In Nepal, an inspired teacher trainer, Babita Sharma Chapagain, wrote her own texts and also encouraged older children to write texts for younger children.

Here is an example of a story by Chapagain:

I'm sorry

My name is Muna. I study in grade III. I am not perfect. I make mistakes. Sometimes when I feel bored I want to do something to amuse myself.

I can't help it. I happen to do some mischief like jumping around in the class, hopping like a frog, asking silly questions to the teacher, pulling friends' hair, making funny faces, blowing a whistle and swinging on the door. But then when I see my pretty teacher's sad face, I feel that she is hurt. So I smile and say, 'I'm sorry, teacher. I will not do it again.' She forgives me. I try not to repeat my mistakes.

It is clear that the story was intended as a model. Others can now write about what they feel sorry for and who they want to apologize to. Some of these texts might be written with a clear focus on certain grammatical patterns or types of vocabulary, as well as a message that is meaningful to the learners. Creative teachers and learners could experiment with writing texts for one another. Texts can be very short and simple and gradually become longer and more demanding.

This is a wonderfully economical way of working with texts, and it is motivating for both writers and readers. Children who write for younger classes learn about constructing good texts in English with the help of the teacher, and they can also use their creative talents as illustrators. Being a writer is very motivating, and it gives children a sense of accomplishment. The younger children will also be more motivated to read stories written by other children rather than by adults, and they can also become interested in writing by following others' examples. Even though this is a practice that is happening in a developing country context where real books are hard to find, children writing for other children in English can be incorporated as good practice in any context. Even in schools where there are lots of books, children might write their own stories for other children. Computers can also be used to create books in contexts where they are readily available.

Reading activities for older learners

Many older children, especially beginners, will enjoy word-level and sentence-level practice with reading. However, they will soon want to progress further. Reading for meaning entails doing exercises which encourage children to skim and scan texts in order to understand the meaning. Older children can be taught that there are many cues that they can use while reading. Semantic cues include those that help them to guess the meaning, for example from illustrations. They will also help as learners look at the structure of sentences and ask questions such as 'Is this a question or a statement?' or 'Is this sentence about the past or the present?'. Phonological cues such as relating spelling patterns to typical pronunciation patterns can also help. Older learners also enjoy dictionary work. They may be introduced to different types of dictionaries, such as English–English dictionaries, picture dictionaries, bilingual dictionaries, or electronic dictionaries.

Working with simplified texts such as 'readers' is a good way to encourage children to read for meaning by themselves. If at all possible, teachers should try to get hold of a class set so that everyone can have their own copy, as this can have an additional motivating effect. Reading a book, even if it is a simplified reader, can help children to stay motivated about English and give them a tremendous sense of accomplishment. Materials extract 6.C is an example of the first two pages from an *Oxford Read and Imagine* reader entitled *The Big Storm* (Oxford University Press). The main characters of the story are introduced here, and interest is created by placing the van in the middle of the picture. The actual story is 18 pages long, and the rest of the book is devoted to additional activities. There are grammar- and vocabulary-related activities, followed by project and picture dictionary pages. Children can read the story alone, together as a class, or in pairs supporting each other. There is also a CD with audio material so some or all of the text can be turned into a listening task. Children can read a few pages at a time and work on the activities at the back of the book. A reader like this works well for mixed-ability classes where faster learners can do additional work.

When children enjoy readers, they are eager to choose new titles to read outside class, and they can even become inspired to write similar stories. As a general rule, it is best not to over-emphasize grammar and vocabulary and learning every word, because enjoyment and a sense of accomplishment come from actually finishing the book in a reasonable amount of time.

Materials extract 6.C (Shipton, 2014, pp. 2–3)

Children who enjoy reading something in their first language, such as the Harry Potter books, typically read these texts very carefully, perhaps more than once, and watch any film versions too. Once they are really familiar with the first language texts, it might be possible to encourage them to read it in their second language as well. It is not uncommon for children who have loved a translated book to want to attempt to read the original English text, after familiarizing themselves with the text in their first language. Familiarity with the text in the first language serves as an important scaffold, and it allows the less experienced reader to make progress with the text in their second language.

There are many digital libraries to explore on the internet. One popular example is *Storybird* (https://storybird.com). This is a great place where readers and writers of all ages can browse stories and try out their creative talents in story or poetry writing. If you want to write a story for your class, you can use existing artwork and add your own words to it. Your story will be read and enjoyed by a supportive community, and you might even get some 'followers'.

Teaching writing in TEYL classes

What do native speaker children write?

Writing is a complex skill progressing from the level of tracing, to copying familiar words and phrases, to developing an awareness of text structures and genres, to the processes of drafting and editing, to writing for an audience. Reading and writing are usually taught in parallel because children who begin to read enjoy writing, too. English native speaker children begin with what we call 'emergent writing'. This starts with pretend writing, and then the children gradually begin to write words and short texts but without knowing exactly how to spell. They utilize their early phonics knowledge from reading, and emergent writing is often combined with drawings. The example in Figure 6.2 was written by a five-year-old over a period of several months. The progress from pretend writing to simple story writing is clearly evident here.

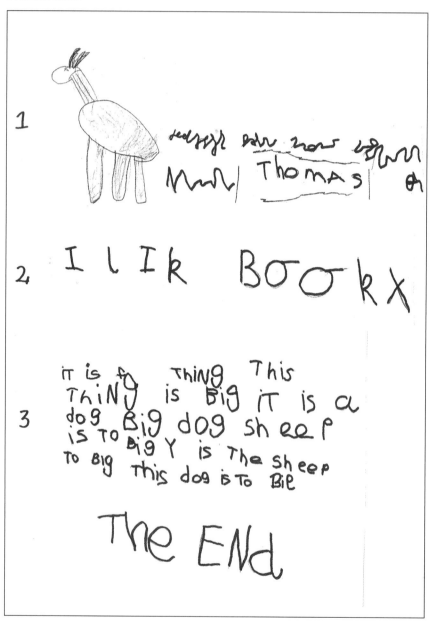

Figure 6.2 Example of a native speaker five-year-old's writing

During the first years of formal schooling, native speaker children learn to trace and connect letters to make words. They learn to use basic punctuation marks and start composing passages such as simple story endings and messages, invitations, or cards, slowly progressing towards creative, independent writing and drafting.

Writing activities for younger learners in TEYL classes

Depending on their specific language background and the type of writing system of their first language, EFL learners may need more or less practice with the mechanical basics of writing. It is useful for these learners to start with tracing and copying. In order to make these early mechanical activities fun, teachers can vary the activities, for example introducing creative copying in which learners select which words to copy from a list, then add one on their own. Other examples include copying only words which refer to some kind of food, or copying only those which contain the letter T, or copying only the names of animals that appeared in the story. Copying can also be done as a follow-up to an oral activity. For example, the teacher might get the learners to brainstorm lists of words or phrases to write on the board, then later ask the class to copy these words into their exercise books.

Moving on from copying, many games and activities popular in the primary classroom involve word-level writing; for example, games which involve pairs of children creating 'word snakes' for each other, correcting words where the letters have been mixed up or written backwards, and creating and solving simple (four- to five-word) puzzles. (See Figure 6.3.) These are also excellent activities for children to design for each other. For example, they could create their own crossword puzzles which can be given to classmates to solve.

Another popular type of writing practice is finger writing, which follows a multisensory approach. This involves writing on different surfaces, which requires children to get up from their chairs and move around. Using their fingers, children can write in the air, on each other's backs, or in the sand outside, and they can either simply copy words or write creatively.

In most contexts, children use an activity book as well as a coursebook. The activity book contains written grammar and vocabulary exercises which practise writing at word or sentence level. These can be gap-fill exercises or those which involve matching pictures with words or sentences. They all help learners to practise writing using familiar language. Many teachers use guided writing of some kind. This means, just as in guided speaking tasks, that there is a framework or some kind of a model for learners to complete with their own ideas and relevant details, for example cards, invitations, letters, stories, or posters. These genres are important because they can be used to introduce the idea of writing for an audience, and learners can begin to see that we write differently depending on who we are writing for. Guided writing activities can be motivating because they allow children to write longer pieces of text by substituting their personally relevant messages into a given frame. These products can also be displayed or taken home.

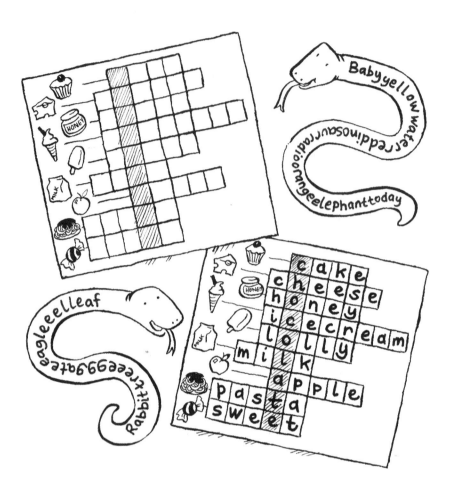

Figure 6.3 Simple word puzzles

Materials extract 6.D is from *New Treetops 3a* (Oxford University Press).
The children are asked to complete a model letter with some missing words which
are provided in the box. It is much easier to write a letter by simply filling in the
gaps rather than writing everything from scratch. The pictures inserted into the
text provide further support and clues about the missing words. Teachers can easily
modify this activity and make it either easier or harder. For example, you could cut
up the letter and ask the students to put the sections back in the correct order, or
take out more words from the letter. Once children have worked with letter frames
such as these, they may be able to move on to writing letters by themselves.

3 Write a letter.

| nine café shops Petal you from |

14 Strawberry Lane

Flower Town

Hello!

My name's _____. I'm _____ Flower Town.

I'm **9** _____. How old are _____?

In my town, there's a _____ and there are lots of

_____. What's in your town?

Write soon.

Love, Petal.

Materials extract 6.D (Howell & Kester-Dodgson, 2012b, p. 16)

Writing activities for older children in TEYL classes

Older learners also need practice with word- and sentence-level writing and spelling, but they may also be ready for freer writing. This can start with filling in captions in speech bubbles in a group cartoon story, or writing instructions, scripts, shopping lists, recipes, and puzzles, or simple diaries or blogs, or short messages within an email group. The introduction of various written genres will further enhance the learners' appreciation of different audiences. They may begin to see clear reasons for writing; for example, to fill in forms, write their own stories, or produce their own class newspaper.

It is good to use word processing because doing so makes it possible to have a good-quality end product and because making corrections in the editing and redrafting processes is easier and less time-consuming. Many teachers nowadays work with secure, restricted-access websites (such as https://padlet.com) where they can upload student work as well as their own input materials.

Encouraging written communication with real people—such as when a group of children in one country writes to a group of children in another country—can be very motivating. Teachers can set up email accounts for everybody in the class and encourage communication within the group both during and after classes. The internet is a great source of information that children can use with a teacher's guidance. For example, they can search for useful tourist information or timetable details. Creating English websites is a great way of getting older children to practise and enjoy writing. Many teaching resource books suggest further ideas for authentic writing.

Researcher Graham Stanley (2013) describes how an Egyptian teacher working with 12-year-old children collaborated with another teacher in Argentina simply by using Skype, with just one computer in the classroom. The children in Egypt were learning about rainforests in their English lesson, their teacher had the idea to interview some similar-aged children and their teacher about rainforests in Argentina via Skype. This interview was recorded by the teacher and used as a basis for further materials and learning in the classroom. The children listened to this authentic recording several times and completed a writing task based on the information they had learned. The children's feedback was overwhelmingly positive and, following the Skype sessions, a closed Facebook group was set up to continue the written interaction between the children. The truly genuine communication on Facebook and Skype was motivating for all learners in the project, and the Egyptian teacher decided to keep using Skype in her classroom.

In many contexts, once children can read and write, teachers give homework which often involves doing exercises from a workbook. It is worth exploring other fun options for homework, such as making writing puzzles for each other or letting children choose from a range of reading and writing tasks. Where teachers are convinced of the positive role of homework in learning, it is important to allocate time to check or discuss this work. Parents/Carers who are aware of how best to support their children can help a great deal with homework.

Research shows that learners who work together in pairs on tasks that ask them to write texts such as stories or letters do much better together than they could have done on their own. This is because, during the process of writing, it is important to focus on both the message and the grammatical correctness of the writing. Children can usefully help and scaffold for each other during this process. The work of Merrill Swain and her colleagues in Canada (see Swain & Lapkin, 1998) clearly shows that interactive writing tasks can stimulate learning. Working on a piece of writing together with a friend is also beneficial in terms of sustaining interest and motivation.

Sharing your plan for a piece of writing with someone is a useful learning exercise, and sharing final pieces for feedback can be equally useful. The example in Materials extract 6.E is taken from *Our World 6* (National Geographic Learning). First, the learners are asked to read the model text carefully and pay particular attention to the connecting expressions. Then, in task 18, the learners are asked to write a short paragraph about a person of their own choice, following the model. Finally, task 19 asks learners to share their writing, providing them with an opportunity to give corrective feedback to each other.

Biographical Paragraphs

A biographical paragraph describes the life of another person. When you write a biographical paragraph, you can make it more interesting for the reader if you connect the dates and events in that person's life. Words you can use to link the dates and events include: *After (that), before, since then, the next year, then, at the time, suddenly* and *afterwards*.

 Read. Read the biography. Underline the expressions that are used to link the events.

High Climber

Before the age of nine, Matt Moniz enjoyed summer holidays like all children do. Then his life suddenly changed. Matt's father invited him to join a climb to Mount Everest. At the time, Matt did not know what to expect, but he said afterwards that the experience was 'the best of his life'. After that, there was no stopping him! The next year, he climbed two of the world's highest mountains: Africa's Kilimanjaro and Russia's Elbrus. Then, at the age of ten, he climbed Argentina's Aconcagua (a height of 6,962 metres). Since then, Matt has climbed more mountains with his dad. In 2010, Matt became the youngest person in the world to climb the highest point in all fifty states in the USA – in record time. He loves the outdoors and often talks to other children about spending more time outdoors.

18 **Write.** Write a short biographical paragraph about someone who has an exciting job, does an exciting sport or has travelled to exciting places. Remember to link the events and dates with connecting expressions.

19 **Work in a small group.** Share your writing.

Materials extract 6.E (Cory-Wright, 2014, p. 16)

Writing in the second language, even for older children whose proficiency may be higher, often remains a challenging task. Materials extract 6.E clearly illustrates the types of support that can be built into writing tasks to help learners to stay motivated, such as giving them model texts and getting them to collaborate when planning, while writing, and/or after the first draft is finished.

In fact, one of the most important sources of support is collaboration with a peer. Collaborative writing tasks are fun, and they allow learners to pool their knowledge. Moreover, research shows that collaborating with a peer may take away some of the pressures of second language writing. One good way to encourage creative writing is to start small and do it in groups. For example, the teacher might put learners in groups of four and give each group the beginning of the same cartoon story. The story might be quite simple, with just two pictures and two paragraphs relating to the pictures. Then the children in the groups can continue the story by adding two more pictures and some additional sentences or paragraphs. It is likely that different groups will complete the story in different ways, therefore making it particularly meaningful to share the stories between different groups. This task will be genuinely motivating to children because they will be curious about their friends' responses. As a next step, teachers could encourage children to come up with their own brief story beginnings and let their friends finish their stories. Over time, stories can become a little longer and more sophisticated. The basic structure of the activity will remain similar and yet still be attractive to learners.

In addition to writing stories, descriptions, or letters, children also enjoy writing poetry. Materials extract 6.F gives an example activity sequence from *Oxford Discover 3* (Oxford University Press). Poems can be as short and simple as you like, and they can motivate children to write more. Poetry is also ideal for uploading and sharing. Poems are always unique and personal, and there is no right way of writing them, and this may liberate children from the need to always write to meet set criteria.

Summary

Reading and writing can be useful skills in the TEYL classroom, provided the children are interested and ready to begin the process of familiarizing themselves with the English writing system. Knowing about the process of learning to read and write in English as a first language can be a useful starting point for teachers to make informed decisions about when and how they feel reading and writing should be tackled in their classrooms.

Writing

A Read this cinquain poem written by Sara. She explains why she wrote the poem and chose the words.

Topic	Sun
2 adjectives	Warm, bright
3 action verbs using -ing	Shining, glowing, smiling
1 sentence	I like to play in the sun.
1 new noun	Friend

Why I Wrote My Poem

Topic sentence — I chose the topic word SUN because I love to be outside in the warm sun. The sun

Supporting sentences — makes our world warm and bright. I love sunlight. I like to know that the sun is always shining and glowing somewhere in the world. Of course, the sun doesn't have feelings, but I wrote that it is "smiling" at me like a friend. A sunny day is always a happy day for me.

B Answer the questions.

1 Why did Sara choose the topic word *sun*?
2 What is the sun doing in the poem that friends often do?
3 What kind of day is a happy day for Sara?

Learn How to Write a Poem

• First choose the type of poem you want to write. Look back at pages 58–59 to review the rules.
• Then write your poem.
• After your poem is written, write a paragraph telling why you wrote it.

WRITING PROCESS STEP 3
Write a Paragraph

• Remember to organize your ideas before you write your paragraph.
• Write your topic sentence first. This tells the reader what your paragraph is about.
• Then write three or four sentences that support your topic sentence.

 Write Now go to the **Workbook** to plan and write your own poem and paragraph. page 56

Materials extract 6.F (Kampa & Vilina 2014, p. 64)

Suggestions for further reading

Arnold, W., & **Rixon, S.** (2014). Making the moves from decoding to extensive reading with young learners: Insights from research and practice around the world. In S. Rich (Ed.), *International perspectives on teaching English to young learners* (pp. 23–44). Basingstoke: Palgrave Macmillan.

This is a research-based paper focusing on the challenges of teaching children to read and write in a second language in general. The authors discuss debates about first language literacy and establish that second language approaches cannot simply be based on first language findings. They stress the importance of bridging activities to help young learners make transitions from one stage of development to another. This is illustrated by introducing the reader to an extensive reading programme for children in Hong Kong.

Campbell, R. (2002). *Reading in the early years handbook, second edition.* Buckingham: Open University Press.
This is an introduction to how native speaker children learn to read in English. It covers many useful topics such as emergent writing, the role of storybooks and reading schemes, shared reading, whole-word approach, and phonics.

Fu, D., & **Matoush, M., M.** (2015). *Focus on literacy.* Oxford: Oxford University Press.
This book explores research on the second language literacy development of learners aged 5–18. The discussion throughout makes links between theory and practice, and implications for teachers are clarified through 'classroom snapshots'. Chapter 3 in particular focuses on theory and practice relevant for young learners. Online resources and free sample material can be found at: www.oup.com/elt/teacher/fol

Geva, E., & **Ramírez, G.** (2015). *Focus on reading.* Oxford: Oxford University Press.
This is a research-based handbook exploring the multiple skills involved in reading in a second language. It is particularly relevant for teachers working with learners aged 5–18. It offers practical ideas for teaching and assessing second language reading. Examples are taken from real classrooms, and reflective activities help teachers to make links with their own practice. Online resources and free sample material can be found at: www.oup.com/elt/teacher/for

Griva, E., Tsakiridou, H., & **Nihoritou, I.** (2009). *A study of FL composing process and writing strategies employed by young learners.* In M. Nikolov (Ed.), *Early learning of modern foreign languages: Processes and outcomes* (pp. 132–148). Bristol: Multilingual Matters.
This is an interesting empirical account of young learners' writing development in Greece. The study attempted to investigate how children aged 12 years went about planning their writing task and what strategies they used to complete the task. Both questionnaires and interviews were used, and results helped local teachers better understand what aspects of writing were causing particular difficulties to these learners.

Tasks

If you would like to explore your own practice related to the content of this chapter, you can try the following tasks:

Task 6: Working creatively with materials (page 186)

Task 14: Collaborative writing and reflection (page 191)

Task 15: Good language learner booklets/blogs (page 192)

Task 20: Cultural self-portraits (page 196)

Task 21: Exploring cultural content in books or other materials (page 196)

Task 22: Making class posters (page 196)

Task 24: Get the children to decide (page 197)

7

TEACHING VOCABULARY AND GRAMMAR

Introduction

This chapter looks at teaching language systems to young learners, focusing in particular on vocabulary and grammar. This discussion overlaps to some extent with ideas and principles from previous chapters. For example, in Chapter 5 there was mention of getting children to listen to songs, rhymes, or stories. These activities aim to practise listening but can also be used to teach new vocabulary and/or grammar. Similarly, in Chapter 6 there were examples of word-level reading and writing games such as matching words with pictures. Such activities can, of course, also be used to practise or recycle vocabulary. Teaching language skills and language systems are inseparable processes.

Teaching vocabulary and grammar

Vocabulary and grammar are interdependent

Fluent speakers and writers put together the component parts of the language system quickly and efficiently. To be able to do this, they need to know a large pool of vocabulary items and a long list of grammatical structures. However, it is not enough to know these in isolation; language users also need to understand the complex interaction between vocabulary and grammar. Native speakers put words together quickly in typical combinations, and this is what makes them fluent. Such building blocks are often called chunks. (See Chapter 5.) Speakers store and retrieve phrases such as 'What have you been up to?' as chunks rather than taking each word in isolation. Native speakers also know word collocations, i.e. how words go together naturally, such as 'tall' rather than 'high' to describe trees, or 'take' medicine rather than 'drink' or 'eat'. Vocabulary and grammar are stored together in the mental lexicon in typical combinations rather than in isolation. The implication of this for teaching is that vocabulary and grammar should be taught and learned together. When teaching vocabulary, teachers may need to consider grammatical choices and environments for the words, and when teaching grammar they may need to consider meaningful contexts and typical lexical combinations. For example, when we learn the verb 'write', we have to learn other related words such as 'a writer', 'a piece of writing', the past tense form 'wrote', and the past participle form 'written'. These words related to 'write' might not all be learned in primary school, but the principle of connecting words to their networks is still important.

From picking up words to knowing words

Vocabulary and grammar are difficult to divide into two distinct areas because lexical choice is always dependent on grammar. When children learn their first chunks of language, these often combine both grammatical patterns and lexis. Younger children in particular are not interested in thinking about language systems or manipulating the language so as to separate lexical items from structures. They take a more holistic interest in the meaning and function of language—in order to play a game, sing a song, or act out a story. As they grow older, their awareness of language and its component parts grows, and the separation and careful analysis of grammar and lexis can begin to take place.

When children pick up new words, they might be able to recognize a vocabulary item without knowing the exact meaning. For example, they might recognize the word 'anteater' in a story or song and infer correctly from illustrations and the accompanying mime that it is some kind of an animal. Recognizing 'anteater' in such a context does not mean that children will be able to remember and use the word later in conversation without some deliberate practice and use. Children can learn concepts or words in the second language that they do not yet know in their first language. This is natural in a rich linguistic environment. At a more advanced level, knowing an item of vocabulary will also include being able to spell it correctly and knowing grammatical information about it—for example, that 'weather' is uncountable as a noun and collocates with 'nice' rather than 'pretty'. Knowing a word can also extend to knowing its most common synonyms, such as 'expensive' and 'costly' or 'dear', and antonyms such as 'expensive' and 'cheap'. It is easy to see that the more we know about a word, the more we enter the world of grammar.

Learning grammar is a messy process

All teachers will agree that teaching grammar in isolation, for its own sake, can be a dry and boring activity. It is better if grammar is noticed and learned from meaning-focused input. This means that grammar emerges from meaningful contexts embedded in appropriate lexis, and that there is some sort of meaningful communication that leads to focus on grammar. Children need to be able to see the relationship between form and function—what form is used to express what functions and meanings. For example, in the sentence 'Can I have a piece of cake, Mummy?', 'can' functions as a modal auxiliary of permission, while in the sentence 'Mummy, I can count to 100 in English', 'can' is used to express ability. It is important to emphasize that some grammar rules are more consistent than others.

Learning grammar is not a linear process, and a lot of intermediate forms are used by learners before they are ready to conform to target language rules. This means that it is natural for children to make mistakes and acquire grammatical forms only partially at first. It is only with continued practice and careful attention that children will finally learn to use correct forms. Children from different language backgrounds go through the same processes and make similar mistakes when learning grammar. This means that the learner's first language is not the only cause of errors in second language production. As was suggested in Chapter 2, some mistakes are universal. Learning grammar is a messy process requiring the teacher to provide plenty of meaningful practice, recycling, and guidance in attending to language structure.

The role of deliberate practice

In both vocabulary and grammar teaching, there is a stage when deliberate practice of words or grammatical patterns is used in order to commit the new language to the learners' memory and help them to automatize it so that they can retrieve it quickly and efficiently when needed. Learners will have opportunities to reproduce patterns and vocabulary in a controlled way before expressing their own meanings more freely. Encouraging memorization strategies is an important way to practise new vocabulary. However, it is equally important that learners have the chance to use new language (both vocabulary and grammar) in meaning-focused output in situations where they have control over the choice of language.

Recycling and revising both vocabulary and structures are important in TEYL classrooms. It is essential that recycling remains fun and that children do not experience it as a simple repetition of activities from previous classes. For example, board games, class surveys, project work, and various digital games provide excellent opportunities. Recycling grammar and vocabulary will offer natural opportunities to integrate the language skills.

Vocabulary and grammar for younger learners

Learning grammar in a holistic way

For younger children, vocabulary and grammar should be learned in a holistic way, and only when they grow older and begin to show interest in language analysis should separation begin, with the powerful tool of analysis being introduced while they continue to learn from rich input. Stories are an excellent vehicle for teaching vocabulary and grammar together in a holistic way. For example, in the story of 'The Enormous Turnip' teachers can revise or teach new vocabulary such as 'turnip', 'old farmer', and 'seed', but these lexical items are learned in the context of relevant grammatical structures such as the past tense for narrative: 'The old farmer planted a seed, he looked at it, he couldn't pull it out, a dog walked by, they pulled the turnip out, they cooked some soup, they ate the soup'. The past tense will not be analyzed or broken into component parts, or manipulated in any way, but it will be recognized as a natural tense for stories. In this way, children will be exposed to the grammar without the pressure of using it.

In Materials extract 7.A, taken from *New Treetops 2a* (Oxford University Press), the structures to learn are 'I like' and 'I don't like'. Food items are a natural choice to accompany these structures. Once the children have been introduced to the structures, they listen to a recording about who likes what and put ticks in the correct boxes. Then, in the next activity, they draw a picture of themselves and write two sentences about what they like and don't like. The skeleton structure is provided so that they can simply fill in the gaps. These are deliberate exercises that expose learners to both receptive and productive practice.

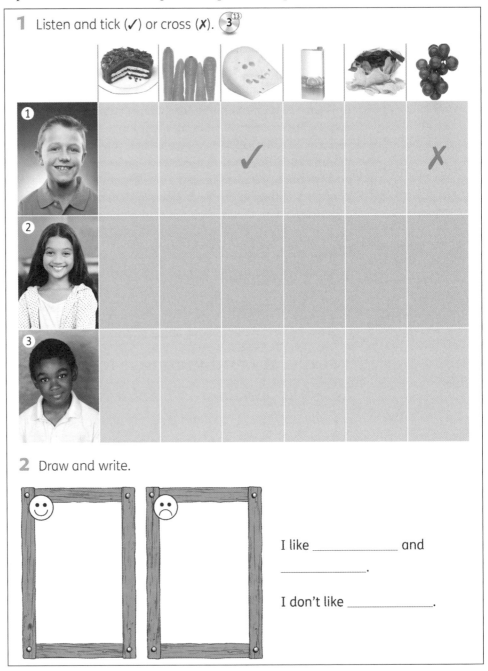

Materials extract 7.A (Howell & Kester-Dodgson, 2012a, p. 59)

Children enjoy vocabulary learning. They pick up new words at an astonishing pace in both their first and second or foreign language, and they can understand the concept behind words well before the concept of grammar. It is a good idea to make deliberate presentation of vocabulary as varied as possible. When presenting vocabulary to the youngest children, teachers can first introduce things they can see, feel, play with, touch, and experience every day. Meaning can be made apparent without the use of the first language. Teachers can use toys, such as dolls, to present parts of the body, or puppets to act out a dialogue. They can also use classroom objects such as the desks and chairs, pictures, and posters. Occasionally, when appropriate, teachers can bring in real objects such as apples, carrots, baskets, bags, hats, bottles, and cups: anything that is easy to pack in a bag or store in the cupboard. Pictures and picture cards are often supplied with young learners' coursebooks, together with a set of games and exercises to use. These can also be made at home, or teachers can ask children to help make them. Another technique is Total Physical Response (see Chapter 5), which is also used for presenting vocabulary, especially actions and movements (get up, turn around, pick something up, etc.). TPR activities allow children to hear the new vocabulary in a meaningful context and respond non-verbally first.

The role of rhythm and music

Rhyme, repetition, and TPR have been discussed more fully in Chapters 1 and 5. Research shows that, in addition to rhyme, mime, and repetition, rhythm and music also aid vocabulary learning for children. A recent article by Spanish researchers Yvette Coyle and Gómez Gracia (2014) indicated that teaching new vocabulary through songs, by making use of melody, rhyme, and rhythm, seems very effective. In this study, a group of 25 children aged five to six years of age were taught new vocabulary using the well-known song 'Wheels on the bus'. The results indicated that even though there were great differences across the board in terms of how many language items the children actually learned, most children did particularly well on the receptive tests, i.e. they could readily recognize the new words from the song. In order to produce rather than simply recognize the new words, children needed more sustained practice. The authors recommend that teachers introduce new vocabulary through songs, using gestures, and encourage children to participate in various ways such as finishing lines, singing a karaoke version of the song, and even dictating the text back to the teacher to write it on the board. These activities all encourage the productive use of new vocabulary.

Incorporating new vocabulary into children's existing knowledge

One important question is just what kind of vocabulary or grammar is suitable in the early years of learning English. In a research article published in 1999, Shelagh Rixon, a prominent British researcher in the field of teaching English to young learners, examined seven major international children's coursebooks and compared their approach to vocabulary teaching. All seven books were intended for beginning stages of learning with children of around eight years of age and for a total of about 90 hours of teaching. Interestingly, in terms of the number of words, the books proved to be very different indeed. The amount of vocabulary taught within the given time ranged from just under 200 items to just under 500 items. There did not seem to be common core vocabulary, in that only approximately 50 percent of all the words appeared in all books. Rixon also found that there was little attention given to working on meaning relationships such as synonyms, subordinates, or categorizing words in useful ways. The majority of words were presented and practised in a static manner without the opportunity for the children to see how words interacted with other words in a dynamic way, or how the same word can mean different things. For example, if we take a word such as 'chocolate', it can be used as a noun with adjectives or it can be an adjective itself. It can be used to refer to a drink—a 'hot chocolate', or 'a bar of chocolate'—it can describe a type of cake or ice cream, as in 'chocolate cake' or 'chocolate ice cream'. It can even describe a shade of colour, as in 'a chocolate brown carpet'. Such richness of meaning was never explored with words in the books that Rixon examined. Vague words such as 'person', 'thing', 'place', or structures such as 'a place where' were not introduced, even though they would be very useful for beginner speakers for paraphrasing and explaining. Rixon's conclusion is that teachers may want to identify such gaps in their coursebooks or discover opportunities to seek patterns and notice links between vocabulary items so that lexis can be taught, practised, and recycled in dynamic and meaningful ways. For example, if children learn the word 'sandwich' in the unit called 'Parties', this is also an excellent opportunity to recycle possible types of fillings they might know, such as jam, ham and cucumber, cheese and tomato, chicken, etc., or even silly ones such as frog or snake. (See Figure 7.1.) As a follow-up, children can invent different sandwiches and put them on the menu of a coffee shop. Activities like this will illustrate to the children that when they learn a new noun such as 'sandwich', it can interact with language they already know. This kind of dynamic view makes vocabulary come alive and paves the path to explicit grammar learning.

Recycling vocabulary and grammar can be a good opportunity to explore words and structures dynamically. For example, children can create 'mind maps' on topics already covered, such as 'holidays', or create poster displays with drawings and words. There are vocabulary games and activities to explore online, too. A popular example is *text2mindmap* (www.text2mindmap.com). This is a free device which allows even the youngest learners to work with mind maps.

Various board games, card games, and digital games also offer excellent chances to revise and revisit vocabulary or grammatical structures. Memory games, such as 'I went to the market and bought …', can be an enjoyable way of revising food or animal vocabulary. The same underlying principle of memory practice can be used to revise other vocabulary, such as presents in 'For my birthday, I would like …', wild animals in 'In the zoo, I saw …', or household objects such as 'In my cupboard, there are …'.

Figure 7.1 A semantic network for the word 'sandwich'

Vocabulary and grammar for older learners

For older learners it is possible to introduce explicit activities which focus on separating vocabulary and grammar. The right time to do this will be when children show an active interest in grammar forms, such as by asking the teacher why the verb 'drink' changes to 'drank', but 'think' doesn't change to 'thank' in the story or song. Another factor to consider is what grammar the children are learning in their first language. They may be familiar with some metalinguistic terms, that is, terms which allow them to talk about grammar, and which will help them to access similar concepts in English.

Vocabulary activities for older learners

With regard to vocabulary, children can continue building their semantic networks mentioned in the previous section. They can also begin to move away from the 'here and now' and learn words that are not visible or touchable—perhaps abstract nouns such as 'friendship' or 'freedom'. Older learners can be encouraged to look up words in dictionaries and begin to interpret dictionary information.

They can be introduced to explanations, paraphrasing in the target language, and analytical methods to compare first and second language equivalents, synonyms, and definitions. Recording vocabulary can become more sophisticated and older learners can use a great many useful strategies to help them to remember new vocabulary, such as practising with cards that have an English word on one side and a synonym or first language equivalent on the other. One activity that can be introduced regularly is 'word study'. For example, in Materials extract 7.B, taken from *Oxford Discover 5* (Oxford University Press), the word-study activity focuses on the prefix *in-*. All the explanation is given in English, relying on the learners' ability to use second language **metalanguage**.

Word Study

D **Learn** Prefix *in-*

Remember: A prefix is added to the beginning of a word. It changes the meaning of the word. The prefix **in-** means "not" and makes an opposite.

If your brushing is inadequate, you could get a cavity.

in adequate

Listen and say the words. Write the opposites by adding *in-*. 1·22 **A-Z**

1 visible _____

2 complete _____

3 accurate _____

4 credible _____

E Work with your partner. Write a sentence for each word above and its opposite.

Materials extract 7.B (Bourke, 2014, p. 35)

Many children regularly use electronic readers, such as Kindles, or tablets. When using these devices it is easy to look up unknown words or annotate the text. These electronic readers have a translator function and vocabulary tools where definitions appear within the text. An example from *The Heron and the Hummingbird* (Classic Tales, Oxford University Press) is shown in Figure 7.2

There are also some excellent websites for looking closely at vocabulary from a given text. One of my favourites is WordItOut. (http://worditout.com). As a teacher you can simply upload any text you are working with and the site will produce a word cloud as shown in Figure 7.3 overleaf.

The word cloud was generated after uploading the story 'The Princess and the Pea'. The words printed in larger font size represent the words that occur most frequently in the story. Children and young teenagers will enjoy using the website

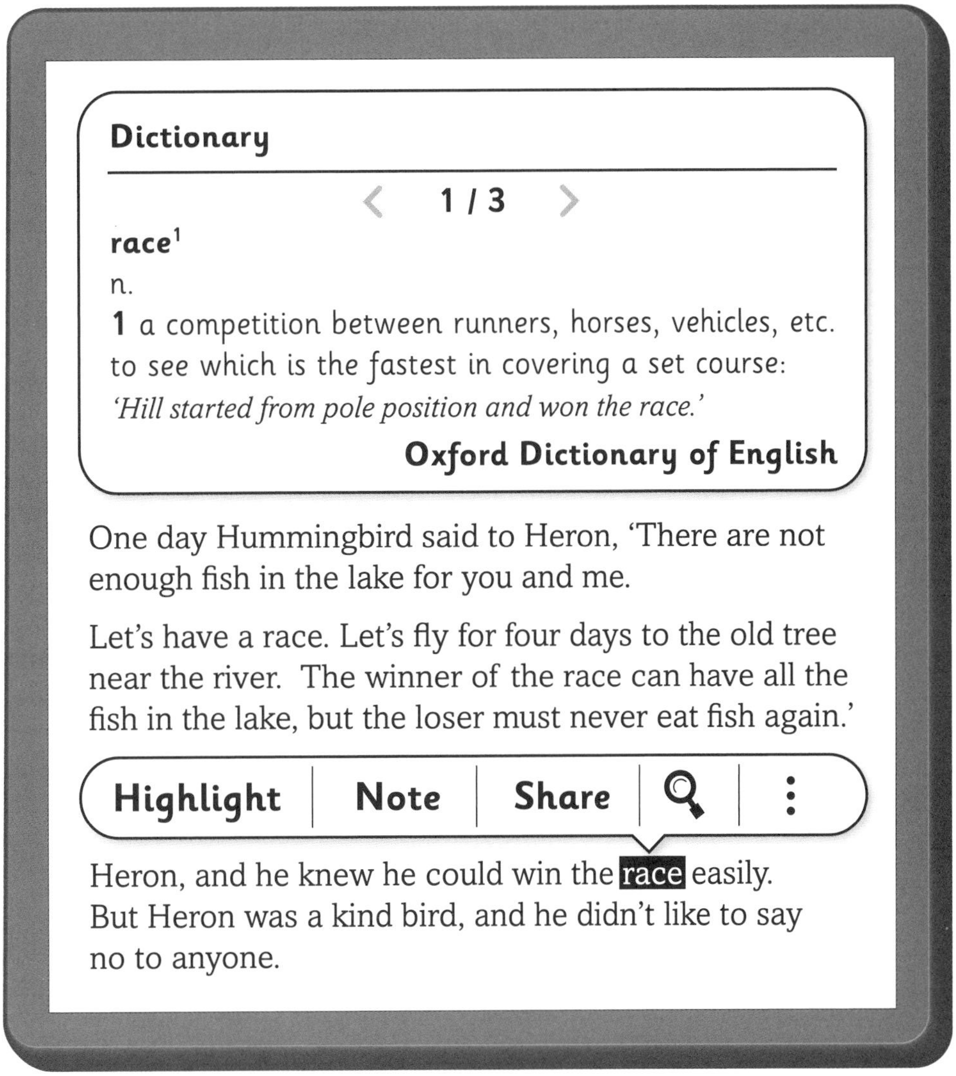

Dictionary

⟨ **1 / 3** ⟩

race[1]

n.

1 a competition between runners, horses, vehicles, etc. to see which is the fastest in covering a set course: *'Hill started from pole position and won the race.'*

Oxford Dictionary of English

One day Hummingbird said to Heron, 'There are not enough fish in the lake for you and me.

Let's have a race. Let's fly for four days to the old tree near the river. The winner of the race can have all the fish in the lake, but the loser must never eat fish again.'

Highlight | **Note** | **Share** | 🔍 | ⋮

Heron, and he knew he could win the race easily. But Heron was a kind bird, and he didn't like to say no to anyone.

Figure 7.2 Using an electronic reader (extract from Bladon, 2013)

themselves to upload their favourite pop songs or texts that they are interested in. You can organize simple competitions whereby students create word clouds and the rest of the class guess which song the cloud might represent. You can also create sentences and organize or categorize the words according to their part of speech, or offer a definition, or cover up one of the words and let the children guess what it is. Word clouds can be designed according to the individual learner's taste, using different colours, font sizes, and shapes.

Figure 7.3 Word cloud of 'The Princess and the Pea'

Grammar activities for older learners

Language analysis and the introduction of metalanguage can start with simple examples. The extract in Materials extract 7.C is taken from Sarah Phillips' (1993) resource book, *Young Learners*, where children are encouraged to study the component parts of the structure aux + pronoun + verb + noun, as in 'Do you like pizza?' In the activity, the words are jumbled up and the children have to create sentences similar to the model. The activity introduces different colours for the different parts of speech. This gives the teacher the opportunity to teach useful metalanguage. Children can make sentences in groups, in pairs, or on their own. As a next step, in order to contextualize this practice, they will make a questionnaire about their eating habits for another class at school or for parents/carers.

	5.8 Colour parsing
LEVEL	2, 3
AGE GROUP	B, C
TIME	30 minutes
AIMS	**Language:** to learn how a sentence is constructed.
MATERIALS	Coloured chalk, coloured pencils.
PREPARATION	1 Decide which structure you are going to focus on (in this example questions with *like*).
	2 Decide on the colours you are going to use. In this case you only need four:

red	*like, love, hate* (verbs)
blue	*I, you, he, she, etc.* (subject pronouns)
yellow	*do, does* (auxiliary verbs)
green	*pizza, coffee, tea, bananas, tomatoes* (nouns)

IN CLASS

1 Divide your board into two halves. On the left write some words that fit into the sentence structure you have chosen, like this:

2 Underline the verb in red and invite the children to find and underline other 'red' words. Do the same with the blue, yellow, and green words.

3 Write your model sentence on the right of the board and ask the children to underline the words in the appropriate colours.

4 Show the children how to make other sentences like yours, using the words on the left. Then they make some of their own, either individually or in groups.

5 Ask the children to tell you their sentences and write them under the model.

FOLLOW-UP

Ask the children to select sentences that would be suitable for a questionnaire about favourite foods.

Do the questionnaire (for the technique, see 2.6, 'A questionnaire on health').

COMMENTS

If you are going to use this technique regularly in class, it is worth devising a more complete colour scheme so that you are consistent. Make a poster of it for the classroom wall. Remember that the technique has its limitations and is best used with single structures—if you are not careful the colour coding becomes more complicated than the structure itself!

Materials extract 7.C (Phillips, 1993, pp. 77–78)

Fun grammar activities for older learners include puzzles where students are encouraged to discover grammar rules for themselves, such as describing the differences between two pictures, which can be used to practise prepositions. For learners who also do some writing in English, it is very important to learn about grammar above sentence level. In the 'writing study' section of *Oxford Discover 3* (Oxford University Press), we have an explanation of how to use 'but' to connect two sentences. (See Materials extract 7.D.)

E Learn *But*

We can describe how two things are different in one sentence.

We use the word **but** to separate the things.

In Korea people often eat rice, but in Germany people often eat potatoes.

In India the summers are rainy, but in Minnesota the summers are sunny.

Materials extract 7.D (Kampa & Vilina, 2014, p. 35)

Collaborative writing, such as story-writing in pairs, can be a very fruitful way of focusing on grammar, accuracy, and, above all, grammatical rules above sentence level. Getting children to work with drafts and incorporating feedback from others into their drafts is a good way to progress and become more accurate. (See Chapter 6.)

Summary

This chapter started out with the idea that grammar and vocabulary were very difficult to divide into two neat categories. Younger learners are simply not ready for, or interested in, analyzing and discussing component parts of the language, so vocabulary and grammar are better taught in combination. For older learners it is possible to begin to separate vocabulary and grammar and include more explicit and analytical exercises as well as more use of metalanguage. Recycling is key in both vocabulary and grammar teaching for all children.

Suggestions for further reading

de Oliveira, L., & **Schleppegrell, M. J.** (2015). *Focus on grammar and meaning.* Oxford: Oxford University Press.
This is an up-to-date source that brings together the theory and practice of teaching the language system in a meaningful way for teachers. In particular, Chapter 3 is devoted to classroom-based research and practice relevant to young learners. The authors draw on classroom snapshots and discuss aspects of learning grammar with much clarity. Online resources and free sample material can be found at: www.oup.com/elt/teacher/fogm

Legutke, M. L., Muller-Hartmann, A., & **Schocker-v. Ditfurth, M.** (2011). *Teaching English in the primary school.* Stuttgart: Klett Lerntraining.
This is a comprehensive guide to primary English teaching covering a range of topics from task-based learning to working with texts, culture, media, and skills development, and it has a particularly accessible chapter on teaching grammar and vocabulary.

Thornbury, S. (2000). *How to teach grammar.* London: Pearson Longman. This book explains what grammar is in theoretical terms but also offers ideas for grammar teaching and sample lessons, including a storytelling session with focus on grammar for young learners. It also contains photocopiable training tasks.

Thornbury, S. (2002). *How to teach vocabulary.* London: Pearson Longman. This book discusses both the theory and practice of vocabulary learning and teaching principles. It explains how we learn words and offers techniques and strategies that teachers can use to deal with real-life challenges in classrooms.

Tasks

If you would like to explore your own practice related to the content of this chapter, you can try the following tasks:

Task 5: Exploring materials (page 186)

Task 6: Working creatively with materials (page 186)

Task 15: Good language learner booklets/blogs (page 192)

Task 17: Getting the children to record themselves regularly (page 195)

Task 21: Exploring cultural content in books or other materials (page 197)

8

LEARNING TO LEARN

Introduction

Learning to learn is one of the most important objectives for all learning and teaching contexts for all ages. In our fast moving world, it is simply impossible for learners to acquire all the knowledge and skills they need while they are at school. It is the school's responsibility to teach learners how to learn, i.e. to equip them with strategies that they can use outside school. This process needs to start as early as possible, preferably at the beginning of schooling. Rapid developments in information technology have meant that independent learning opportunities are becoming available all the time through the internet.

Learning to learn is also closely related to the so-called '21st century skills' mentioned in Chapter 1. Various aspects of learning to learn can be introduced into the day-to-day practice of any language classroom without changing many of the usual classroom practices. This chapter will discuss explicitly some opportunities that teachers of English for young learners can take to promote the principles of learning to learn. Most of the suggested techniques and ideas can be adapted to all contexts and can work in both large classes and mixed-ability classes.

What is learning to learn?

The overall aim of incorporating some kind of learning to learn is to begin to raise children's awareness of the various factors that influence their language learning and to give them some time and space to start to think for themselves. Learning to learn is a broad concept which can encompass a great variety of different activities, tasks, or discussions between children and the teacher.

In this chapter, learning-to-learn activities are divided into three main categories. These categories offer some ideas to begin to explore learning to learn, but are by no means complete. Teachers are invited to add or adapt as they see fit.

The categories in Table 8.1 have been listed to illustrate the order in which they can be introduced. Teachers can start with emotions, feelings, and boosting self-esteem (so-called **social/affective strategies**). They can then introduce metacognitive strategies which can be made applicable to any unit of learning.

Finally, the **cognitive strategies** can be added with older or more experienced learners. This, of course, does not mean that this order must always be followed. Teachers are encouraged to judge for themselves what is appropriate and feasible and can also combine different strategies from the very start. Some schools may be fostering learning-to-learn strategies in other areas of the curriculum, which gives teachers a good chance to integrate English into an existing framework.

What types of strategies can be developed?

1 Social and affective strategies: to raise awareness about how learners' own emotional states and feelings, as well as those of others, can influence their learning. Activities in the classroom can include teacher-led discussions (usually in the mother tongue) about the social aspects of learning, such as the importance of listening to each other, turn taking in games, or controlling shyness and fear of speaking out in front of others. As part of developing awareness about affective factors, teachers can give plenty of praise and positive feedback to children to raise their self-esteem and self-confidence as well as boost their motivation. These discussions with children may also involve topics about why it is beneficial to learn foreign languages, how long it takes to learn a language, why it is important to practise, and why everyone makes mistakes. These regular awareness-raising discussions help children to better understand what language learning entails.

---

2 Metacognitive strategies: to introduce and develop the ongoing process of reflection through planning, monitoring, and evaluating language learning.
Activities in the classroom can include encouraging children to think about what they did well and why, and what they enjoyed and why. At later stages, children can be prompted to think about the reasons for doing various activities and tasks and about lessons that can be learned from each learning experience. A 'plan–do–review' cycle can be incorporated into most activities in language classrooms.

---

3 Direct or cognitive strategies: to develop children's ability to deal with linguistic information in an effective way, i.e. to organize, categorize, or memorize linguistic information.
Activities in the classroom can include training strategies such as how to remember a list of words, how to guess the meaning of unknown words in a text, or how to link unrelated language to aid memory.

Table 8.1 Types of strategies

Developing social and affective strategies and raising awareness about language learning

Activities for younger learners

This aspect of learning to learn can be the foundation for all children. In terms of the affective factors, all teachers of children are concerned with issues such as building confidence and raising self-esteem. This links well with training about tolerance and diversity in Chapter 11. Without these, and a positive learning environment full of encouragement, it is impossible to achieve the goals related to fostering positive attitudes. The younger the children are, the more important these considerations become. The teacher can be an important role model, displaying positive, cheerful behaviour, and friendliness at all times. This is particularly important because younger children see the teacher as a source of motivation. (See Chapter 4.) All teachers can foster children's self-esteem by emphasizing what children can do rather than what they can't. Asking children's opinions about the English lessons and their own progress are fundamental parts of building self-reliance and awareness. Gaining experience in expressing their opinions is a good foundation for self-assessment. (See Chapter 10.) Children's simple reflection notes about their progress should focus on what has been achieved rather than where the gaps are. Evaluation sheets should always be phrased in a positive way, as shown in Table 8.2.

NAME:			
I can …	say the alphabet	write a short story	say a rhyme
I am proud of …	my project	my homework	my blog
I enjoy …	listening to stories on the internet	playing games in class	singing English songs

Table 8.2 Reflecting on progress

Teachers should provide positive reinforcement and use plenty of praise when commenting on children's work and performance in English. They can also show their appreciation by displaying children's work on the wall or by giving feedback to individuals. It is important for teachers to encourage children to express their feelings and to listen to those who have something important to say before the lesson begins. Younger children are often much more affected by events at home than older ones. Teachers of very young children might find it useful to listen to children talking about falls, lost pets, or the birth of a baby brother or sister. The fact that the teacher knows about their concerns will give younger children a sense of security.

In terms of social development, it is important for teachers to be sensitive to individuals and friendship groupings. They can promote co-operation, listening, and turn taking in order to train children specifically in developing skills for working effectively in pairs or groups. This also links with 21st century skills. Even younger children can begin to learn to collaborate with one another, first in pairs and then in small groups. Children will begin to understand that different people see things differently and that it is important to be tolerant of others. Drawing up class rules together is an effective way to start establishing what is acceptable during English classes and, in particular, in pair and group work. Children should be involved in this process so that they can feel they have some control over what is happening.

With regard to the nature of language learning, it may be appropriate, for example, to talk about general expectations in learning languages. How much can we learn in a week, a month, or a year? What will we be able to do in English by the end of the school year? These discussions can happen in the mother tongue and do not need to take up a lot of time, perhaps just five to ten minutes a week. However, once they are introduced, it is a good idea to incorporate them regularly. Teachers can share anecdotes and interesting facts about language learning. Many children will be fascinated by this and will have their own insights to offer.

Activities for older learners

For older learners, rather than just focusing on the English language, it is also possible to raise awareness about other languages—how languages are different, or how many languages are spoken in the world. Such an extension of their understanding about languages and language learning can feed into other areas of the curriculum, such as geography or history.

With older groups, teachers can further develop children's skills in working collaboratively—they can consider affective factors in some detail, or encourage children to continue their discoveries about language learning, for example through the comparison of their mother tongue with English. Regular discussions can help children to become more aware of what is involved in language learning as well as help them to cope with ups and downs, or days when they find it less exciting. Such self-motivation was also discussed in Chapter 4. With older children, teachers can include discussions about the need to practise regularly and the need to be patient when you are learning a new language.

To help children to learn to collaborate effectively with each other in groups, it is a good idea to teach a set of useful phrases that help children to manage group work in English. These can be recorded on cards or on a poster for display (see Figure 8.1). These visuals can serve as useful reminders any time group work happens. New phrases can be added to the set as groups get more accustomed to working together.

WHAT TO SAY WHEN WORKING IN A GROUP

Shall we ...?

What do you think?

What have you got?

I'm next.

I think we should ...

Let's decide about ...

Let's check everybody's answers.

How's it going?

How much time is left?

What do we need to do first?

Figure 8.1 What to say when working in a group

More sophisticated social strategies can also be taught to help children when they are stuck with a task. For example, older children might need strategies to find answers to a quiz, to use a dictionary to look up unknown words while reading, or to ask a friend or a teacher to repeat or paraphrase what they said.

Developing metacognitive strategies

Learning to reflect

Learning a foreign language at school means being actively involved in a range of different activities, such as listening to a story or to the teacher talking, answering questions, creating dialogues with a friend, or writing a short paragraph. It is important that children begin to understand why these activities are used in the classroom and how they can participate in them effectively. Such reflection on the learning process is a natural part of effective learning and can be adapted at the level of individual activities, tasks, or lessons, or even larger units such as terms and school years. In other words, learners can reflect about why and how well they answered a question, and why or how well they carried out the dialogue or role-play. In the latter example, it would be possible to think about whether each speaker contributed fully, listened to others, rehearsed effectively, or managed to control their nervousness in front of the class. Reflection is also important when teachers and learners take stock of what has been achieved at the end of a school term or year. Developing metacognitive awareness is, of course, directly linked to developing self-assessment, which will be discussed in Chapter 10.

Explicit reflection is often fostered in coursebooks as well. Materials extract 8.A is an example of an activity from *Cross-Curricular Resources for Young Learners* (Oxford University Press) that focuses on reflecting on an aspect of learning in any one lesson. This can be adapted by teachers to make it suitable for different groups of learners and also to reflect on slightly longer periods of learning, such as a month or a term.

STUDENT'S SELF-ASSESSMENT FORM

Class: _____   Name: _____

Date: _____   Activity: _____

☐ What I liked doing most: ....

....

☐ What I didn't like or found difficult: ....

....

How I worked:

☐ on my own   ☐ with the help of the teacher   ☐ with the help of the other students

☐ with commitment   ☐ without much commitment   ☐ with difficulty   ☐ without difficulty

In the group

☐ I participated actively in the work of the group

☐ I let the other students take the initiative and decide

☐ I accepted all the suggestions of the other students without discussion

☐ I tried to contribute my own ideas and suggestions to the work

☐ ....

WHAT I CAN DO	☺	😐	☹

Materials extract 8.A (Calabrese & Rampone, 2015, p. x)

Activities for younger learners

For the youngest age group, the reflection process may start by asking children to think and decide which activities they liked in a lesson or unit. At the end of a lesson the teacher can simply ask children to put their hands up to show the activities they enjoyed most. Simple but creative illustrations (for example, smiley faces or rabbit ears, where the position of the ears, up or down, means good or bad) can be used to represent categories such as 'I like it very much', 'I'm not sure', or 'I don't like it'.

Teachers can ask children at the end of a lesson or unit to think about different activities (such as playing games on a whiteboard, singing the ABC song, or creating a dialogue with a friend) and to think about what they enjoyed and why.

These simple activities will encourage children to pause, think for themselves, and come up with reasons why they like or dislike certain tasks. If such reflection is carried out on a systematic basis, the children will get used to having to think for themselves and the teacher will gain insights into their motives and developing opinions.

The above examples are restricted to reflecting about a learning experience after it has happened. However, the 'plan–do–review' reflective cycle can be extended to thinking ahead before doing an activity, or thinking while doing the activity, not just thinking about how it went and why. This three-step process is often referred to as the 'metacognitive' cycle. (See Figure 8.2.) It is possible to introduce a general methodology for developing a 'plan–do–review' cycle in most learning situations.

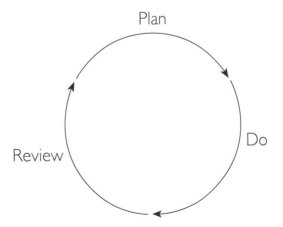

Figure 8.2 'Plan–do–review' cycle

Activities for older learners

Older children can think more explicitly about the process, using questions at each stage of the activity. When a group of children are planning a mini-project they may consider the questions in Table 8.3 with the teacher's help.

Before:

Planning stage: What do we have to do here?

- Have we done this before?
- How can we build on what we already know?
- How many ideas have we got to start with?
- Which shall we do first?

During:

Monitoring stage: How are we doing so far?

- Have we got enough time?
- Do we have to change our plan?
- Have we got a problem?
- How can we sort out the problem or get help?

After:

Evaluating stage: What did we learn?

- What did we enjoy about this project and why?
- What did we find easy or difficult and why?
- How can we do it better next time?

Table 8.3 The 'metacognitive' cycle

An Iranian teacher, Samira Hazari, was interested in developing metacognitive strategies with a group of children. She decided to implement a 'plan–do–review' cycle in her classroom and observed the impact on her students' learning (Hazari, 2013). The children were 10–12 years old and working at a pre-intermediate level of English. She asked the children to work in pairs to carry out three collaborative writing tasks in English. The first task was to write a short booklet about Iran. The second task was to write a magazine about their school, and the third task was to write a poster about their experiences in the two projects.

Hazari introduced the 'plan–do–review' cycle through some strategy cards. First she introduced the cards and talked to the children about the 'plan–do–review' cycle. When the children started working on their writing tasks, they were regularly prompted to look at the strategy cards. Hazari observed that the children got used to these cards very quickly, and after a while they were able to remind each other of appropriate strategies without even looking at the cards. When the three writing tasks were completed, she also asked the children about their experiences and feelings of writing together, and the feedback indicated that the children were aware of the effectiveness of the strategies, and also of how their writing improved as a result of reflection and of completing the writing task three times.

One helpful way to foster metacognitive growth is to encourage explicit analysis of tasks and games in order to learn to play them better. The teacher can talk children through how to play a game. This is a kind of 'scaffolding' referred to in Chapter 1. For example, let us imagine that a teacher wants a group of ten-year-olds to play a guessing game in which they ask questions to guess what the teacher has got in a 'magic box'. Before starting the game, the teacher might want to think together with the children about how to play the game. What types of questions would help them to succeed? For example, considering the size of the box or the bag, certain objects would be excluded. They can ask themselves: 'What sort of things are of that size?' It is also important for them to listen to other people's questions and the teacher's answers in order to put all useful information together. The teacher should also support the children through clarification checks because if they miss some important clues then they have no chance of guessing the object.

For older groups it might be possible to start recording learning by building up a 'learning tree' or a 'learning wall' at the back of the classroom. (See Figure 8.3.)

Figure 8.3 'A learning tree'

At the end of every week the teacher can ask the children to think about the vocabulary they learned that week, and then the suggestions can be put up on the tree as leaves. Depending on the children's ability to read, it is possible to use drawings instead of writing on the leaves. The tree will grow more and more leaves as the weeks go by, and the children will have an explicit record of what they have done. The leaves can be moved around to show how learning different things can link to previous knowledge.

Developing cognitive strategies

Language learning often requires manipulating linguistic information in an effective way. There are specific strategies to help language learners, such as organizing, rehearsing, using different visual and other meaningful clues, predicting, and using deduction while listening or reading. For example, children will have to memorize and categorize words, learn rhymes by heart, or predict information while listening to a story. Teachers can help them to learn effective ways of doing so.

Activities for younger learners

For the youngest age groups, teachers may start developing cognitive strategies slowly and carefully. For example, in classes where children often perform short dialogues in front of their friends, teachers might want to begin to encourage rehearsal strategies. Children can be given explicit advice as to how to help each other and what clues they can use to remind themselves of what comes next. Another early strategy is the development of predicting skills during storytelling sessions. Teachers can start by simply asking the children to say what they think will happen next. Carried out systematically, this training will help them to make predictions in other situations as well. It is also a good idea for children to have their own English vocabulary picture books. They can begin to explore and personalize ways in which they can organize new language.

One very effective problem-solving activity that requires careful language analysis can be seen in Materials extract 8.B—'How many words?', taken from *Teaching Young Learners to Think: ELT Activities for Young Learners Aged 6–12* (Helbling Languages). This activity can be played with any age group of children if they can already read and write.

In this activity, children have to search for different words using the same letters in different combinations. This search will focus and motivate learners if it is organized as a competitive game, but it is also a perfect challenge for those early finishers who need an extra task. Activities like this develop children's analytic skills; in particular, spelling skills in this case.

6 How many words?

Language focus	Revision of vocabulary; spelling skills
Thinking skills	Analysing; moving letters around in one's visual short-term memory; risk taking
Age	Any
Level	Post-beginner / A1 upwards
Time	10–15 minutes
Preparation	Write words in block letters on big sheets of paper; examples:

HOLIDAYS   CHOCOLATE INTERNET FOOTBALL

MOBILE PHONE COMPUTER BIRTHDAY HANDBAG

There should be enough space between the letters so students can easily cut out the individual letters of the word. Bring in one pair of scissors per group of 4–5 students.

In class

1 In block letters, write the word ELEPHANT on the board. Ask students to use any number of letters from the word in any order, and try to make as many new words as possible. Give them some help if necessary. Examples:

HEN   NET   HAT   TEN   EAT   LET   ANT   PEN

2 Put students in groups of four or five. Give each group one of your words.

3 Tell the students to cut up their word. The students should try and make as many new words as possible out of any number of the letters from their word, used in any order.

4 Whenever a group thinks they've found a new word, they present it to you by standing in a line, with each student holding one letter. If the word is correct, the group can write it down on a piece of paper. If a word they want to present has more letters than there are students in a group they can 'borrow' as many students as they wish from another group.

Variation The task is more difficult if the students don't cut the letters up but have to visualise the words contained in the big word.

Puchta/Williams | Teaching Young Learners to Think | © Helbling Languages

Materials extract 8.B (Puchta & Williams, 2011, p. 194)

Activities for older learners

With older children it is possible to do sophisticated organizing and categorizing of strategies; for example, vocabulary learning strategies. Hanne Thomsen (2003), a classroom practitioner working in Denmark, has written about training children in their fourth year to develop vocabulary learning strategies. Throughout several lessons her learners were encouraged to reflect on their own ways of organizing and recording vocabulary as well as their own strategies for memorizing words. With the help of the teacher, the learners started compiling lists on posters, which included strategies that individual learners used either inside or outside the classroom. All the strategies were discussed as they were added to a poster, and good strategies were highlighted. For example, one learner suggested recording new vocabulary in a book together with synonyms and example sentences. Learners were encouraged to choose a vocabulary recording system to suit their taste, but good models were discussed and shared by everyone. Such discussions can be very useful in children's first language, too, if their language level does not permit them to be in English.

Making links between general thinking skills and language learning strategies

The categorization of language learning strategies (into social, affective, metacognitive and cognitive strategies) is inspired by second language researchers, such as Rebecca Oxford (2011), who have developed their frameworks using second language related strategies, often based on observations about successful second language learners' experiences in particular.

However, learning a second language cannot be separated from other useful thinking and learning skills relevant across the whole of the curriculum. There are, in fact, many so-called 'general' programmes that encourage the development of 'thinking skills' for children. For example, Herbert Puchta and Marion Williams' book (2011) about teaching young learners to think is based on the principle that general thinking skills can and should be incorporated into everyday language teaching. These thinking skills build on a range of basic concepts that all learners have to acquire. The most basic concepts include time, space, size, hierarchy, and position. These concepts will help children to make sense of the world around them. In addition to these basic concepts, children also need to acquire skills to solve problems by comparing, visualizing, describing, and classifying information. These skills allow learners to select relevant information, then memorize it, and finally retrieve it for later use. Finally, children, like all learners, also rely on knowledge and experience about the world, and they work with shared conventions and rules such as how to collaborate with others. Thanks to this type of knowledge, children can interpret information according to contexts and situations and can communicate their thoughts effectively. Since children's knowledge of the world is limited, teachers need to be aware of the need to help them by continually extending it.

When teaching thinking skills, most authors recommend starting with basic concepts and then moving to higher-order thinking skills such as complex problem-solving. Another aspect of effective thinking is creativity. Creativity can be defined in various ways, but, simply put, it is the ability to look at something in a new way. It is also important to foster creativity in children's language classrooms. Predicting different endings for a story or making up your own song can both be labelled as creative. Teachers can foster both creativity and the learning of new words through activities such as 'How many different ways can you use a paper clip?' or 'How many objects can you make out of a circle?' (See Figure 8.4.)

Figure 8.4 How many objects can you make out of a circle?

Giving space to children's choices

In order for children to be able to put their developing strategies into practice, it is a good idea to give them more space and time during lessons. This means that teachers will have to let go of their total control of the classroom and involve children in the decision-making process. Allowing children to make some choices and initiate ideas during class is motivating for them because this will lead to more active involvement and more enjoyable learning. Listening to children's voices also sends out the clear message that their interests and opinions are valued and appreciated by the teacher.

It is, of course, important to offer only limited choices at the beginning. For example, for the youngest groups, when teachers introduce vocabulary such as 'wild animals' it is a good idea to let children brainstorm in their mother tongue the names of animals that they want to learn, rather than presenting them with a predetermined list—they may have their own favourite animals. It is possible to prepare two or three similar tasks and give children a choice of which animal they want to read or write about. Even if there is hardly any difference between these texts and tasks from the teacher's perspective, the children will experience it as a real choice.

There are many other ways in which teachers can encourage children's involvement through recognizing and respecting their choices. They can try to set freer homework tasks. For example, children can learn three new vocabulary items of their own choice every week on top of what is learned by everybody. They can look words up in a picture dictionary, ask their older siblings for ideas, or choose words or phrases from their favourite comics, books, or even the internet. In class, they can make displays of their words and/or keep a personal vocabulary book. What matters is that their own involvement in choosing these words will make the language more relevant to them, and this will increase the likelihood of remembering and learning. At the beginning of the next lesson, children can be put into small groups to tell each other what new words they learned.

Another small step towards giving children choices is to start a modest self-access corner in the classroom, with activities and exercises organized systematically in a cupboard or a box. For a start, there could be some crossword puzzles in the corner, and later on teachers could add some picture books and then, perhaps, games to be played in teams or pairs. It is possible to allow just 15 minutes each week when children can choose something from the corner to look at and work with individually or in small groups. It is possible to build this up gradually and change the tasks and activities as needed. Children can help to build it up by creating tasks and activities for each other, such as word snakes, crossword puzzles, or other tasks. Teachers may find it very beneficial to collaborate with others to pool their resources.

One online activity that encourages choice is Fotobabble (www.fotobabble.com). This is an easily accessible web tool that allows each child to choose and upload a picture and record a short description and audio file about it. The pictures and descriptions can then be placed on a secure website where both the children and the teacher can see them, listen to the audio files, and make comments. The element of choice will be motivating for children and they will be eager to upload pictures and drawings of their own choice, but in my experience they will also be eager to see and comment on other children's work.

Figure 8.5 shows an example by a seven-year-old child from South Korea who decided to upload a photo of her new watch, accompanied by a short audio file.

Transcript: *This is my watch from the Milano airport, and my mommy bought it for me because I've been really good at Italy. And I know how to tell the time, and it's twenty to five now. And I've choose this because the colour is so nice and, you know, the small hand and the big hand is the girl and boy, it's so cute and nice.*

Figure 8.5 An example of a Fotobabble picture and a transcript of the accompanying audio file

Playing back their own recording of the description will help children to notice any inaccuracies in their own language because they are focusing on listening, rather than production. When mistakes are noticed, most children will want to re-record their description, which means extra practice. Simple Fotobabble pictures can be developed further into talking photo albums with a range of sequenced pictures and uploaded audio files.

Offering choices to children and encouraging their independence in small ways is also consistent with the principle advocated in this book—that all children's needs are different, and it is important for teachers in language classes to cater for individual learner differences, interests, and requirements. For example, a motivated high achiever will find it exciting to be able to rise to the challenge of his or her own choice. Equally, learners who are progressing more slowly might need the time to consolidate something quietly while the others are engaged with more demanding tasks.

Raising awareness about the learning process, developing language learning strategies, and giving children some freedom in their learning are all principles which, taken together, can foster independent learning in classrooms. This means systematic awareness-raising, preparing children for future learning, and encouraging a reflective attitude to learning without much change to the usual content and procedures.

Summary

In young learners' classes there will, of course, be great differences between age groups as to what it is possible to achieve. The younger the learners, the less they are able to stand back and reflect on their own learning, choose for themselves, plan, or evaluate their performance. However, even the youngest children will be able to respond well to small steps taken in the direction of learning to learn. Incorporating some learning-to-learn activities into language learning is beneficial for both the children and the teacher. The children gradually learn useful skills that can be applied to other areas of learning and become more aware and self-confident, and the teachers can discover more about their learners. The internet offers a wide variety of tools for linking classroom learning and outside classroom learning and for practising enjoyable tasks with a specific focus on developing learning and thinking strategies.

Suggestions for further reading

Dam, L. (2014). *Learner 3 autonomy: From theory to classroom practice*. Denmark: Askeladden.
This is a classic text about learner autonomy. Based on many years of work as a classroom teacher, Dam explains what learner independence means in her classrooms, what the teachers' and the learners' roles are, what sorts of problems occur in these classrooms, and what the benefits are of working this way.

Ellis, G., & **Ibrahim, N.** (2015). *Teaching children how to learn.* Peaslake, Surrey: DELTA Publishing.
This is a handbook that gives a brief introduction to the principles that underline the activities offered in this book or online. Learning to learn is defined for teachers and learners. Teaching and learning activities all follow a 'plan–do–review' cycle and readers are invited to select activities that fit with their own aims and contexts. Teachers are also invited to follow the 'plan–do–review' cycle in the process of pursuing their own professional development.

Fisher, R. (2009). *Creative dialogue: Talk for thinking in the classroom.* Abingdon: Routledge.
This is a practical book that helps teachers to become more skilled at encouraging creativity and thoughtfulness in their classrooms. The book contains more than 100 ideas about how to stimulate effective dialogue in classrooms and increase children's concentration.

Jesson, J. (2012). *Developing creativity in the primary school.* Maidenhead: Open University Press.
This books discusses major theories and current thinking about creativity. It offers ideas about to how to promote group creativity and individual children's creativity in addition to focusing on the teacher's own capacity to become more creative.

Puchta, H., & **Williams, M.** (2011). *Teaching young learners to think: ELT activities for young learners aged 6–12.* London: Helbling Languages.
This book provides a brief overview of the main approach promoted in the activities, which centres on the development of thinking skills. A strong rationale is given as to why it is important to promote children's thinking skills in ELT. A categorization of the different types of thinking skills is offered, followed by practical photocopiable ideas.

Tasks

If you would like to explore your own practice related to the content of this chapter, you can try the following tasks:

Task 7: Observing children choosing tasks (page 188)

Task 8: Getting children to reflect on their learning (page 188)

Task 14: Collaborative writing and reflection (page 191)

Task 15: Good language learner booklets/blogs (page 192)

Task 16: Developing skills towards self and peer assessment (page 193)

Task 17: Getting the children to record themselves regularly (page 195)

Task 19: Exploring group presentations (page 195)

Task 23: Conversations with children based on drawings (page 197)

Task 24: Getting the children to decide (page 197)

9 MATERIALS EVALUATION AND MATERIALS DESIGN

Introduction

The most important teaching and learning material that guides teachers' and learners' activities in many classrooms seems to be the coursebook, whether in a traditional or a digital format. Modern coursebooks come with useful accompanying material such as a teacher's resource book or resource pack, audio and video material and digital packages, and additional online materials or 'apps'. Young learners' coursebooks are well designed with attractive features, such as colourful visuals, fun games and tasks, crafts, and projects, yet it is important to note that no coursebook can be perfect for any teaching and learning situation, and this is why teachers find materials evaluation and materials design very useful skills.

Using coursebooks

In some contexts, teachers follow a set coursebook very closely, lesson by lesson and exercise by exercise, while in other contexts teachers are able to select their own materials and activities more freely. Realistically, most teachers are somewhere in the middle, where there is a coursebook to follow but there is also some scope for individual contributions. Most countries have national syllabus guidelines and objectives for primary English. Ministries of Education often identify a list of recommended books that schools can choose from. Since many international young learners' coursebooks cannot meet special local expectations or needs, individual countries develop their own materials.

Syllabuses: four skills and more

Children's course materials typically contain attractive authentic materials, stories, and fun games, and they are consistent with some of the educational goals discussed in Chapter 4. The syllabus outline in Materials extract 9.A, for example, from *Oxford Discover 1* (Oxford University Press), indicates that the main organizing principle here is the authentic topic and the 'Big Question', which is related to extra-curricular themes such as science, music, or art. The column on the left-hand side indicates that out of the four language skills reading takes the most important role and each unit is indeed introduced with a piece of reading.

Scope and Sequence

Billy   Gus   Layla   Dot

UNIT	READING	VOCABULARY	GRAMMAR	LISTENING	SPEAKING	WRITING	WRAP UP
BIG QUESTION 1		**Who are your family and friends?** Social Studies: Community					
1 Page 6	**Families and Friends** Informational text (Nonfiction) **Reading Strategy** Predicting from details	**Reading Text Words** mother, father, brother, sister, grandmother, grandfather, family, friend **Word Study** Opposites	**Verb be** I am, You are, He / She is, We are, They are He's eight years old.	**Different Families** People describing their families **Listening Strategy** Listening for details	**Introducing People** This is my brother. It's nice to meet you.	**Tasks** Talk about your family and write about them. (Workbook)	
2 Page 16	**Elliot's New Friend** Story (Fiction) **Reading Strategy** Predicting from Pictures	**Reading Text Words** elephant, tortoise, lonely, sad, scared, eat, play, sleep **Listening Text Words** hamster, goldfish, bird, rabbit, lizard, kitten	**Demonstratives: This, That, These, and Those** This is zebra. Those are lions.	**Friends and Pets** People describing their friends and their pets **Listening Strategy** Listening for details	**Describing Friends** This is Tim. He has a hamster. We play together.	**Capitals for Names** My friend's name is Sun. **Tasks** Talk about your friend and write about him or her. (Workbook)	**Project** Family and Friends Collage **Review** Units 1 and 2 (WB)
BIG QUESTION 2		**Where can we see colors?** Art					
3 Page 26	**Who's In The Tree? Roses are Red I Like Colors** Rhyming poems (Fiction) **Reading Strategy** Predicting from Titles	**Reading Text Words** yellow, red, blue, green, purple, black, brown, white **Listening Text Words** fireworks, dark, light, gray, orange, pink **Word Study** Nouns	**There is ... / There are ...** There's a black spider. There are two white kittens.	**Fireworks** A conversation while watching fireworks **Listening Strategy** Listening for color details	**Inviting and Making Suggestions** Do you want to play with me? Let's roller! OK. Good idea!	**Tasks** Talk about rhyming words and write a poem with animals and colors. (WB)	
4 Page 36	**Let's Make Colors!** Informational text (Nonfiction) **Reading Strategy** Predicting from Titles	**Reading Text Words** mix, mural, ocean, sand, seaweed, seashell, jellyfish, starfish **Listening Text Words** jacket, shorts, sneakers, T-shirt, hat, pants	**Prepositions of Place: In, On, Under, Next To** The starfish is under the seaweed. The seashells are on the sand.	**My Favorite Clothes** A conversation about clothes on a clothesline **Listening Strategy** Listening for color and place details	**Describing Using Colors** I have a yellow hat. There's a starfish next to me. It's orange.	**Capitals and Periods in Sentences** The starfish is under the seaweed. **Tasks** Talk about your favorite clothes and write about them. (WB)	**Project** Color Mix Chart **Review** Units 3 and 4 (WB)
BIG QUESTION 3		**Where do animals live?** Life Science					
5 Page 46	**Animal Homes** (Nonfiction) **Reading Strategy** Predicting from Titles and Pictures	**Reading Text Words** eagle, chick, nest, opossum, tree hollow, honeybee, hive, cash **Listening Text Words** woods, field, pond, squirrel, mouse, frog **Word Study** irregular plurals	**Where Questions with Verb Be** Where's the eagle? Where are the chicks?	**Animal Homes** A documentary about animal homes in different habitats **Listening Strategy** Listening for details	**Warning People** Watch out! Be careful! OK. Thanks!	**Tasks** Talk about animal homes and write about one. (WB)	
6 Page 56	**My Friend, Anak** Realistic Fiction **Reading Strategy** Identifying Characters	**Reading Text Words** orangutan, rainforest, reserve, teach, take care of, miss, take a nap, put out **Listening Text Words** day, night, morning, midday, afternoon, evening	**What and Who Questions with Verb Be** What's that? Who's this?	**Animals on a Reserve** Descriptions of animals' eating and sleeping habits **Listening Strategy** Listening for time details	**Describing Animals** It's small. It's brown. It lives in the woods.	**Question Marks** What is it? **Tasks** Talk about animals and their habits and write about one. (WB)	**Project** An Animal Booklet **Review** Units 5 and 6 (WB)
BIG QUESTION 4		**How are seasons different?** Earth Science					
7 Page 66	**The Four Seasons** Informational text (Nonfiction) **Reading Strategy** Using Captions to Clarify Ideas	**Reading Text Words** warm, hot, cool, cold, rain, snow, long, short **Listening Text Words** weather, cloudy, sunny, windy, snowy, rainy **Word Study** Compound nouns	**Simple Present (It)** It gets hot in the summer. It snows in the winter. It doesn't snow in the summer.	**Weather and Seasons** Conversations about the weather in different seasons **Listening Strategy** Listening for details	**Inviting People** Do you want to play in the snow with me? Sure! Great! Let's go!	**Tasks** Talk about your favorite season and write about it. (WB)	
8 Page 76	**The Seasons of Arnold's Apple Tree** Realistic Fiction **Reading Strategy** Using Captions to Clarify Ideas	**Reading Text Words** watch, build a snowman, build a tree house, make a swing, make apple pie, grow, fall, bring **Listening Text Words** ride a bicycle, go to the beach, eat ice cream, drink hot chocolate, fly a kite, plant flowers	**Simple Present (I / You / We / They)** In the summer, I build a tree house. Do you watch honeybees? No, I don't.	**Seasonal Activities** Conversations about what we do in different seasons **Listening Strategy** Listening for details	**Asking and Telling about Activities** What do you do in the spring? I ride a bicycle.	**Commas** The four seasons are spring, summer, fall, and winter. **Tasks** Talk about what you do in different seasons and write about it. (WB)	**Project** A Seasons Journal **Review** Units 7 and 8 (WB)

Materials extract 9.A (Koustaff & Rivers, 2014, pp. 2–3)

The other three skills and vocabulary and grammar also deserve their separate columns, but are all derived from the reading skill. In addition to these organizing principles, there is also a wrap-up column which indicates that there is systematic review and recycling incorporated into the materials. The units also focus on collaborative skills, critical thinking, and creative thinking, all of which resonates with the 21st century skills emphasized in earlier chapters. The content is presented as questions to ponder on, and this facilitates inquiry-based learning and a student-centred approach to teaching. Teachers and learners are further supported by additional materials, such as posters, cards, iTools, a teacher's website, an audio CD, a Big Question DVD, online practice materials, and a parent website.

Evaluating coursebooks

Coursebooks are evaluated and adapted informally all the time by both teachers and learners. Teachers monitor what works and what does not work, and add their own style and interpretation to the book. Coursebooks can also be evaluated formally. One obvious aim of such evaluation could be for teachers to put a case to school administration to change an old coursebook or to identify ways in which the given coursebook can be supplemented. Coursebook evaluation usually starts with examining the author's claims about the book. For example, if it is claimed that the coursebook gives all four skills an equal balance, includes systematic learner training, or teaches reading with authentic, fun texts, these claims can be checked easily by examining the relevant units in the book. In addition to the coursebook author's original claims, each and every teaching/learning context will generate a set of additional criteria that are important to the specific teachers, children, and schools. These criteria can be divided into three sets of factors, as shown in Table 9.1.

Learner factors	These factors include the age, cultural background, cognitive maturity, interests, and needs of the learners.
Teacher factors	These factors include teachers' professional background, whether they are native or non-native teachers, their experience in a given context, typical workload, way of working, difficulties and interests, and their access to professional development opportunities.
Institutional and contextual factors	These factors include the number and frequency of hours English is taught per week, how English is integrated into the rest of the curriculum, whether there are curricular guidelines, the resources available to teachers and learners—such as computers, access to the internet, tapes, videos, storybook collections—and restrictions such as furniture that cannot be moved in the English classrooms.

Table 9.1 Drawing up criteria for coursebook evaluation

Teachers will evaluate and select coursebooks according to how appropriate they seem for the given context. For example, where the learners are very young (four to five years of age) and the teachers are inexperienced, it may be advisable to look for a coursebook that 1) contains songs, rhymes, and action stories with drama and hands-on crafts for this very young age group, and 2) supports the inexperienced teachers by providing detailed teacher's notes which include sample language used in the classroom, tips, explanations, answer keys to exercises, full audioscripts, ideas, and activities in photocopiable or downloadable sheets to use in the classes. Well designed teacher's books can support inexperienced teachers a great deal because they act as training materials.

Coursebooks can also be evaluated by exploring teachers' and children's experiences and opinions of them as used in the classroom. It is possible to give questionnaires to or interview children or colleagues to find out what aspects of the book they like or do not like and why, and what does or does not suit their contexts. Findings from such interviews and questionnaires—and possibly from classroom observations by teaching colleagues—can reveal interesting results about the effectiveness of a coursebook. Children's and teachers' opinions about the same coursebook can sometimes be different or change over time, so it is important for teachers to monitor their own experience as well as the children's opinions and experiences. Since it is impossible to find the perfect coursebook, most teachers will engage in activities to supplement and refresh the one they are working with.

The following data extract is from a small-scale study conducted by Jennifer Joshua (2015), a South African researcher and teacher. She decided to interview her learners about the materials she designed. The children first drew pictures of the most enjoyable activities and then talked about these with the researcher. The short extract in Figure 9.1 indicates that children can provide very clear reasons why they like or do not like certain materials. This can be an invaluable source of information for future planning.

Another teacher and researcher in India, Maduri Modugala (2012), also asked her learners their opinions about their current English coursebook. The children were working in groups and they discussed what they liked and disliked about the coursebook. They were then given disposable cameras to take photos of things they wanted to appear in their new coursebook. The children also designed their dream coursebook units.

Here is some of what the children said:

- All the coursebook is just writing. If someone cannot understand what the teacher is telling, if they make into a story, and put it in a DVD, they can see it and understand it.
- Reading these texts, it is so long and boring! They should give us research like Google and project work or go out on a real picnic.
- Funny things, crazy things, we should be excited, we should be eager to know what's next.
- Real topics like real life, like stop child labour.

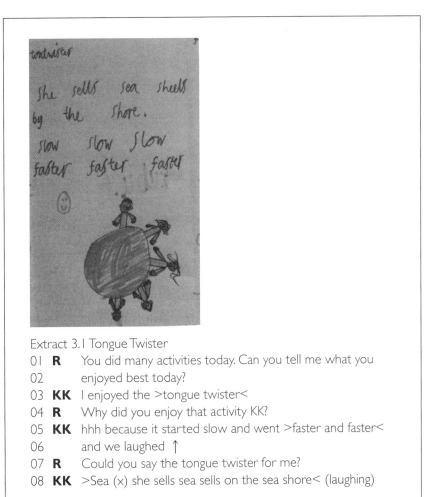

Extract 3.1 Tongue Twister

01 **R** You did many activities today. Can you tell me what you
02   enjoyed best today?
03 **KK** I enjoyed the >tongue twister<
04 **R** Why did you enjoy that activity KK?
05 **KK** hhh because it started slow and went >faster and faster<
06   and we laughed ↑
07 **R** Could you say the tongue twister for me?
08 **KK** >Sea (x) she sells sea sells on the sea shore< (laughing)

Figure 9.1 Interviewing learners (Joshua, 2015)

As these examples illustrate, children do have opinions and ideas about materials. When children are asked about their opinions, they often come up with unexpected views. Teachers might want to ask their learners about coursebooks and encourage children to design new, exciting units or chapters for their existing coursebooks. The most successful units or materials could then be taught in class.

Supplementing coursebooks

All coursebooks have attractive features but, equally, they are all restrictive in some ways, and it is important that teachers can take time to identify gaps in them. Having done this, they can begin to adapt and rewrite materials to fill these gaps so that the content becomes better suited to their class. Teachers may want to supplement the main coursebook for a number of different reasons. When, for example, an international coursebook is used, local teachers may feel that the cultural input is not entirely appropriate. They can adapt existing activities to broaden the cultural perspective by including concerns of local or international interest. For example, rather than discussing festivals in English-speaking countries only, they can compare and include festivals in their own or other countries as well. Another reason to supplement a book may be that the teacher wants to experiment with encouraging children in learning to learn. If learning to learn does not feature in the coursebook, teachers may plan activities to introduce the 'plan–do–review' cycle into each unit (see Chapter 8), or teach specific vocabulary learning strategies. Yet another common reason for supplementing a coursebook is to use attractive, authentic materials to motivate learners. For example, a teacher may decide to include authentic stories or storybooks to supplement the predictable language of the coursebook. Storybooks, children's magazines, and other children's publications, as well as the internet, are great sources of authentic materials for teachers.

Authentic texts

Many authentic materials such as picture books can be used in English classes without any adaptation. The original language is often rich and attractive and, because of the excellent visuals, it is actually quite easy to guess specific meaning from context. Children generally do not mind if they do not understand every word in a story as long as following the plot is still possible. Repeated opportunities to listen to the same story will also help learning new language embedded in the story.

In some cases, however, teachers may have a good reason to decide to adapt a piece of authentic material. One commonly experienced difficulty, especially at lower levels, is associated with the linguistic demands of authentic texts. Children would be very interested in the authentic stories teachers come across, but their language level in English is often not adequate to access these texts in their original form. One useful skill that the teacher can easily develop over time is making judgements about changing and adapting authentic or difficult texts to suit the competence level of the class. In this process, it is important to make sure that the original appeal of the text does not suffer. In some cases, changing and simplifying can destroy the original.

Adapting a well known-fable

Fables are particular types of animal stories with moral lessons applicable to human life. These can be simplified quite easily. Materials extract 9.B shows the start of a traditional fable attributed to Aesop, 'The Grasshopper and the Ants'. In the fable, while the grasshopper sings and dances all summer, the ants work hard and collect food for the winter. When winter comes, the grasshopper has no food and has to beg the ants to give him some. This fable could be a good source of language learning for children but, as the teacher has indicated in the extract, the traditional fable is far too difficult for her class of eight-year-olds with very little English.

Fables

The grasshopper and the ants

One winter day, when the sun came out unexpectedly, all the ants hurried out of their anthill and began to spread out their ~~store~~ of grain to dry. *food ?* *bring out*

Up came the grasshopper who said: 'I am so hungry. Please, will you give some of your grain?'

One of the ants stopped working for a moment and replied:

'Why should we? What has happened to your own ~~store of~~ food for the winter?'

'I have not got a ~~store~~ *any*' - said the grasshopper. 'I did not have time to collect any food last summer because I spent the whole time singing.'

The ant laughed and all the others joined in.

'If you spent the summer singing, you will have to spend the winter dancing for your supper.'

The grasshopper went on his way, hungry.

Materials extract 9.B A traditional fable (Clark, 1990)

This teacher has crossed out words and phrases such as 'unexpectedly', 'spread out', and 'store', and also replaced some phrases with simpler ones such as 'began to bring out food' instead of 'began to spread out their store'. After crossing out the words, she has made further changes to the text by inserting repetition to make the content more accessible to her learners. The text now resembles the cumulative stories described in Chapter 5. In the new version (see Figure 9.2), the grasshopper talks to several ants, and each time the conversation is the same. The grasshopper says he is hungry and asks for food, and the ants ask him what he was doing in the summer. When they find out that he was idle, they do not give him any food. This pattern is repeated with predictable language. The teacher has also changed the story ending. The ants refuse to give the grasshopper any food but when the queen ant comes along she suggests a solution. They give him food but they make him promise that he will help next year and will play music for them all year round.

One winter day the grasshopper met an ant. The ant was eating some nice food.

The grasshopper said, 'I am so hungry. Can you give me some food, please?'

The ant said, 'I worked hard all summer. What did you do in the summer, grasshopper?'

'I was singing and dancing.'

The ant shook her head and did not give him any food.

The grasshopper was very sad and hungry. He met another ant.

The grasshopper said, 'I am so hungry. Can you give me some food, please?'

The ant said, 'I worked hard all summer. What did you do, grasshopper?'

'I was singing and dancing.'

The ant shook her head and did not give him any food.

The grasshopper was sad and hungry when he met a third ant.

The grasshopper said, 'I am so hungry. Can you give me some food, please?'

The ant said, 'I worked hard all summer. What did you do, grasshopper?'

'I was singing and dancing.'

The ant shook her head and did not give him any food.

The grasshopper was sad and hungry when he met the queen of the ants.

The grasshopper said, 'I am so hungry. Can you give me some food, please?'

The queen said, 'I worked hard all summer. What did you do in the summer, grasshopper?'

'I was singing and dancing.'

The queen said, 'I see. We will give you some food but you have to promise to help us next summer and play music for us all year round.'

The grasshopper was happy and he promised to help and play music for them.

He had a nice dinner with his new friends.

Figure 9.2 Adaptation of 'The Grasshopper and the Ants' for storytelling

This adaptation, although in the end quite dramatically different from the original, still works for a number of reasons. First of all, the story is still a good source for learning new vocabulary, structures, and functions. Children can learn names of animals, listen to the past tense used in narrative, and learn the question-and-answer routine from the conversations between the grasshopper and the ants. The traditional moral lesson taught by this fable about the need to work for your food is still there, although changing it slightly makes the message less harsh. Children can listen to or read the story about the grasshopper and the ants with enjoyment; they can act it out, and certainly learn some English from it.

Creating own materials

Topic-based planning

In many primary schools where English is integrated with other areas of the curriculum, teachers integrate planning for English into their general planning. Many primary schools use what we call 'topic-based planning', which means that a topic is chosen for a term and all the activities in all areas of the curriculum will be related to that one broad topic. For example, if the topic is 'Water', in a maths class children might measure how much water goes into different containers, in a geography class they might take a trip to the local pond and observe the life of water creatures, in an art class they might look at famous paintings of the sea, and in an English class they might write simple poems about water. Topic-based learning is beneficial and meaningful because all new learning experiences are deeply rooted in the same theme and children can see the links between various learning tasks and areas of learning. This is conducive to a holistic approach to learning. The difficulty from the perspective of teachers is that this type of planning is very time-consuming, and without a clear linear outline it is difficult to ensure that all objectives are covered by the end of the year.

Topic-based planning and teaching is also popular among teachers who have the freedom to plan their own materials. Once the topic is selected, teachers will typically brainstorm activities and games that can be used to introduce the new language related to that topic in a natural way. Table 9.2 and Figure 9.3 illustrate how teachers might start brainstorming ideas for the topic of 'Families' in their English class.

Younger learners	Older learners
Cross-curricular activity Crafting: a family tree: make the tree, decorate it, display it, and talk about it	**Reading** Sections of an authentic book: Children like you in the world (an information book)
Vocabulary Members of the family (with extended family)	**Speaking** Future of families in our societies
Structure 'have got'	**Mind maps** Advantages and disadvantages of having big families
Listening Short description of families in different parts of the world	**Structure** 'When I grow up, I will'
Speaking Dialogues: Sharing photo albums: 'This is my brother. He is two here.'	**Listening** Extraordinary families
Listening Animal families	**Writing** Introduce your family – create a webpage
Crafting Making cards for Mothers' Day or Fathers' Day	**Speaking** Play a game: Find someone who … in their family.
Games Playing online vocabulary games related to family	**Writing** Writing a blog about the adventures of an imagined family

Table 9.2 Ideas for younger and older children on the topic of 'Families'

Figure 9.3 Activities on the topic of 'Families'

Lesson planning

Once some ideas for activities have been brainstormed, the next step is to think carefully about the objectives for each activity and begin to sequence them. Table 9.3 shows a draft plan to teach three consecutive lessons to children aged seven using some of the ideas from Table 9.2. Each lesson is 40 minutes long, and has a main objective and a number of steps. Each step takes about ten minutes, which leaves time for a warmer at the beginning and a closing activity at the end. All three lessons are focused on listening and speaking because these children do not yet do any reading or writing.

Lesson I (40 minutes)	Lesson 2 (40 minutes)	Lesson 3 (40 minutes)
Objectives(s)	**Objectives(s)**	**Objectives(s)**
Introduce members of family vocabulary (mother, father, sister, brother, etc.) and 'have got'.	Further practice of 'have got' + family members + introduce question form 'have you got'?	Introduce vocabulary for animal families and consolidate language from lessons I and 2.
Steps	*Steps*	*Steps*
I **Listen** to a short text where a child describes a photo album: **match pictures with names of family** members in Paris (exposure to 'have got')	I **Family chant:** joining in.	I **Song: Animal families** joining in with miming.
2 **Snap card game:** (introduce sample language): practise names of family members in groups ('I have got' + family members).	2 **Team game: Listen to descriptions of families** two teams: children listen and run to stick cards on the board when they hear the names of family members (model rules).	2 **Gap speaking task:** children are given cards with pictures of family members and pets to describe for each other to complete families (model question and answer routines).
3 **Drama:** (model) acting out family members (ask children to freeze when music stops).	3 **Mingling game:** find somebody who (has two sisters, has a brother, has three cousins, etc.). Model sample question/answer routine.	3 **Craft:** making family trees or family posters including pets (provide models). Each child can choose one craft activity. In the next lesson they will talk about their posters and family trees.

Table 9.3 Lesson planning

During the process of planning it is a good idea to keep these questions in mind:

1 Do the lessons fit together well? (Is there a logical progression from one lesson to the next? Does my second lesson build on my first lesson?)

2 Do the lessons look balanced in terms of variety of activities, skills, and interaction patterns? (Is there a range of activities, are both listening and speaking practised, and is there any group or pair work?)

3 Do I have a progression from receptive to productive practice (listen first and then speak)?

4 Are the activities meaningful for the children? Why will they want to do them?

5 Is the language outcome real, natural? Is the sample language planned for the activities real and meaningful? Would children use the language like this in the real world?

6 Are all the activities different? Check that no two activities do exactly the same thing.

7 Have I thought of optional activities for those pairs/groups or individuals who finish early?

8 Have I included my usual warmers/closing activities such as a homework check?

9 Have I included timing for each activity?

Immediately after teaching a lesson, it is a good idea to take a few minutes to think about how the plan worked out, what went well and why, in order to improve the planning process on subsequent occasions.

Writing own texts

As part of working on a topic, it is possible to exploit stories, poems, songs, and rhymes, too. Many teachers enjoy writing their own material.

According to Brian Tomlinson (2015), a researcher interested in materials development and evaluation, young learners' English materials need to be engaging and enjoyable, and they should give children real opportunities to use the second language. One very inspiring example he cites is about a teacher he observed in Vanuatu, in the South Pacific. This teacher told the children in the break that in the English class they were going to watch television. She asked them to go into the classroom and sit down in front of the new television. The children rushed in and sat down in front of the large cardboard box, i.e. the television that the teacher had made. The teacher then 'switched on the television' and in the cut-out screen, using a rolling pin and a roll of paper, began to 'roll' a story. The story was stopped every now and then and the children predicted what might happen in the next scene. The teacher then got them to 'watch the drawings' and to read the words on the screen. She rolled the paper faster and faster as the children got better and better at understanding and following the story. After this, each lesson was started by watching a story on 'television', and the children soon wrote their own stories, created poems, and had lively interactions related to the stories with each other in

English. Tomlinson comments that such simple, yet meaningful, and fun materials can be excellent vehicles to lead to natural second language acquisition in young learners' classrooms.

Children can also create materials for each other. (See Chapter 6.) For example, in some contexts it is often the case that older children write stories or poems for younger ones to work with. In very large classes, teachers divide learners into groups which can create learning materials for one another. Children can also contribute ideas to add to or change texts such as story endings. With some support, they can create their own poems, rhymes, or stories. Practice leads to enjoyment and more creativity for both teachers and children.

Summary

In this chapter materials evaluation has been discussed, taking coursebooks as a starting point. Teachers might want to supplement their coursebooks with authentic materials taken from storybooks, the internet, or other sources. Teachers' creativity and their confidence is the real driving force to supplement the coursebook or write new materials for the class. The involvement of children is important both in evaluating coursebooks and choosing and creating new materials.

Suggestions for further reading

Dudley, E., & **Osváth, E.** (2016). *Mixed-ability teaching*. Oxford: Oxford University Press.
This book contains ideas for teachers who work with mixed-ability groups. First, the characteristics of mixed-ability classes are examined, and then suggestions are offered for ways in which teachers can get everyone engaged in a positive classroom atmosphere. It also focuses on assessment and evaluation of learning in such classrooms. Online resources and free sample material can be found at: www.oup.com/elt/teacher/itc

Garton, S., & **Graves, K.** (Eds.). (2014). *International perspectives on materials in ELT*. Basingstoke: Palgrave Macmillan.
This book offers international perspectives on ELT materials from a variety of educational contexts. Each chapter offers a theoretical background as well as practical concerns relevant for teachers. Several chapters are specifically relevant for young learners and classes, and many of the chapters deal with ICT.

Moon, J. (2000). *Children learning English*. Oxford: Macmillan.
This book contains many useful ideas for teachers in primary English classes who are in the position to create their own teaching materials. Chapter 7 offers a checklist for creating language learning activities and Chapter 9 introduces the idea of topic-based planning with its benefits and disadvantages. There is clear advice about sequencing activities, too.

Tomlinson, B. (Ed.). (2003). *Developing materials for language teaching*. London: Continuum.

This is a comprehensive overview of the role of materials in ELT. The content covers evaluation, adaptation, and ideas for designing materials for different learner groups, as well as ideas for training materials designers in ELT. Each chapter is a research-based account written by various experts in the field.

Tasks

If you would like to explore your own practice related to the content of this chapter, you can try the following tasks:

Task 1: Exploring different age groups (page 183)

Task 5: Exploring materials (page 186)

Task 6: Working creatively with materials (page 186)

Task 7: Observing children choosing tasks (page 188)

Task 8: Getting children to reflect on their learning (page 188)

Task 9: Planning lessons (page 188)

Task 10: Exploring authentic materials (page 189)

Task 11: Designing your own assessment tasks (page 191)

10 ASSESSMENT

Introduction

All teachers need to know how effective their teaching is, and all learners are interested in how well they are doing. Assessment of the learning process is therefore an integral part of teaching and learning. In many contexts children are also assessed in some standardized way, by, for example, having to do a national English language test at the end of primary school. Teachers need to be familiar with different purposes and means of assessing learners, and they also need to be aware that in the case of younger learners, some traditional assessment methods can be problematic. This is why it is important that assessment in language learning for children is handled with care. This chapter will introduce some basic background about testing and some child-friendly methods that can be used in a variety of different contexts, preferably in combination with each other.

Purposes of assessment

Assessment refers to the process of data analysis that teachers use to get evidence about their learners' performance and progress in English. In terms of purpose, assessment is carried out because head teachers, school authorities, and parents/ carers require evidence of learning, but it is also the right of the children to know how they are doing.

Assessment can be carried out by authorities outside the school, i.e. by national or international bodies, to check that certain standards have been achieved. Testers in this case typically use materials that have been developed over a careful process of piloting, and the final scores or certificate issued carry high status and may influence children's progress to new contexts of learning.

Learners can be assessed in a **summative** way, i.e. to find out what they achieved after covering a unit, or a term's or year's work; in this kind of assessment there is a focus on the final product. Alternatively, learners can be assessed in a **formative** way. Formative assessment is more focused on the process of learning, and it is aimed at diagnosing learners' stages of development on an ongoing basis.

Norm referencing versus criterion referencing

There are two main approaches to assessment: **norm referencing** and **criterion referencing**. Norm referencing means that teachers compare their learners' achievements with the norm, i.e. the class average. If someone is below average, they will get a low mark. One problem is that this approach to assessment fails to take into account small steps in individual progress and achievements, and it encourages comparison and competition among children. Criterion referencing, on the other hand, means that learners have to meet certain set criteria. Teachers make a note of where each learner is according to the criteria and then track their progress. All children can progress at their own pace. Comparisons among children are discouraged because individual achievement is the focus. Children's results and achievements are compared with their starting point. In criterion referencing, teachers of young learners tend to favour success-oriented assessment, i.e. they encourage and praise everybody and value both efforts and achievement. Children carry out tasks in familiar learning contexts in an environment that encourages confidence and builds self-esteem and, as a result, they are not worried about being assessed.

Standardized large-scale testing

With more and more children learning English worldwide, many more governments have introduced national tests, and many more organizations offer international certificates to children. There is also a global trend to align assessment practices to the Common European Framework of Reference (Council of Europe, 2001).

The CEFR and young learners

More recently, the CEFR has been adopted worldwide to describe learners' foreign language competence using overall communicative proficiency on six levels. A1 and A2 describe the basic user, B1 and B2 the independent user, and C1 and C2 describe the proficient user. There are specific descriptors associated with each level. These are always positive in that they describe what the learner *can do* with the language. The most well-known document that is strongly linked to the CEFR is the European Language Portfolio (ELP), which is intended to make the language learning process more transparent and also encourages self-assessment and learner autonomy. More about **portfolio assessment** for children is covered later in this chapter.

Even though the CEFR was not intended for children/younger learners, it has been used increasingly as a reference point for assessing children in EFL classes. Many counties have designed their own ELP materials for schools, and there is growing evidence that, in many contexts, children and teachers enjoy working with the ELP. However, in 2015, Carmen Becker reported on the evaluation of a large-scale implementation of ELPs in Germany and her results were only partially positive. Her study revealed that, even though teachers and learners had positive attitudes to this assessment tool, the uptake by teachers was rather low and they did not integrate the ELP into their practice. Teachers reported that they did not have confidence in their learners' ability to assess themselves, and teachers tended to focus on the coursebook and assessment suggested by the coursebook. Teachers also felt that the ELP tool was not flexible enough and that they needed more training and support.

The Cambridge English: Young Learners tests

Many other international tests are available on the market, such as the Trinity or the TOEFL Junior tests, but perhaps one of the most popular is the Cambridge English: Young Learners tests. These are designed at three levels for learners aged 7–12 years of age. The three levels are called Starters, Movers, and Flyers. The test papers are available for children internationally to do either online or in a 'paper and pencil' format in designated testing centres. The tests are described as fun to do and motivating, and the three levels represent gradually more complex tasks. The test tasks are interactive and meaningful. Many publishers provide practice materials that teachers and learners can use in preparation for taking these tests. Materials extract 10.A is a typical interactive task from a practice book, showing a speaking task at Flyers level. The candidate has one picture and the examiner has another. There are a number of differences between these two pictures and the candidate's task is to ask questions to find the differences. The extract is taken from *YLE Tests Flyers* (Oxford University Press).

Materials extract 10.A (Cliff, 2010, p. 23)

As a result of the popularity of the CEFR and its international impact, publishers use the CEFR level descriptors in their courses, and there are ongoing efforts to link young learners' tests to the levels and descriptors specified by the CEFR. For example, a study published in 2009 by Szilvia Papp and Angeliki Salamoura describes efforts to align the Cambridge English: Young Learners tests to the CEFR. The study reveals that the test components have been verified as being pre-A1 (Starters), A1 (Movers), and A2 (Flyers) levels, except for the writing element, which is pre-A1 for all three levels. This means that the Cambridge English: Young Learners tests are more focused on language development in speaking and listening, as the writing skills in primary are mainly concerned with spelling, copying, and writing short phrases rather than producing coherent discourse. Language comprehension levels are generally higher in children than language production levels. Many descriptors in the current CEFR are not appropriate for children; for example, those describing work routines or studying, or applying for jobs, or discussing current affairs. Additional topics have also been suggested specifically for children, such as stories, fantasy, and animals. Overall, the researchers conclude that the CEFR descriptors in speaking and listening are largely appropriate with some adaptations, while the scales for reading and writing would need further work before the Cambridge English: Young Learners tests could be aligned to the CEFR.

In some contexts, international English exams for children are very popular. Many parents/carers are keen to push their children to get these certificates. While these tests and certificates can be motivating for children in terms of confirming their abilities in English, questions do arise about those children and families who cannot afford them and about the value of these certificates as children grow older and make important choices about schools, universities, and careers.

Teacher assessment

While standardized assessment is generally concerned with summative purposes, assessment in the classroom might be more focused on diagnosing learning needs and, therefore, more focused on formative assessment.

It is important for teachers to think about ways in which they may measure learning and development in their classes. This begins with setting learning goals. For example, after completing a unit on 'Families', the children will be able to talk or write a short paragraph about their own families. They may also be able to answer questions about their families and talk about their photo albums. They will be able to recite a rhyme or sing a song from the same unit. It is important for teachers to identify these objectives at the beginning of each unit of teaching so that they can check children's performance against them. Teachers will be able to see where the gaps are, what seems easier or harder for a group of learners, and what objectives have been achieved by everyone. These findings will feed directly into everyday teaching. For example, teachers may spend more time on those aspects of the unit that proved to be harder, or they might spend some time looking again at an activity which was seen to be problematic in an assessment exercise. The main aim of this process is to inform and improve teaching.

In relation to effective teacher assessment, Peter Edelenbos and Angelika Kubanek-German (2004) coined the phrase **diagnostic assessment**. This is defined as teachers' ability to interpret foreign language growth in children through one-to-one attention to individual learner production. In their paper, they describe various diagnostic activities, which include careful scaffolding of learners and a general ability to exploit each learning/teaching situation fully. Some of these techniques, for example, are

- guess what a child might want to say and motivate them to say it
- interpret silence
- group children according to their needs
- evoke children's prior knowledge
- recognize from children's facial expressions whether they understood something
- adapt teacher language readily depending on each child's level of competence.

Teachers who possess high levels of a diagnostic ability can also describe stages of linguistic growth in children and can analyze and evaluate different assessment tools, appreciating both their strengths and weaknesses. The authors conclude that teacher education in the area of classroom assessment is crucially important.

In 2005, Angela Hasselgren, a Norwegian researcher, also wrote about the importance of teacher education in the area of assessment. She argues that children need to experience assessment as fun and appealing. At the same time, teachers need to understand the links between assessment and learning, and the criteria they are using for assessment must be clear. In Norway, there is intensive work ongoing about linking the CEFR by extending the currently used descriptors to young learners. There, every teacher is given at least one day of professional development in testing specifically relevant to the CEFR. Teacher development programmes worldwide could benefit from including more training in the area of teacher assessment.

Traditional methods of assessment and young learners

Assessment of adult learners is full of challenges, but there are some additional challenges to consider with children. Young children's knowledge of English is often hard to pin down, as it often comprises, for example, being able to sing songs, participate in stories and games, or mime an action story, i.e. things that are not easy and straightforward to assess objectively. Traditional 'paper and pencil' tests typically include activities such as filling in gaps in sentences, answering multiple choice questions, or translating vocabulary lists. They are often favoured by teachers because they are relatively easy to set and correct and they reduce language knowledge to points, marks, and grades, i.e. quantifiable results. However, in the case of younger children especially, these tests often do not work because such isolated exercises do not show what children know and can do with confidence. They might also have a negative influence on teaching so that instead of singing, reciting rhymes, listening to stories, and playing games, children will have to spend time answering multiple choice questions in class in order to prepare for the test. This is often called the negative **washback effect** of tests. Children are often not yet very good at writing and this means that traditional tests can be stressful and tiring. There is the danger that inappropriate assessment methods and possibly lower grades would discourage children and cause them to lose their motivation to learn English. Given that many programmes aim to develop attitudinal goals such as positive motivation towards language learning and broadening cultural horizons, these tests could do more harm than good.

It is important for teachers to use assessment techniques that are child-friendly and compatible with the activities used every day in their classrooms. In order to understand what children have learned, teachers may need to use a variety of assessment methods. If traditional 'paper and pencil' tests need to be used because of institutional restrictions, they should be considered together with other methods, such as self-assessment, portfolio assessment, or observations, in order to get a more complete and more reliable picture of children's achievements.

Restrictions and opportunities in individual schools and coursebooks

Within a school context, whether English is integrated into the primary curriculum or taught separately, the assessment culture of the school will influence the assessment practices in English. For example, in schools where eight-year-olds are assessed in every subject with a single grade (1–5), it is unlikely that it will be possible to follow a different system for English. In these contexts, it is often the case that teachers work on compromises such as respecting the grade system but awarding only good grades for both effort and achievement. Teachers can choose from a range of alternative assessment tools, most of which can be incorporated into the teaching practice of any context. Most modern coursebooks recommend their own set of assessment materials and these, more often than not, represent a cluster of different approaches to, and tools for, assessment. This type of support is helpful to teachers but, at the same time, teachers need to be critical and careful about implementing them.

Child-friendly methods and a variety of assessment tools

Teachers will discover more about their learners' second/foreign language abilities if they use a variety of assessment methods. This will help to formulate a more holistic picture of what the learners can do. Below are some alternative assessment methods and tools that can be integrated into almost any context.

Observation

Teachers can use systematic observation as a tool to assess children's performance. Observation is non-intrusive because children are often not even aware that they are being assessed. The same sort of task is given to children in class again and again until they are used to it, and then the teacher observes the performance of a particular group. Depending on the goals of the observation, teachers can assess children in a variety of situations, such as working in pairs, or in groups, or independently. Observation is also good for checking the performance of non-linguistic skills (such as engagement, interest, motivation) which make up some of the core objectives of primary English programmes. Simple observation checklists can be created for these purposes.

The two observation schedules in Materials extracts 10.B and 10.C are from *Cross-Curricular Resources for Young Learners* (Oxford University Press). Extract 10.A is focused on progress made by individual children in relation to different assessment tasks, whereas extract 10.B is focused on children's general participation and attitudes to English. These are simply examples and they can be readily adapted by teachers according to their specific focus in different classrooms.

RECORD OF CHILDREN'S ABILITIES

School .... Group/Class/Age .... Teacher .... Topic ....

Is capable of ... (list skills)	Name .... Date			Name .... Date		
	Achieved	Progressing	Not yet achieved	Achieved	Progressing	Not yet achieved
Forms of assessment used						

Materials extract 10.B (Calabrese & Rampone, 2015, p. ix)

RECORD OF CHILDREN'S STRATEGIES AND ATTITUDES

Date: ....   Group/class: ....   Topic: ....

Description of activity: ....

Students	INTERACTION				COMPREHENSION				PRODUCTION			
	S/he is interested in the activities carried out	S/he works with the other students in carrying out the activity	S/he can work autonomously to complete activities		S/he can understand the general meaning of the subject	S/he can understand simple questions about the subject	If s/he does not understand, s/he asks for explanations in L1 or L2		S/he can answer simple questions on the subject	S/he participates and asks questions only in L1	S/he participates and asks questions in L2 as well as L1	
1.												
2.												
3.												
4.												
5.												
6.												
7.												
8.												
9.												
10.												
11.												
12.												
13.												
14.												
15.												
16.												
17.												

Key: ☺ always   😐 sometimes   ☹ never

Comments: ....
....

Materials extract 10.C (Calabrese & Rampone, 2015, p. viii)

Self-assessment and peer assessment

Another method that teachers can experiment with is self-assessment and peer assessment. Initially this would have to happen in the first language, but as children progress with their English competence some reflection can be recorded in the second language. Encouraging children to assess themselves is an integral part of a learner-centred approach. Self-assessment means that children are asked to think about their own performance and achievements on a regular basis. Once children have experienced self-assessment, they may be interested to try peer assessment based on clearly defined criteria. In some sense, it is easier to make judgements about someone else's performance than one's own, although children often find it hard to apply the criteria when they work with their friends. It is hard to give critical comments to one's best friend. The skills used in self- and peer assessment are clearly linked to the principles of learning to learn. (See Chapter 8.) It is important to emphasize that careful and gradual training is needed, and the ability of children to assess themselves cannot be taken for granted. Self-assessment works best if it is restricted to certain well-known tasks and situations. In the same sort of task, the same sort of criteria can be used and this gives children confidence and a sense of safety. Younger children in particular may find this harder at first, so it is important to take it slowly.

There is growing empirical evidence from research which shows that children, especially those beyond the age of eight or nine, are able to assess their own performance. For example, in a study in 2010, Yuko Butler and Jiyoon Lee explored the effects of self-assessment among 254 young learners of English in South Korea. They found that sixth-grade children were able to improve the accuracy of their self-assessment over time, and self-assessment had a marginal but positive effect on the students' foreign language learning and confidence. However, they also reported that teachers and students perceived the effects of self-assessment very differently in different types of schools. In the heavily exam-oriented contexts, teachers felt it was not realistic to emphasize self-assessment. This result indicates that specific cultures of assessment are particularly powerful in certain contexts, and changing the assessment system may therefore be very difficult.

Portfolio assessment

One method of assessment gaining popularity with teachers of young learners is the portfolio. A portfolio contains a collection of a student's work and evidence of student achievement over a period of time. As mentioned previously, the CEFR has many examples of locally used ELPs and teachers can explore those specifically designed for their own contexts, but it is also possible to design one's own version.

A portfolio can include drawings, pieces of writing, examples of crafts, or even recorded oral performances. Children can be encouraged to select their best work to go into the portfolio with the help of the teacher. It is important that teachers work out criteria for selection together with the children, otherwise some children might want to put in everything without developing the ability to differentiate between samples of work. Children's growing ability to choose examples they think show their performance at its best is linked to their ability to reflect about their learning. If children are used to reflecting about their work on a regular basis, as part of the learning-to-learn activities integrated into the English class, then they will find using a portfolio both natural and meaningful. In addition to the sample pieces of work, portfolios can be used for collecting information about children's activities outside the classroom. Pages can be inserted to prompt them to think about what they want to learn next and why. These may include pages which ask them to summarize and reflect on what they can do in English, i.e. self-assessment pages.

Portfolios link teaching and assessment very clearly since they offer concrete evidence of what a learner can do. This method of assessment can also motivate learners by getting them to focus on what they are good at and develop ownership of the learning process, thus promoting learner independence. However, portfolios are arguably labour-intensive from the teacher's point of view, especially if the teacher helps with the process of selection and gives ample and regular feedback, both in writing and sitting down with individual children. In the case of younger children, teachers may have to take more responsibility for helping to choose appropriate pieces of work. Portfolios can be bulky and they need to be stored somewhere the children can have easy access to them. It is also important that rules are worked out about taking them home. Parents/Carers can take an active part in promoting their children's learning by taking an interest in their portfolios.

Project work

Many teachers like to use project work as an alternative tool for assessment. If children often work in groups during the lesson then it is logical to assess them in groups, too. The advantage of this tool is that it combines all four language skills and the joint effort of several children. Working with others and completing a substantial task can be very motivating for weaker learners because of the opportunities to learn from friends. It is also beneficial for stronger learners because they have a chance to display their knowledge and skills. Projects can work well in mixed-ability classes if the members of the groups are carefully selected and all have appropriately defined roles and tasks and adhere to agreed rules. In addition, project work is an opportunity for children to demonstrate other non-linguistic strengths such as drawing or acting. There is, of course, the disadvantage that it is very difficult to assign grades to project work because of the need to acknowledge both individual endeavour and group effort, and it is virtually impossible to be completely fair to everyone. One solution is to give children praise and general feedback rather than grades, and use project work as part of formative assessment. Teachers might want to experiment with grouping children in various ways to find out which groups work best for collaborative learning. This could easily lead to an **action research** project and interesting discoveries. (See Chapter 12.)

Materials extract 10.D Designing a poster

Materials extract 10.D shows as an example of a project where children will design their 'green city' on a poster. Children can work in groups of four or five. The first step is planning. They can brainstorm ideas and then research different sites on the internet related to the environment and green technology. As a next step, they can share their ideas in class and get some feedback before designing the posters. Children can take different roles in the group such as taking responsibility for drawing, labelling, writing, proofreading for spelling, and designing the overall layout of the poster. When the poster is complete they can present it to the class. (See Materials extract 10.D.)

When children are new to this kind of project work, teachers can break down the steps involved and help groups to allocate roles and make decisions at every stage. Once children are more used to working this way, they may enjoy managing the process by themselves and will need less direct help.

Teachers and learners can collaboratively decide on the criteria to assess the end products. For example, in this case:

- Are the green ideas clearly explained and illustrated?
- Did everyone in the group participate and contribute?
- Is the poster attractive and clear to look at?

Summary

In the case of children, traditional scores and 'paper and pencil' tests do not work, especially if they are used as the only method of assessment. A variety of principles have been suggested for introducing alternative assessment methods into TEYL classrooms. Assessment does not have to be stressful and competitive. Instead, it can contribute to fostering positive self-image and self-esteem in a collaborative environment.

Suggestions for further reading

Ioannou-Georgiou, S., & **Pavlou, P.** (2003). *Assessing young learners*. Oxford: Oxford University Press.
This is a collection of imaginative assessment ideas and activities to use in primary classrooms. The book contains multiple assessment techniques such as portfolio, self-assessment, and project work, but also more traditional assessment techniques are carefully explained and classified for different age groups.

Jang, E. E. (2014). *Focus on assessment*. Oxford: Oxford University Press.
This is a comprehensive introduction to language assessment for teachers with theory and practice relevant to classrooms. The book helps teachers to develop skills in designing and critically evaluating assessment tools in school contexts. Chapter 3 specifically concerns issues for young learners' classes. Online resources and free sample material can be found at: www.oup.com/elt/teacher/foa

McKay, S. (2006). *Assessing young language learners.* Cambridge: Cambridge University Press.
This book offers an excellent background chapter on how children learn best and therefore what approach to take when it comes to assessment. The detailed framework for assessment suitable for second language learners, both EFL and ESL, is fully explained and illustrated. The assessment is task-based and centred around techniques suitable for children. The book covers both underlying theory and practical ideas for assessment. It also refers to examples from around the world.

Nikolov, M. (Ed.). (2015). *Assessing young learners of English: Global and local perspectives.* Switzerland: Springer International Publishing.
This book contains 14 articles by various assessment experts around the world. The editor has written an excellent introductory chapter about the challenges of testing and assessment with young language learners. Each chapter takes either a local or global issue and presents some empirical data. Topics include young learners' testing and the CEFR, testing the different skills, peer- and self assessment for children, and large-scale standardized test production, as well as teacher development in the area of testing and assessment.

Tasks

If you would like to explore your own practice related to the content of this chapter, you can try the following tasks:

Task 11: Designing your own assessment tasks (page 191)

Task 16: Developing skills towards self- and peer assessment (page 193)

Task 18: Using diagnostic assessment (page 195)

Task 19: Exploring group presentations (page 195)

Task 23: Conversations with children based on drawings (page 197)

11 INTERCULTURAL AWARENESS

Introduction

Intercultural awareness is about making children more aware of intercultural issues, such as the importance of accepting and celebrating diversity within their own contexts and the need to cultivate curiosity and openness about other cultures and languages. These have become priority issues for teachers, especially language teachers. Today's children come into contact with different cultures more than previous generations: through the internet and other media, and through the effects of global travel and migration. Classrooms all over the world are increasingly multicultural, and therefore there is, more than ever, a need to integrate intercultural content into the primary curriculum. This chapter will look at what intercultural adaptation means and will then explore aspects of intercultural education, including strategies and materials that teachers can exploit to increase intercultural understanding in their own classrooms.

Children relocating to a new country

Children all over the world experience the effects of global travel. Families might be relocating to escape violence or economic hardship, or to find better career opportunities. Once arrived in a new country, these families send their children to local schools where they have to cope with learning a new or second language, and learning a new curriculum through this language. Many children are affected by this global relocation because, while very large numbers of children may be relocating in new countries, even larger numbers of children will be welcoming such new arrivals in their schools and communities. It is important to recognize that all these children will be affected and they will all experience the day-to-day effects of what we call **cultural adaptation**. Rather than perceiving this as a problem looked at in rather negative terms, cultural adaptation can also be looked at as a challenge and an excellent opportunity for schools and individual teachers to exploit for general learning and development. New arrivals, wherever they come from and however long they stay, will bring a wealth of rich cultural knowledge and new resources to any school or classroom.

Children's cultural adaptation

When culturally disparate groups come into contact with one another, they have an impact on each other. Cultural adaptation can be a stressful experience. When the decision to relocate is taken by a family, children usually have little say as they simply follow their parents/carers. Empirical research about the experiences, challenges, and well-being of adult newcomers is abundant, but only a few studies are focused on younger people and almost none on young children. One well-known study was conducted by John Berry, Jean Phinney, David Sam, and Paul Vedder in 2006. In this large-scale international study, Berry et al. examined the complexities of teenagers' adaptation processes in 13 countries. They concluded that it was extremely important for these young people to learn to fit into the new host environment by establishing close ties with its members, i.e. to make local friends and be accepted by them. At the same time it was equally important for them to retain their heritage cultural identities. The balance between these two goals is hard to strike, and many teenagers experience conflict between what they want to do to fit in with their peers and what their parents/carers want them to do to preserve heritage cultural values.

Much literature suggests that overall, compared to adult migrants, children have an easier time because they are more malleable and better exposed to the new culture through the school system itself. When newcomers arrive at a young age, before primary school, the process seems smoother because young children have not fully **enculturated** into their parents'/carers' own culture yet, and because flexibility and adaptability are maximal during these early years. With regard to the nature of social attachments, a young child considers a friend anyone who is available to play with. Consequently, younger children have fewer problems leaving their friends and making new friends in the new environment. School-aged immigrant children show a more varied picture than preschool children, but on the whole they still **acculturate** faster than their parents/carers.

Children as cultural mediators

Most children who stay in a new country longer than a year or two will, eventually, successfully adapt to the new environment. Children's experience of full-time schooling with the associated practices helps them to grasp cultural phenomena that might be hidden from their parents/carers. Many children explicitly teach their parents/carers phrases and words learned at school and educate them about what is or is not appropriate in situations in the new country.

In 2014 Zhiyan Guo, who worked with Chinese families living in the UK, collected some interesting data from Chinese parents/carers documenting their own English language learning that occurred when they simply talked to their own children. Their children often pointed out important words for them, corrected them, and taught them new phrases and concepts they had picked up at school. Figure 11.1 is an example of a diary entry by Mrs Zhao, one of the parents in the research project.

> Today while I was in the kitchen, Lin sat on the top of the sofa. Hanging his legs from there, he said to me: 'Mum, do you know what I am doing.' I said: 'what is that'. 'This is called dangling, you know?' I immediately learned this word, much more quickly than I learned it in other ways.

Figure 11.1 Translated diary entry 12/01/05 (Guo, 2014)

Children also teach parents/carers about important practices around everyday events in their lives, such as how to organize birthday celebrations, how much pocket money is appropriate, and what to wear when going out. These new, often seemingly unusual, cultural practices can of course cause conflict with parents/carers, but the research project above indicates that children are real experts at persuading parents/carers of the value of these newly learned cultural practices.

Temporary relocation

Some travel or relocation is only temporary. Once the period of study in a new country or a work contract is up, the family often go back to their country of origin. Depending on whether families intend to stay in the new environment temporarily or to settle down for good, their motivation to invest in the new culture will vary. I have worked with some international families in the UK who were temporary visitors and intended to return to their home countries after a year or two of study in the UK. The children of these families were in a particularly difficult situation because they joined a local primary school without any English at all and had to fit in quickly, and yet they knew that by the end of the academic year they would leave their new friends behind. I observed great differences between how these families coped with the pressures of settling their children at school.

Figure 11.2 recounts the very positive story of a young child from South Korea (May, aged eight) who came to the UK for one year while her mother was studying at a university and was an excellent example of someone who seemed to make the most of her time in her new school. The data in Figure 11.2 is from my own notes after I interviewed Sook, May's mother, about how her daughter was getting on at school.

On the whole, May constructed herself as an independent, competent child who not only coped well but took charge of her year in England. She finished her school year in the UK very happy and with an excellent school report that praised her enthusiasm and achievements. Her ability to adapt to life in a UK school significantly surpassed her mother's expectations, and Sook felt that bringing her children over to the UK while she was studying was an excellent decision, a really worthwhile financial and cultural 'investment'.

When asked about how May settled down at school, Sook was very positive. In fact, she was amazed at the speed with which May set about the task of settling in and making new friends. She mentioned that in the second week of school May was already invited to a party. She also made friends at school very quickly. In fact, in the morning as soon as she saw her friends she went off to play leaving Sook alone with the other parents. Not only did May acquire some friends early on but she soon became the leader of her friendship group. She organized simple games to play with her friends and always took something for them such as cards or sweets. Sook was genuinely surprised by her daughter's confidence and her coping strategies. She reported that May practised English phrases at home. When nobody was listening, she was often looking in the mirror and she practised saying things she heard at school. If her mother tried to correct her pronunciation she did not accept feedback from her. In addition to practising phrases, Sook suggested that May was coping well because she worked out a way of dealing with her lack of comprehension. Whenever she did not understand something, she simply ignored the situation and quickly moved on. Sook also mentioned that her daughter was from the start very eager to participate in classes whenever she saw a chance. She often took risks, raised her hand and tried to participate at school as much as possible.

Figure 11.2 A South Korean child's temporary stay in England

Overall, the work I have been doing with international students and their families shows that not all children enjoy the first six months at school—or even the first year—as much as May did. However, in the case of those who do, there is a range of factors that seems to make a difference. First of all, it helps to have a parent who has time and energy to support a child fully in addition to their own academic or work pressures. It also helps to have an inclusive school environment where international children are looked after well and where staff understand about their need to be included. It is beneficial to have friends to play with and to be invited to parties and other after-school activities, too. These extra-curricular activities seem even more important than participating in class. On a personal level, good coping strategies, perseverance, and wanting to be the centre of attention also helped May.

Intercultural education

Teachers may have permanent or temporary newcomers in their classes, or they may have homogeneous classes where maximizing opportunities to do with raising intercultural awareness might be a priority. This section is therefore focused on intercultural education in a broad sense. Given the diversity of classrooms, what materials and resources can teachers and schools make use of, and how can they adjust available resources to their own needs?

The fact that learning a second or foreign language will involve learning cultural input means that foreign language lessons are particularly suitable for providing intercultural training or awareness raising, but there is generally a lack of resources available to language teachers and they may find it challenging to teach intercultural awareness. For the beginning years in the primary school, intercultural awareness simply starts with instilling positive attitudes about other cultures. (See Chapter 4.) For the teacher, the most important first step is to overcome their own monolingual disposition, if this is relevant.

In 1997, Michael Byram, a researcher interested in intercultural issues, identified three different concepts within intercultural education: intercultural attitudes, knowledge, and skills. Attitudes include positive predisposition, such as openness and curiosity, but also a readiness to compare one's own culture with others. Knowledge comprises facts about cultural groups and their products and practices in one's own and other countries, and it also includes understanding of processes of societal and individual interaction. Finally, skills comprise interpreting and relating to cultural phenomena, discovering and interacting with cultural concepts, and having a 'critical' cultural awareness. These concepts link with cognitive abilities and, as a consequence, younger children are less ready to compare and contrast cultures because of their less developed cognitive states, whereas children in middle childhood identify with others' perspectives and views of the world more readily.

Two central aspects of the attitudinal level are an openness towards others and curiosity. These can be successfully cultivated even in the youngest of learners. Genuine experiences with members of other cultures invited to the classroom, or handling authentic materials and objects from other cultures, can provide good initial opportunities to open up horizons and begin the journey towards de-centring, i.e. seeing others' and one's own cultures as equally legitimate ways of looking at the world. Activities in coursebooks that encourage this process by drawing comparisons across cultural phenomena are abundant. Materials may focus on similarities and differences between school systems, meals, birthday customs, and other cultural content that is deemed of interest to learners of certain ages.

Cultural content in language learning materials

Cultural content has always been an integral part of coursebooks for all ages. Traditionally, cultures (mainly target cultures such as North American or British) were represented in coursebooks in a static way, such as knowledge to be learned about institutions, customs, or holidays. In modern coursebooks, the focus is more on the parallel development of language and cultural content in an integrated way, through a process of dynamic discovery that involves familiarizing learners with a range of cultures and deepening understanding about their own cultures.

For example, in a popular coursebook for young teenagers *Teen2Teen Plus 3* (Oxford University Press), the teenage characters of the book come from different countries in the world. These characters appear in all units and are connected online, making intercultural communication a central feature of the book. The diverse geographical contexts represented by the main characters allow for the introduction of interesting information from these countries, such as special birthdays in South Korea, Peruvian food, village life in Africa, and many other themes. All these aspects of life can then be contrasted with the learners' own lives, whichever country they come from. The cultural content is embedded into 'Topic snapshots', and these are full of 'real' photographs depicting attractive cultural content. A 'blog post' appears as a reading text, contextualized as a response to a question one of the teenage friends has asked the other. For example, in Materials extract 11.A Charlotte, who is from the USA, is answering the question 'What is the most popular food in your country?', and she mentions her favourite lunch.

Another example comes from *Incredible English 5* (Oxford University Press), aimed at younger children. The cultural content of the book covers topics such as street parties, food, castles, and kings and queens—these are all relevant to Britain but other parts of the world are also represented, such as Thanksgiving in the USA, food festivals, and the Chinese New Year. There is also a regular feature 'Me and my world' where two children's lives are contrasted in a reading passage. Here, in Materials extract 11.B, we have Sunil from Sri Lanka and Holly from California writing about animals in their neighbourhoods. These texts are also illustrated with real photographs.

Learners of English in different parts of the world are then encouraged to think about their own countries and write similar paragraphs to introduce their contexts, or explore a new country using the internet to find out about animal life somewhere else. If your class is multicultural, these activities can be followed up by describing habits, customs, and facts about those countries and cultures that are represented in the class, as well as exploring countries of interest from the learners' point of view.

Reading A blog post

1.28 **1.** Read Charlotte's answer to the open question on Teen2Teen Friends. What's Charlotte's favorite lunch?

2. **Identify the main idea** After reading Charlotte's answer, circle the number of the statement that expresses its main idea.

1. Claire doesn't like peanut butter.

2. Peanuts and peanut butter are very popular in the U.S.

3. French bread is the best bread in the world.

Snails are a popular food in France.

Open question: What's the most popular food in your country?

Charlotte:

Some people think we're crazy, but we Americans <u>love</u> peanut butter, especially in peanut butter and jelly sandwiches. For me, the totally best lunch is a peanut butter and jelly sandwich on white bread with a glass of milk. Yum!

My cousin Claire is from France. She likes some of our typical dishes, especially hot dogs and hamburgers. But Claire thinks many American foods are terrible. She thinks our worst food is peanut butter and jelly sandwiches. She says, "No offense, but I don't think sweet foods and salty foods go together. And I don't really like American white bread either. Come to France if you want to taste the best bread in the world!"

Well, I <u>do</u> go to France sometimes and Claire is right about the bread. French bread is delicious. But a few of the things they eat in France are (to me) a little gross, like snails!!

Americans love peanuts, peanut products, and peanut butter. Here's something I found on a website about peanuts in American food:

In the U.S., more than 90% of all families eat peanut butter. More than 40% of American candy bars have peanuts or peanut butter in them. And the average American eats more than 2.5 kilos of peanuts and peanut butter a year.

That's a lot of peanuts and peanut butter!

Materials extract 11.A (Saslow & Ascher, 2015, p. 26)

Which text has these words and phrases? Write *E* (elephants) or *B* (bears).
Read and check.

| 1 | watersports | | 2 | carry wood | | 3 | scared | | 4 | intelligent | | 5 | to the river |

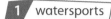

Hello. My name's Sunil. I'm from Sri Lanka. I often visit the elephant refuge near my home on Saturdays. Elephants are a very important animal here. Some elephants carry wood in the jungle and others take part in festivals. More than 10,000 lived in the jungle 100 years ago. But then people hunted them and also cut down the jungle to make farms. The elephants did not have enough space to live in and in 1993 there were only 2,000. This was sad, nobody could imagine Sri Lanka without elephants.

Elephants are protected now and there are about 7,500 in the country. In the elephant refuge the oldest elephant, Udara, is 62. There are some baby elephants too.

Some of the babies are born in the refuge and others are rescued after hunters kill their mothers. They have a good life here. Their favourite activity is going to the river. They love playing in the water!

Hi. I am Holly and I live near Lake Tahoe in Californa, USA. It is an enormous lake and there are huge pine forests near it. Lots of people come here for their holidays. They do watersports, camp and go walking in the forests around the lake. The forests are the home of black bears too. It is funny because they are called black bears but they are not usually black. They are often brown or even white!

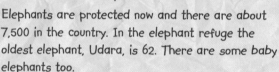

People are scared of black bears because they do not understand them. We learned about bears at school. They are not dangerous, but they are always hungry. If they find food in a rubbish bin or a garage, they think it is for them. The bears are intelligent and they will return the next day for more. Bears won't cause you any problems if you remember one thing; do not feed them!

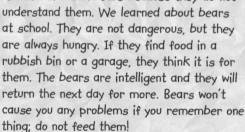

Materials extract 11.B (Phillips, Grainger & Redpath, 2012, p. 80)

Cultural encounters and intercultural training

Authentic encounters with speakers of other languages from other cultures are now readily available in many classrooms, thanks to technology such as Skype, and there are many initiatives that teachers can take advantage of through school 'twinning' projects. In school, twinning projects—where children become friends with another class from another country—create genuine reasons to learn English and motivation to practise English.

It is important for teachers to find out what the children in their classes consider meaningful, interesting, and relevant. For example, schools that are close to a national border may be more interested in communicating with children just across the border than those schools that are geographically further away. It is important to take into account any micro-factors and local realities, and make the most of the children's immediate environments and intercultural encounters. For example, Elżbieta Sowa (2014), a researcher interested in intercultural awareness, reports on practices of some European teachers who were keen to incorporate some locally appropriate and meaningful intercultural training in their primary classrooms. Ana, a teacher in Poland who had a sizable minority of Romani speakers in her classroom, wanted to sensitize both Polish and Romani students to each others' cultures and decided to work with both Polish and Romani fairy tales and legends in her class. Ana also invited some Romani parents/carers and representatives of the local Roma Institute to share traditional stories with the children. The project was aimed at widening the horizons of the Polish children about the Romani culture, but it was also intended to increase a positive attitude to schooling for the Romani community. Some schools may have a more heterogeneous population than others, but cultural awareness is an important topic everywhere and there are locally meaningful ways to exploit this.

Multilingual schools

Two researchers writing about Mexican schools, Caroline Linse and Alina Gamboa (2014) propose that schools can play a key role in promoting a positive approach to opening doors into different cultures and also to multilingualism, which means that more than one language would be promoted and accepted at school. The first step is a description of the linguistic capital available both at regional and national levels. This means taking stock of all the cultural and linguistic resources available outside the school context. Then the next step is the development of a language contact survey that each family will fill out, to gain insights into both the linguistic variety and the practices that exist within the school. The design and administration of such a questionnaire needs to be sensitively handled, of course. Based on all the information collected from the community and families, the actual development of a multilingual policy in the given school could be adopted. Schools may decide to introduce strategies such as labelling things in different languages, creating bilingual texts for literacy activities, or creating opportunities for involving parents/carers to help with specific language input. In a multilingual school, all languages are equally important and respected the same way.

Introducing a truly multilingual approach in a primary school can work in schools with high proportions of migrant populations. If all teachers embrace the multilingual approach, children will continuously strengthen both their first and second languages (or even their third and fourth languages in some cases), relying heavily on both peer support and parental support. For example, a child whose first language is Polish would continue using Polish in the English-medium classroom, have regular chances to use Polish with other Polish peers, and would be encouraged to complete most of their writing tasks in both Polish and English, relying heavily on the support of their Polish-speaking parents/carers. In this way, all children's first languages are respected, developed, and appreciated, and this makes for a healthy development of a bilingual identity. If there are many languages practised at school, children will also have regular opportunities to hear and pick up a third language.

The examples in Figure 11.3 are from a primary school in Ireland where a large proportion of the school population is made up of immigrant children. The head teacher, has been promoting a multilingual approach to education in her school. The pieces of writing below are by the same girl, Ying (a pseudonym), who wrote these pieces when she was almost 12 (11 years and 11 months). The subject of the writing is 'Marceline', a fictitious character. The children in this class had devised and organized a fashion show to which all the classes in the school were invited. The children acted as models, commentators, and sound technicians. Each model was introduced by two classmates, one of whom described the model's clothes using either English or Irish. The second commentator used either French (introduced in the penultimate year of primary school) or their home language for their description. When the fashion show was over, the children were required to invent a model and to describe her, in writing, in as many languages as possible. Ying was able to do this in four languages. She had learned English and Irish all the way through her primary schooling, she was in her second year of learning French, and her family had been encouraged to support and develop her home language all through school as well.

This is perhaps an ambitious example but it does indicate that a multilingual policy can work in a school where the staff are convinced of its value and concrete benefits in terms of learning, where the children are from different language and cultural backgrounds, and where they all contribute to actively celebrating their respective languages.

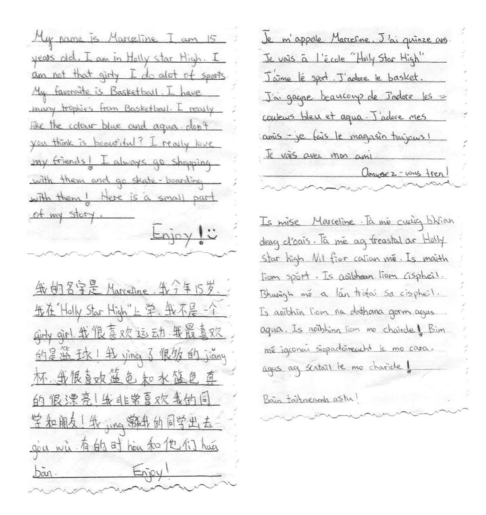

Figure 11.3 Example writing from a multilingual learner

Learner benefits: Multilingual identities

In an interesting study by Canadian researcher Gail Prasad (2013), a group of Grade 5 students were invited to explore their own multilingual and multicultural identities. These children were using both French and English, as these are the official languages in Canada, and in addition to these two languages also regularly used other languages in their communities, such as Spanish, Farsi, Russian, Serbian, and Hebrew. The researcher was keen to introduce a methodology which allowed the children to become co-investigators. (See Chapter 12.) As a starting point for the project, the researcher invited the children to use creative arts to express their own perspectives on their own identities, without being limited to talking by a conventional interview. The children created their linguistic and cultural self-portraits (collages) that reflected on the roles of all the languages and cultures that they brought to the classroom. In these collages, the children associated different languages with different colours, shades, and textures, and thus creatively represented the purposes these languages played in their lives. This kind of explicit focus on children's identity development related to their languages is important because one's positive identity development is directly related to successful language learning. (See Chapter 2.)

This creative activity allowed for a reflective process and the children were able to express their feelings freely, in an artistic way. The collage was then used as a prompt for further discussion as the children answered questions from their peers and the researcher. Finally, the children also talked freely about their self-portraits. This then led to reflective writing in journals and video-recorded presentations about themselves. Next, the children used digital cameras to take photos to represent the linguistic landscapes of their school and their homes and neighbourhoods. As co-researchers, the children themselves selected photos and analyzed them by categorizing them for the interview with the researcher. Finally, the children worked on their 'identity texts'. The identity text is at the heart of this project because it integrates all the resources the children identified through the development of the creative activities.

As a next step the children worked in groups, making sure that at least three languages were represented in each group, such as French, English, and another language, for instance Spanish. They created multilingual e-books for a launch to which all families were invited. Products and events involving audiences outside school are very attractive to children. The stories they wrote were translated into all relevant languages used at the school. This made all students curious about other languages and cultures they were less familiar with. The teachers noted that all students benefited from the project in terms of language awareness, i.e. understanding about the differences between languages. Parents/Carers reported increased levels of interest in languages and cultures in their children. All students responded positively to the opportunity to direct their own learning and were proud of publishing a real book. The researcher refers to this project as a 'transformative experience' because these bilingual/multilingual learners were able to take pride in their languages and cultures and this pride will carry forward into all other aspects of their lives.

Tolerance and diversity

Developing awareness and tolerance about cultures goes hand in hand with broader educational goals such as developing and promoting tolerance, equal rights, and diversity around us. David Valente, a teacher trainer and materials designer, has developed a diversity-focused acronym, PARSNIP, for primary language teachers. (See Figure 11.4.)

P is for Positive thoughts and words

Use age-appropriate activities to enable learners to talk positively about each other and their differences. Use stories and language games to encourage children to think positively about people's differences. Help them to understand that name-calling and being negative about classmates' differences is not caring or friendly. Praise children who talk positively by using a rewards chart and have clear consequences for name-calling. When the children do writing activities, for example, post their work around the classroom—they read each other's and stick stars/smiley faces on the ones they like best. Then they say why, for example, *I really like Joost's poster because it's colourful and interesting!* Encourage equal participation of all children and make sure all children feel included, rewarded, and proud of their English work.

A is for Age and abilities

Read stories, watch short clips, and talk positively about what people can do, including children with disabilities. Use listening and reading texts about caring for parents, grandparents, and other family members as they grow older. Celebrate individual achievements by doing lots of personalized speaking and writing activities. Include photographs and clips of children with disabilities (ensure there is a balance of genders) doing everyday activities to help your class to see disability positively.

R is for Religions, ethnicities, and cultures

Use stories about people from a variety of different backgrounds. Give each learner an opportunity to talk about their home life and own experiences. Do mini-projects about festivals and special events to help children from all backgrounds and religions to feel welcome and valued in the English language classroom.

S is for Sharing with classmates

Make an 'Our Classroom Rules' poster with positive statements about learning together: *We take turns when we play games in English./We say please and thank you when we ask for things./We pass equipment gently.* Make an 'Our Classroom Jobs' chart and the learners take turns each week/month to do different jobs. Help children to work well together as a classroom community by giving team names, mascots, and use lots of encouragement to promote motivation when completing team tasks and activities.

N is for Neighbours and communities

Take the children on mini-excursions with a project, for example, picking up litter from the beach or the park. Organize a class visit to a museum or an interesting place and make a worksheet to find out more about the local community. Encourage the children to talk and write about their class visit back in the classroom. Use the child-friendly sites *Kiddle*, *SearchyPants* and *Kid Rex* and help them to search online for information to complete a simple WebQuest and write group fact files about the communities in your village/town/city. They share what they discover with the whole class and talk about ways to help their neighbours.

I is for Individuality and interests

Do lots of personalized activities and enable learners to talk about their preferences. For example, a class survey *Find someone who likes/doesn't like… (food, sports, free time activities)* and in whole-class feedback they report on each other's likes/dislikes. Ensure different genders have a safe space to express genuine preferences and that traditional gender stereotypes around sports and other interests are not reinforced. After singing a song or reading/listening to a story in English, encourage children to say if they enjoyed it or not, and why. Respect different ideas in your classroom by teaching the children to give opinions using *I think…*, and teach language to accept each other's opinions using: *That's interesting!/I like your idea./Piotr likes this, but Deepti doesn't, we like different things and that's OK!*

P is for Peace and kindness

Help children to think about friendship and how good friends are kind to each other, sing songs and tell stories about friendship and peace. Make flower posters for groups in the class with a cut-out petal for each child. Help them to write simple definitions of a friend on their petals and stick on the group posters to make a wall display entitled 'Our Friendship Flowers'. Point to the definitions on the flowers to praise the children when they are kind to each other, or to remind them if someone is unkind. Use stories in English to help children to understand *'What is a bully?'*. After the story, they work on computers in groups to make 'No Bullying' posters with pictures to display. Refer to these posters when promoting peace and harmony in your English language classroom.

Figure 11.4 Tolerance and diversity PARSNIP (Valente, 2015; Valente, personal communication with the author)

Embracing diversity and tolerance of difference can apply in all lessons. For example, when learning about families, a teacher may want to bring in photos of different family types and describe all of these rather than just the stereotypical family of mum and dad with two children. Further activities can include exploring different family types represented in class, then actively and explicitly promoting pride in all family types without judgement. Children can also look at examples of families from all over the world.

Other immediate consequences of the PARSNIP principles might be that the class draw up a list of agreements as in Figure 11.5. If the language proves to be difficult, this can be drawn up in the first language initially and then translated into the second language or, indeed, it can be drawn up in two languages, or as many languages as are spoken by the children in the class.

We will try our best to give positive feedback to classmates.

We will not laugh at mistakes of others.

We will share materials.

We will celebrate differences in views, opinions and likes and dislikes.

Figure 11.5 Example classroom agreement

Summary

As the world changes at a fast pace around us and with us, it is every language teacher's duty in the primary school to think about what aspects of intercultural awareness might be suitable to introduce into everyday teaching. It is always advisable to start from local opportunities and the interests of the children, but the creativity of the teacher and the children can take these initial explorations in interesting unexpected directions.

Suggestions for further reading

Byram, M. (2008). Intercultural competence and foreign language learning in the primary school. In M. Byram (Ed.), *From foreign language education to education for intercultural citizenship: Essays and reflections* (pp. 77–86). Clevedon: Multilingual Matters.
The overall book is a comprehensive volume about intercultural education. It explores the purposes and possibilities of foreign language education and links it to intercultural competence training. The discussion also covers links between foreign language learning, intercultural education, and citizenship training. In particular, this is an insightful chapter that is particularly relevant for primary schools anywhere in our globalized world.

Guo, Z. (2014). *Young children as intercultural mediators: Mandarin-speaking Chinese families in Britain.* Bristol: Multilingual Matters.
This book is an excellent introduction to the role children play in relocated families when it comes to learning about local culture, peer culture, and school life in general. There is a very well written chapter about childhood, and then the author introduces some families as case studies, with rich data illustrating reciprocal learning between parents/carers and children.

Spencer-Oatey, H., & **Franklin, P.** (2009). *Intercultural interaction:*
A multidisciplinary approach to intercultural communication. Basingstoke: Palgrave
Macmillan.
This is a comprehensive introduction to intercultural interaction drawing on a
range of disciplines. Concepts such as culture and adaptation are fully explained
and authentic data illustrates the meaning of theoretical concepts. The book also
covers current research issues and debates.

Tasks

If you would like to explore your own practice related to the content of this
chapter, you can try the following tasks:

Task 20: Cultural self-portraits (page 196)

Task 21: Exploring cultural content in books or other materials (page 196)

Task 22: Making class posters (page 196)

12 RESEARCH IN THE PRIMARY ENGLISH CLASSROOM

Introduction

Research can be interpreted at various levels, but whether it is research by academics, by teachers, or by children themselves, it involves deliberate, systematic action and it involves finding out something new. As part of their teaching, most teachers reflect on what they and their learners are doing and why, and thus continuously explore their own classrooms and practice. They may take a mental note of what did and did not work and what the children seemed to enjoy. Such initially informal explorations, if undertaken on a systematic basis, can naturally lead teachers to engage in **classroom research** to discover more about themselves, their learners, and their classrooms. The main aim of this chapter is to give some guidelines to teachers who wish to engage in explorations of their classrooms in a systematic way. Considering the role of children in research, this chapter will also argue that it is possible to give children the opportunity to work alongside their teachers as co-researchers in classrooms, rather than just becoming and remaining 'objects' of adult research interest.

Classroom research and action research

In previous chapters, it has already been emphasized that the teacher plays a crucial part in the process of children's foreign language learning. Teachers can and should be encouraged to take initiatives, make decisions for themselves, and adapt materials and activities for their specific circumstances. This approach, of course, also implies that teachers monitor and develop their own understanding of teaching and learning on an ongoing basis. Trying to find answers to questions that arise in the classroom is part of everyday teaching. Explorations, reflections, and readiness to change are, therefore, principles that remain at the core of all good teaching.

Classroom research and **action research** are types of research that are typically initiated by teachers. The special characteristic of this type of research is that the results provide answers that are of immediate relevance to teachers. They explore their own practice with the aim of improving some aspects of their teaching and thus positively influence the quality of learning in the classroom. This type of research is context-specific and small-scale and, as such, cannot be generalized beyond the given context or classroom. Teachers often work collaboratively with colleagues on research projects of common interest. Many teachers find that in collaboration with others they can learn more, encourage each other, and sustain motivation for their chosen focus. During the process of exploring a question, they engage in critical reflection about their teaching and their classrooms, and share and develop ideas together. Figure 12.1 shows the 'reflective' cycle, which contains the following steps: a teacher or a group of teachers will start by selecting a focus, a question, an issue, or a problem. The next step is to find appropriate instruments to investigate that focus. Then they collect and analyze data from their classrooms. After that, they reflect on the results and develop an action plan for what changes need to be made. The next step is to implement the change and observe the effects. Often the process cannot finish here because new issues and questions arise from the new situation and the teacher(s) have new questions to ask, thus initiating a new cycle of research. This is why action research is often described as a cyclical process.

Figure 12.1 The 'reflective' cycle

Teachers can explore their own classrooms in various ways depending on what they are interested in, what they have time for, and what is realistic in their contexts. The next section will introduce some tools for exploration, although in no way is it intended as a complete list.

Recording classrooms

There is a lot that teachers may say or do in a classroom that they may be unaware of. Recording either one lesson or a series of lessons can provide the teacher with an objective record of exactly what was said, what questions were asked, or what instructions were given. In addition, teachers may choose to write an action research diary to note down thoughts, feelings, and insights during the process of investigation.

It is impossible to concentrate on everything in every lesson and, therefore, it is helpful occasionally to focus on and explore specific aspects of one's own practice. In the case of interaction patterns, a colleague might be invited to observe some classes and do a simple count of how many learners answered questions, which learners the teacher nominated, or which learners initiated their own comments. Recording the patterns for one or several lessons will help the teacher to become more aware of what is happening in the classroom. Findings from general, open-ended projects such as 'What is happening in my classroom?' are often followed up by more focused questions such as 'How can I involve weaker, more reluctant learners?' The outcomes of this type of exploration may trigger the teacher to think of ways in which interaction patterns can be used more effectively in class. This may lead to observing colleagues, reading articles or books, or simply trying out new ideas.

Observing children

Observation is one of the most commonly used research methods with children. Many questions and issues in the TEYL classroom can be explored by using systematic observation. In addition to the traditional paper-based observation instruments, teachers in many schools can use tablets in their classrooms to take pictures or short videos of classroom events and keep records of groups working together, or individuals making progress on certain tasks, or any other aspects of the classroom. Children themselves are often very keen to help with such recording.

Here are some possible questions for observation:

- When they can choose partners, who do children choose to work with? Does this pattern change over the course of the year?
- What types of pair-work tasks are suitable for younger age groups, for example six-year-olds?
- What types of tasks do six-year-olds and ten-year-olds enjoy?

Asking children about their views and opinions

Asking about children's views and opinions is consistent with the philosophy advocated in this book, i.e. that teachers need to find out as much as possible about their learners so that they can adjust their teaching to children's changing needs. It is important for teachers to talk to children informally to find out about their needs, interests, and views. In addition, teachers can attempt to explore children's ideas and opinions on a systematic basis rather than just during informal conversations.

Using questionnaires

Questionnaires are suitable for quick factual surveys, but they require a good level of literacy, i.e. reading the questions and responding to them in writing. Responses can vary from ticking the answer that best describes one's views or opinions to filling in spaces left for open-ended answers. Although the aforementioned demands may suggest that questionnaires are not suitable for children, they can be made attractive to children using creative design.

Figure 12.2 is a short extract of a questionnaire that has been successfully used with ten-year-old children by a researcher, Samaneh Zandian, in both Iran and the UK (Zandian, 2013). In this questionnaire, Zandian wanted to ask children about their ideas with regard to how to help a newcomer in their classroom. 'Contextualization' was used to get the children to imagine a scenario before asking them questions such as 'Would you like to sit next to the new girl?', 'How can you help her if you do not speak the same language?', and 'Would you invite her to your birthday party?'

Imagine a new student has come to your class in the middle of the term. Her name is CoCo. She is from another country and she only speaks the language spoken in her country.

Now please answer the following questions.

Figure 12.2 Questionnaire extract (Zandian, 2013)

It is important for teachers to check the language used in questionnaires. Children may simply misunderstand a question because they are puzzled by the language. Even in the first language, the phrasing of the questions needs to be considered very carefully. Even 10–11-year-olds can still experience considerable difficulty with complicated concepts such as 'disadvantage', 'benefit', or 'value', even in their first language. Another difficulty inherent in questionnaires is the amount of writing and thinking that has to be done. If there are open questions which invite children to give their own examples and comments, the actual process of writing may be time-consuming and tiring for them, who may be inexperienced writers. When possible, questionnaires are best administered with the teacher present to help children to fill in their responses.

In order to design suitable questionnaires for children, it is a good idea to elicit help from the children themselves. They are usually quite happy to help the teacher researcher with ideas to design a questionnaire for another class. Those children filling in the questionnaires will also be motivated by knowing that the questions were suggested by other children like themselves. In the process of helping the adult to design a questionnaire, children can become interested in learning about principles of questionnaire design, such as what makes a good question, what a biased question is, or even what a Likert scale might be. Children who notice that their views and opinions are taken seriously take a genuine interest in understanding more about such technical matters. Children also take great interest in the data that is generated with the instruments that they helped to design. Real data and real responses to their own questions seem to trigger motivation to be involved more.

Using interviews

In addition to questionnaires, different types of interviews can also be used with children to elicit their views and opinions. When teachers or 'outsider researchers' interview children, in the great majority of cases children's first language will, of course, have to be used. One issue to be aware of is that children may find it difficult to explain if something is not clear to them and, under pressure, they might give a nonsensical answer rather than saying 'I do not know', or 'I am not sure', or 'Can you explain this again?' Children might not be able to make sense of the context of the interview, a point raised in Chapter 1 with reference to the work of Margaret Donaldson. Another common problem is that in an interview, children often want to please the adult and thus give answers that they think the adult wants to hear. Questions, therefore, need to be phrased in ways which do not readily reveal expected answers. Many children, especially younger ones, may find answering questions individually too overwhelming. Indeed, some children may refuse to say anything at all.

In order to overcome this difficulty, researchers working with children emphasize the importance of making children feel at ease and getting them to relax and enjoy these conversations. In interviews, it is important that children should be able to ask questions, and have time and repeated opportunities to make sense of the purpose of the research. Interviews should also be flexible, in the sense that children should have different opportunities to express themselves in a variety of ways through drawings, games, drama, and other inclusive tools, not just through words. This means that even younger children, or those with less developed oral skills, can also contribute. In a project with my colleague Harry Kuchah Kuchah (Kuchah & Pinter, 2012), we found that for the children to open up and feel at ease, it was important to build good relationships, negotiate the identity of the researcher, and reassure the children that there were no expected or right answers. If appropriate and applicable, it is also important to reassure the children that all their responses remain confidential with the researcher.

When interviewed in groups, children need to feel confident and comfortable with the others in the group. Teachers will need to consider issues of gender, group dynamics, and friendships or other important relationship patterns. Children should never be pressed for answers. Some children in the group might choose not to say anything at all and this has to be accepted by the interviewer. On the other hand, in safe friendship groups, they will more easily open up and offer ideas and thoughts, and bounce ideas off each other. There is, however, always the risk that they may respond to peer pressure by saying what the group leader or the most popular child thinks. (See Chapter 1 about children's friendships.)

Children as researchers

The previous sections have already alluded to the fact that children can take more active roles in research, especially in classroom research, through, for example, helping adults to design questionnaires that are likely to be attractive to other children, or through suggesting their ideas to influence the direction the classroom research might take.

But how realistic is it to put children at the very centre of classroom research? In many contexts, the idea of inviting children to voice their opinions and encouraging them to take an active role in decision-making that concerns their lives is not that new or unusual. Since the United Nation's Convention on the Rights of the Child (UNCRC, 1989) was passed and ratified worldwide, children's status has changed and there has been a shift towards involving them as active agents in research so that their perspectives could come to the fore. It has been repeatedly emphasized that children are the experts of their own lives (although of course not the only experts) and, therefore, they can provide fresh and unexpected insights, which are often surprising from an adult point of view.

For those teachers and researchers who believe that the children they work with are capable, responsible, and able to make decisions for themselves, a real opportunity opens up in working with children as co-researchers in their classroom. It is possible to give children, over time, more and more control and responsibility in deciding what to explore, how to go about it, how to make sense of the data, and where to take classroom explorations next. Children may be involved first in a small way and, over time, as they gain confidence, they might be interested in taking more and more responsibility. Table 12.1 describes four ways in which children may be involved.

ON	ABOUT
Children are passive, unknowing objects	Children are research subjects
Interest is in large numbers, averages, and trends	Interest is in individual learners
Everything is adult-motivated and understood from an adult point of view	Focus on smaller groups and cases of individual children
	There is an attempt to understand children as unique individuals but still from an adult perspective
WITH	BY
Children are partners in research	Children are researchers
Collaboration between adults and children	Questions are asked by children and all decisions in the project are made by children
Children contribute to some or all stages of the research/classroom investigation	This offers a unique insight into children's perspectives

Table 12.1 Different ways in which children can participate in research (adapted from Kellett, 2010)

Some scholars, such as Mary Kellett (2005), believe that the most effective way to help children to become researchers is by offering them training. As her work illustrates, ten-year-old children can be taught about research methodology, data collection, and data analysis. One of the children described in her book explored how parents'/carers' late working hours affected children's lives in her school. This child researcher prepared a questionnaire to give to Year 5 and Year 6 children in her school, and she analyzed the questionnaires and presented the results. The researcher child also gave a presentation about the findings, i.e. how many children found the working hours of their parents/carers too much and how many found it OK. Finally she reflected on her experience and came up with some critical comments about her work and made suggestions for a new study. Kellett concludes that children—not just those identified as able or talented, but many others, too—could become active researchers with the appropriate level of support and encouragement to research something they are interested in.

Children working with own questionnaires

Figure 12.3 is an example of a questionnaire designed by a nine-year-old who took part in a 'research club' that I organized for a group of nine-year-old children in a UK school. The children learned about constructing a good questionnaire, filled in questionnaires themselves, and saw other children's presentations about their own research. Then they all designed their own questionnaires to explore a topic of interest. The teachers in the school helped with administering the questionnaires in their classes. Some questionnaires were filled in by teachers and some by children in the school. After the completed questionnaires were returned, the research club participants enthusiastically engaged with the analysis of their data and recorded presentations about their findings on tablets and voice recorders. The example was produced by a child who designed some questions for teachers about homework.

I found that, once children got their own data, they were particularly motivated to work with the data analysis and report their findings. Children enjoy the opportunity to display their work, which in this case meant showcasing their presentations on a website. With a view to displaying the final product, they also enjoy recording their presentations and making them as polished as possible. This is, of course, meaningful language practice that is greatly beneficial for their learning.

Children as peer interviewers

Children can also learn to interview each other. In an interesting study in 2011, the child researcher Vicki Coppock asked children to work as peer researchers. Her 10–11-year-old primary school students were invited to help the adult researcher to evaluate an emotional literacy programme. After some support and preparation,

Hi! I am Dinadi. I am a Year 5 student and I would like to know what you think about 'homework'. Will you please help me by answering this questionnaire? You don't need to write your name but you can if you wish.

Name: ....

How do you feel about homework?
- ☐ Good
- ☐ Bad
- ☐ Other:_____

How many minutes should children do homework?
- Year 1: _____
- Year 2: _____
- Year 3: _____
- Year 4: _____
- Year 5: _____

Do you think you give too much homework to children?
- ☐ Yes
- ☐ No
- ☐ Not sure

Why do you give homework?

_____.

In your class children like doing homework.
- ☐ strongly agree
- ☐ agree
- ☐ I don't know
- ☐ disagree
- ☐ strongly disagree

Do most children in your class do homework?
- ☐ all
- ☐ nearly all
- ☐ some
- ☐ very few
- ☐ no one

When you were at school, did you always do your homework?
- ☐ always
- ☐ sometimes
- ☐ not at all

Thank you for answering my questions!

Figure 12.3 A child's questionnaire

children worked in pairs and interviewed their peers in another class. In each pair, one child worked in the role of the scribe and the other child asked the questions. The children were fully engaged, and their competence as researchers gradually increased as the project went on. The children reported that they had learned a lot and enjoyed the experience very much.

Challenges of research with child participants

So, how far can children be encouraged to become researchers? Returning to the framework in Table 12.1, we might envisage a kind of continuum where, at one end, children are invited to be involved in an investigation, perhaps in a small way (such as by giving insights about an adult-designed tool, or helping the adult to finalize or extend a research question), and then, over time, as they enjoy being involved in small ways, they may take interest in getting involved more and more until they are ready to take full responsibility at the other end of the continuum. Wherever one is situated on this continuum, even with just modest involvement of children, the most important principle is always to think: *How can I involve the children in more ways, and more meaningfully?* Whatever we adults are doing, it is worth asking children about their opinions and views. Whatever our own views are, we need to keep an open eye for alternative ways which may be more authentic for children and which may make more sense from their perspective.

In an English language class, it may be possible for children to explore each others' second language reading habits, or vocabulary learning strategies, or any other aspects of their classroom work. Sometimes some of this work needs to be completed initially in the first language, but it is always possible to find ways to use the second language as well. For example, working on a project in India I observed that six-year-old children in a government school had strong feelings about what they wanted to explore in their classrooms. They wanted to publish a class newspaper that was interesting, as they found real newspapers boring. Preparatory work for the newspaper was initially carried out bilingually, mainly in Hindi, their first language, but they were keen to translate and polish the end product in English so that external audiences could read and enjoy it. We found that the actual interviews the children conducted outside school were in their first language but, again, the final write-up was in English.

Using more than one instrument

Investigating one's classroom is exciting and there are always surprises along the way. It does sometimes happen that a particular tool or question seems not to lead anywhere, or that the answers from two sources seem contradictory, so the general advice is to gather data from several sources. This is often referred to as triangulating data. The word suggests that three angles are used to find answers to a question. For example, a colleague might observe something in a teacher's classroom, then the teacher may decide to record him/her self, and, finally, ask the children's opinions on the same issue. This would mean that the same question or issue would be explored in more depth and any finding confirmed by all three instruments could be presented as convincing evidence. Another way in which teachers can supplement their own data about their classrooms is to involve parents/carers or, indeed, the children as active decision-makers at every stage of the research.

Research ethics

Various issues around **research ethics** are also important to consider. If a teacher is investigating their own practice as part of everyday teaching and the children are co-investigators, official permission and consent may not be necessary. However, if any data is collected with the aim of being recorded, stored, or released, both the children themselves and the parents/carers need to give their consent to the research project. Confidentiality is also more complex with children because adults are ultimately responsible for children's well-being and, therefore, cannot always agree to full confidentiality. Children also need to understand fully about the consequences of research and their involvement, and how this understanding is checked and guaranteed is a challenge. Child-initiated research should benefit children themselves, but in real life this is often hard to achieve. It is important for teacher researchers to explore these and other ethical dilemmas and, since the answers are not black and white, all they can do is to try to find the best possible compromises.

Summary

Investigating classrooms, the learning process, and their own practices are part and parcel of effective teachers' practice. The more teachers know about the classroom complexities and the children they are working with, the better their chance of success. This chapter reviewed some principles and possibilities of exploring young learners' classrooms. Children's views and opinions should be valued, and this is consistent with the principles advocated in this book. The logical consequence of this approach is that we should consider children as active co-researchers of our classrooms so that they can bring a fresh perspective to supplement our adult views.

Suggestions for further reading

Christensen, P., & **James, A.** (Eds.). (2008). *Research with children: Perspectives and practices, second edition.* London: Routledge.
This is an excellent book that explores the challenges of working with children as research participants. There are 14 chapters covering a wide range of topics in international research contexts. These topics include different approaches to working with children, research ethics, the relationship between adult researchers and children, and the challenges inherent in different methodologies.

Eder, D., & **Fingerson, L.** (2001). Interviewing children and adolescents. In J. F. Gubrium & J. A. Holstein (Eds.), *Handbook of interview research*. London: Sage. This article summarizes issues and problems that researchers face when working with child interviewees and offers creative solutions to some of these problems.

Kellett, M. (2005). *How to develop children as researchers: A step-by-step guide to teaching the research process*. London: Sage. This is an excellent and inspiring manual that helps teachers to design their own research methods training aimed at children from about the age of nine upwards. The chapters take you step by step through what content the children need to know to be able to do their own research. It is also possible to adapt these ideas to different contexts; for example, to use only some of the ideas from the book when there is a lack of time.

Pinter, A. (2015). Researching young learners. In B. Paltridge & A. Phakiti (Eds.), *Research methods in applied linguistics* (pp. 113–128). London: Bloomsbury. This chapter focuses on conducting research in the area of language learning and teaching with children, and discusses the key challenges that adult researchers face. It also summarizes principles of good practice and offers further reading and resources.

Tasks

If you would like to explore your own practice related to the content of this chapter, you can try the following tasks:

Task 4: Exploring teaching and learning contexts (page 185)

Task 9: Planning lessons (page 188)

Task 12: Keeping a teaching diary (page 191)

Task 13: Recording your own lessons (page 191)

Task 14: Collaborative writing and reflection (page 191)

Task 15: Good language learner booklets/blogs (page 192)

Task 16: Developing skills towards self- and peer assessment (page 193)

Task 18: Using diagnostic assessment (page 195)

Task 23: Conversations with children based on drawings (page 197)

Task 24: Getting the children to decide (page 197)

Task 25: Getting the children to act as researchers (page 197)

TASKS FOR EXPLORING YOUR OWN PRACTICE

This section contains 25 practical tasks related to the content of the chapters in this book. Some tasks are relevant to the content of more than one chapter. The aim of these tasks is to encourage teachers to explore their own practice. Some tasks suggest observing children in different situations, others invite teachers to explore and record their own thinking and decisions or observe other teachers. Others suggest creating or adapting teaching and learning materials for teachers' own contexts. The tasks may be useful for individual teachers, groups of teachers working in collaboration, or for teacher training sessions. The tasks can be used independently of the chapters of the book, too. Comments after tasks have been included (where appropriate) to indicate possible responses to texts, classroom extracts, and other materials used as prompts for discussion and exploration. This is a bank of ideas but is, in no way, it a complete list. Teachers and teacher trainers may want to use the ideas as starting points for discussion or exploration, or they may want to change or adapt them as they see fit for their contexts.

Task 1: Exploring different age groups

Do you teach different age groups? Think about the types of activities you use with different age groups. Look at the list of activities Table T.1 that might occur in English classes for children. Tick which age group in your context you think these activities would work with. Is it easy to decide? Can you add other activities that you use in your class?

Comments

It is often difficult to decide about these activities without any information about the context, the actual design features, or the way these activities are presented and implemented in class. However, it is possible to say that even the youngest children will enjoy joining in with stories or miming games, while using gap tasks or participating in discussion tasks will be quite challenging for most 10–12-year-olds.

	Under eight years old	Over eight years old
• A counting game which involves adding numbers up to 100 fast.		
• Listening to a story and joining in with repeated lines.		
• An information-gap task where two partners have to create a story together without looking at each other's pictures.		
• A gap-fill task where children have to complete sentences with one word.		
• A guessing game where children have to ask yes/no questions to find out what is in the teacher's bag.		
• A discussion task to debate in groups what present to buy from a limited budget for somebody's birthday in the class.		
• A miming game where children come forward and mime a spare-time activity and the class try to guess the word.		
• A describe-and-draw task played in pairs.		
• Reading a short text and answering comprehension questions.		
• Writing a short paragraph about one's family.		
• Recording a short monologue on a tablet.		
• Filling in a simple self-assessment questionnaire online.		

Table T.1 Activities with different age groups

Task 2: Exploring children's first language performances

Imagine that in your class you would like to try out a new pair or group task, for example, an information-gap task, a 'describe-and-draw' task, or a small group 'role-play'. Ask the children to do the tasks first in their own language and observe what difficulties they have, if any. How can this exercise help you with your planning when it comes to setting up tasks and activities in English?

Task 3: Observing children outside English classes

Observe a group of children in your school in the playground and/or in classes where you do not teach them. If possible, carry on with these informal observations for a period of time. One such opportunity might be observing them playing electronic games, online games, or being engaged in spontaneous play in after-school clubs, but there might be many other opportunities, too.

Take note of what they do, for example:

- Who plays with whom?
- Who is most engaged?
- What language do they use?
- Do you notice anything surprising or unexpected?

Reflect on what you observed and think about the ways in which what you learned about the children could be built on in your English classes. Discuss with them what ideas they have for linking in-class and outside class learning.

Task 4: Exploring teaching and learning contexts

Think about your context. Make a list of all the advantages (such as good-sized classrooms, access to the internet, freedom to choose supplementary materials, cooperative colleagues) and the disadvantages (English lessons restricted to just two hours a week; no English library at school; large, mixed-ability classes).

Do you make the most of your advantages? What is the best way to deal with the disadvantages? Could you turn any of them into opportunities for change or improvement? What else could you and your colleagues do to make the teaching and learning processes more effective and enjoyable in your context?

Focus on one of the restrictions or challenges and explore some possible solutions to implement over a period of time. For example, one of your challenges may be that you need to work with large, mixed-ability classes. Make a plan for the next few weeks such as:

- group the children into six to eight small groups
- brainstorm together and introduce some group rules and select group leaders

- give groups some space to make decisions about which tasks to tackle from the unit you are working on
- note down your observations about how the different groups worked together
- after a few lessons, reflect (if possible, together with the children) on how the group-based learning worked
- change the size or composition of groups and revisit the group rules.

Task 5: Exploring materials

Examine a set of paper-based or digital materials appropriate for the children you are working with. What is the approach to vocabulary teaching in these materials? Choose a unit and check how and where the vocabulary is taught, practised, and recycled. How could you improve the approach taken to vocabulary learning? Design a supplementary activity focused on vocabulary.

Task 6: Working creatively with materials

Figure T.6 is an example of a storyline brief for younger children (taken from Alquist & Lugossy, 2014) which can be easily adapted to different contexts. What kinds of adjustments would be needed in your class to work with this set of materials? Design a set of lesson plans based on this idea.

Toy Inventors

[...] If we look at the levels for the CEFR, we can see that the learners here will be working towards the learning outcomes for A1 in speaking and writing. In speaking, they will interact in a simple way, answering questions, and be able to use simple descriptive phrases. In writing they will write a short descriptive piece. Here is an overview of the topic. First, we will list the Key Questions, [...] This is then followed by an explanation of what the learners did in each KQ.

KQ1: What is your idea for a new toy?

KQ2: What does your new toy look like?

KQ3: How does your toy work?

KQ4: What can we write about the toy in the brochure for the fair?

KQ5: How can we help our English visitor?

The scenario is that a toy manufacturer needs some new ideas for toys, as sales of traditional toys are going badly. There is an additional problem: in a few weeks' time the manufacturer is going to exhibit some of their products at a toy fair, and buyers from all the major toy stores will be there. Can the learners help? When my students did this, one of them took on the role of

---

the manufacturer who came to visit the class throughout the story, initiating the next development. This is the structure of that storyline:

KQ1: What is your idea for a new toy?

Working in small groups, the children think about the kind of toy which might appeal to others of their age, and make a sketch. It is important that, although they use their imagination, they are realistic, because they are really going to make this toy!

KQ2: What does your new toy look like?

Following the manufacturer's second visit, in which the children are thanked for their great ideas, the children set about making their toy. First, they think about the tools and materials they will need and, if these are impractical, then they revise their ideas. This task promotes logical thinking in the form of taking an inventory of what is needed and planning how to construct the toy. It promotes discussion in the group.

KQ3: How does your toy work?

The manufacturer returns to view the children's work in progress, and wants to know how the new toys will work. The children are told that, on the manufacturer's next visit, they will each be asked to explain how their toy works and they should also be prepared to ask questions about each other's toys. The manufacturer is also concerned that the toy must be safe to use and safe for the environment. This KQ, by looking ahead to the manufacturer's next visit, keeps the learners focused and thinking logically.

Showing their work to their peers is likely to have an even more motivating effect than showing it to the teacher, which means that they will want to be sure that they themselves understand how the toy works and that they can explain it to others. Not least, at this stage, the storyline integrates aspects of sustainability at a level appropriate to these young learners in a way which directly touches their own lives (through the focus on toys).

KQ4: What can we write about the toy in the brochure for the fair?

The manufacturer expresses delight at how well the toys seem to work and wants to show them at the toy fair. There will be a catalogue describing all the toys, and the manufacturer asks that the learners write a short description of their toy. We can note here that for some learners, of all ages, being asked to write as a classroom task can be daunting, because they cannot come up with ideas on the spot. But your learners have made their toy and explained to others how it works. They have something concrete to write about—something which they are proud of. These are excellent conditions for reviewing the language of description: present tense, nouns and adjectives, singular and plural, and word order in their L1.

KQ5: How can we help our English visitor?

The manufacturer explains that they had forgotten to tell the learners that there would be a buyer from Hamleys, the well known London toy store, at the fair, so they will need to speak English! But first, the manufacturer would like a short written description of the toy in English. Depending on how much writing the children have done, one or two simple sentences about the toy, based on what they wrote in L1, may be possible. If not, give them a gapped text in which they fill in their details. For example:

Name of toy: _____

This is a _____. **It is** _____ **and has** _____.

It works in this way: _____

It costs: _____

To prepare for the fair, the learners have to think about what they will need to be able to understand and to say in their L1 and in English. The English buyer should be played by a colleague, who will ask the children some questions about their inventions: **What is it? How does it work? How much does it cost?** This is an excellent opportunity for your learners to practise listening to and answering genuine questions in a meaningful context, in which they are likely to be highly motivated to communicate.

Figure T.6 (Ahlquist & Lugossy, 2014)

Task 7: Observing children choosing tasks

Let children choose an activity that they enjoy doing in the last ten minutes of five or six consecutive lessons. Take note of what happens. Who selects what? Do they seem to be interested in their choice of activity? Who needs help? Who surprises you? Who changes their behaviour after the first few lessons?

Task 8: Getting children to reflect on their learning

Before you start a new unit in the book, let the children look through it and comment on the content. Ask them what they think the unit is about and what they think they are going to learn. Ask them what they think they will find easy or difficult and what they will enjoy. Would they like to add anything? Do similar reflections at the end of the unit. Repeat this with three or more units in the book and take note of the changes in their ability to reflect and respond.

Task 9: Planning lessons

Choose one of the topics of Seasons, Holidays, or Sports (or your own choice), and brainstorm activities for one of your classes for three lessons. Use a mind map and put your chosen topic in the middle of the circle.

Lesson 1 Objective(s) Steps	**Lesson 2** Objective(s) Steps	**Lesson 3** Objective(s) Steps

Table T.9 Planning lessons

Then, use Table T.9 to organize the activities for the three lessons, sequencing the activities according to how difficult they are. Think about variety and logical progression. Decide on a main objective for each lesson and make sure each has a clear outcome.

Look at your overall plan for the three lessons. Is there anything missing? Does it look balanced in terms of variety of activities, skills, and interaction patterns? Have you included a variety of ICT tools, if appropriate? If not, make some changes. Do the activities look engaging and motivating? Have you catered for different learning styles and intelligences, and for the needs of both boys and girls? Have you given any space to the children's choices and decisions?

If you get the chance, share your ideas with a colleague and then try them out with a group of learners. Write notes about how the lessons went. Is there anything to change or keep in mind for next time?

Task 10: Exploring authentic materials

The two popular poems in Figure T.10 were written for children whose mother tongue is English. Would you be able to use them for one of your English classes? If yes, for what learning purpose(s)?

Cats

Cats sleep
Anywhere,
Any table,
Any chair,
Top of piano,
Window ledge,
In the middle,
On the edge,
Open drawer,
Empty shoe,
Anybody's
Lap will do,
Fitted in a
Cardboard box,
In the cupboard
With your frocks –
Anywhere!
They don't care!
Cats sleep
Anywhere.

By Eleanor Farjeon

Mice

I think mice
Are rather nice.
Their tails are long,
Their faces small,
They haven't any
Chins at all.
Their ears are pink,
Their teeth are white,
They run about
The house all night.
They nibble things
They shouldn't touch
And no one seems
To like them much.
But I think mice
Are nice.

By Rose Fyleman

Figure T.10 Two popular poems (Webb, 1979)

Comments

Both of these poems are excellent to introduce when children are learning about animals' habits or describing animals. The poem about cats can be cut up and recreated in many different ways by moving the sections that rhyme forwards or backwards. For example, 'top of piano/window ledge/in the cupboard/on the edge' can be moved freely within the poem. Both poems are excellent for practising rhyming words and rhythm in English. Children might want to memorize them. They can also try to write simple poems (not necessarily with rhyming words) about other animals they like or pets they have.

Look out for other authentic materials such as stories, leaflets, information books, comic books, games, internet sites, etc. You can encourage your learners to bring in various English materials they come across outside school and you can make an effort to incorporate those into your lessons.

Task 11: Designing your own assessment tasks

Examine a typical unit in your coursebook and design some assessment tasks to use at the end of the unit to discover what the children learned. Consider more than one instrument. Get the children to design some peer or self-assessment tasks.

Task 12: Keeping a teaching diary

Start a diary and once a week write down one thing that surprised you in class. It could be something that the children commented on or something that they really enjoyed despite what you expected, or any other question or issue. Check your notes at the end of the term. Do you notice any pattern in your observations? How can you use this reflection data for the benefit of your teaching?

Task 13: Recording your own lessons

Record one of your lessons and transcribe it, or simply listen to it. Do you notice anything that you were not aware of doing or saying at the time? Can you learn anything from this exercise to inform your future teaching? If you are able to transcribe it, you could focus on specific aspects of your teaching—for example, on how you give instructions, how you praise the children, and/or what kinds of questions you ask. This focused attention can help you to become more aware of aspects of your teaching that would otherwise have remained invisible.

Task 14: Collaborative writing and reflection

Depending on the literacy levels and the learners' writing background, you might select a particular writing task, such as writing a booklet, a letter, a poster or a story. Once you have selected the genre that the children will be working on, put them in pairs and tell them they are going to write together.

- Show the children some examples of the product (letter, poster, or booklet). You can use previous work from other classes or other children, take examples from published materials or the internet, and/or make some examples yourself.
- Then work together as a class, brainstorming ideas for possible content as well as strategies for writing together effectively (see Table T.14). It is important, though, that the task is not completely controlled; it is best to allow for some freedom so that the children can shape the product; for example, by deciding who the letter is for, which country the poster is about, what shape or type of booklet they want to make.

Content: a poster about a country	Writing together
• where the country is • population • biggest city, capital city • flag • weather, climate • famous sights • animals • food • fun facts	• plan by jotting down ideas • take turns in writing • reread what you have written • work on ideas first • organize the structure

Table T.14 Collaborative writing

- These writing tips or strategies can be displayed in the classroom for everyone's benefit.
- Get all the pairs to start work on the first draft.
- Display drafts on the wall and let children put sticky notes on each one suggesting ideas and improvements.
- Get the same pairs to work on their second draft and encourage them to incorporate those improvements that they agree with.
- Repeat the same cycle one more time if needed.
- Get the children to compare their drafts (first, second, and final version) and interview them (in their first language) in pairs about the changes they made and about their experiences of writing together.

If this procedure is repeated regularly, your learners will develop reflective insights about writing together and also about aspects of the text, such as content, organization, vocabulary, grammar, or punctuation.

While this activity works best with older learners, it can be adapted for younger beginner-level second language writers. For example, they can write a short birthday card, decorate it, and get their peers to give them feedback on it.

Task 15: Good language learner booklets/blogs

As part of your regular teaching, you might like to try to get the children in your classes to reflect on their 'good language learner' strategies.

You can start by discussing with the children what good language learners do and do not do, for example:

- have a notebook for new words they encounter
- proactively seek out two or three new words that they think the others might be interested in and bring those in every week
- listen to a story online every week

- practise English with someone every week
- teach their friend a new word every week.

Make a list of ideas to start with. These can be usefully revisited and expanded later. It is a good idea to have this list handy or have it displayed on the class wall. Then get the children to start a booklet and encourage them to write down each week what good language learner strategies they have actually used. Alternatively, the booklet can be substituted by a blog to be uploaded to a secure website that is shared by the teacher and all the learners.

At the beginning, the children will want to write in their first language, but, later on, you can encourage them to use English for this. Even at lower levels it is possible to use simple English, as exemplified in Figure T.15.

This week I have
- learned ten new words
- listened to a story online
- used a picture dictionary

Figure T.15 Good language learner booklets/blogs

To make it even easier, the teacher can have a list of strategies to choose from and each one can have an accompanying symbol—such as a picture of an owl for using a dictionary—and this way the children can simply tick those that they think they have used.

In class, you might like to focus on these entries from time to time for further discussion. You can ask children to share and compare their strategies with others, and/or conduct a class survey about the most popular strategies. You can also encourage children to try new strategies from time to time. Be prepared to introduce and talk about a variety of different strategies you know about or you use. Regular opportunities to reflect like this will help children to become more aware of their own efforts in language learning.

Task 16: Developing skills towards self- and peer assessment

The success of self- and peer assessment depends on how well your children can work with set criteria to make judgements about their own and others' performance in English. To evaluate oral or written performances (your own or your friends') in English using a set of criteria will require some training and regular practice.

Figure T.16 gives some data from children who tried self- and peer assessment in their English classroom (Vasilopoulou, 2014). In this class of 11- to 12-year-olds in a Greek primary school, self- and peer assessment was new, and the teacher involved the children in developing some criteria for evaluating an activity, which was 'Talking about a picture in English'. The children were then asked to self- and peer assess the task performance. Afterwards, they talked to the teacher about how they felt about using self- and peer assessment.

Consider the quotations from the children in Figure T.16, and discuss them with a colleague.

(What have you learned from your peer?)
Learner 1 The previous time she told me that I was speaking slowly and now she told me that I was speaking fast. […] she made me confused. Miss, can you tell me which one is true?

(Is self-assessment better than tests?)
Learner 2 It is different from tests, I liked it because I wrote down how I believe I did it.

(Did you find peer assessment easy?)
Learner 3 It was easy, yes, because she (my friend) is good and I did not have anything to write about her.

(What have you learned from your friend?)
Learner 4 My friend is very good at English. I like that he is helping me. He has the KET already.

(Have you enjoyed self-assessment?)
Learner 5 Yes, I enjoyed it, I can't wait to learn more words and to pronounce some words better and then put them on the list of my strengths.

Figure T.16 (Vasilopoulou, 2014)

Would using peer and self-assessment work in your context? Try it out in your class.

- Choose an activity that you want to focus on.
- Get the children to practise with the activity.
- Then, based on their experience with the activity, draw up together some criteria for good performance; keep this simple.
- Let the children do the activity again, and get them to self-assess and also assess two of their friends' performances.
- Interview them in groups (in their first language) about their views and feelings right after the experience.

Task 17: Getting the children to record themselves regularly

Get the children in your class to record a short monologue or dialogue in pairs. Even in a large class with just two or three recording devices, mobile phones, or tablets, they can complete this task by taking turns. Then get them to listen to their own performances and think of at least two things to improve when recording next time; for example, they could try to talk a little faster, pronounce something more clearly, work on their vocabulary choices or their grammatical accuracy, or simply add some further detail. If technology allows, upload these performances to a secure, restricted-access website (for example, Padlet (https://padlet.com)). Then you can get the children to log in, listen to each other's performances, and give each other feedback.

Task 18: Using diagnostic assessment

Record yourself teaching two or three consecutive lessons working with the same group of children. Transcribe the lessons, focusing on your own talk (i.e. do not worry if you cannot hear exactly what each child is saying). Identify episodes where you think you might be scaffolding the learners' language use in a way that focuses on learners' growing language development (see concept of diagnostic assessment in Chapter 10).

For example:

- Do you give enough wait time before you answer a question?
- Do you complete learners' utterances?
- Do you build on their first language utterances and reformulate then in their second language?
- Do you praise and encourage learner contributions?
- Do you elicit learner comments?
- Do you modify your language differently when you are addressing different learners?

You will see patterns in your own talk. For example, you may praise learners only occasionally. Once you notice this, you can make an effort to change it.

Task 19: Exploring group presentations

Together with the children, draw up a list of five key criteria when assessing short group presentations or projects. Put the list of criteria on the board or on the wall to refer to. Then listen to one performance and score it together. After this, encourage the children to work in groups to evaluate some presentations by their peers. Compare the evaluation scores, emphasize that differences are likely, and discuss how each group made the decision about their scores.

Task 20: Cultural self-portraits

Explore what languages and cultures the children bring to your English class by getting them to produce a cultural self-portrait. They have to draw and write about themselves, focusing on what the different languages they use mean to them.

First of all, create a cultural self-portrait of yourself and/or search for other examples on the internet, then show some examples to the children. Encourage creativity and the use of colours, textures, and different materials. Encourage questions from peers and give the children an opportunity to talk about their self-portraits. Get them to translate their summaries of the self-portraits into all the languages they know. Display the self-portraits somewhere in the classroom, elsewhere in the school, or online.

Task 21: Exploring cultural content in books or other materials

Choose a book with a cultural message. An example is *Silly Billy* by Anthony Browne (2007) which draws on the Guatemalan tradition of worry dolls as a little boy learns to deal with his worries. Read the book together in class using different activities and techniques mentioned in Chapters 5, 6, or 7. Encourage children to bring stories or legends from their own cultures to work with in class.

Task 22: Making class posters

Talk to the children about diversity and tolerance and make a poster about rules to follow in class. For example:

Our class rules about diversity:

- Respect each other.
- Do not laugh at mistakes.
- Share your things.
- Do not shout.
- Be proud that you are different from everybody else.
- If someone is sad, give them comfort.

These rules can be revisited from time to time and new ideas can be added. You can display them in two languages (both first and second languages) or in as many languages as are relevant for your class. You can work on the language of the posters by playing a memory game (who can remember all six rules?) or getting the children to notice the different language structures.

Task 23: Conversations with children based on drawings

Ask the children to draw a picture of what they enjoyed most in a particular unit of work. Then ask them to talk about their drawings and record these conversations. You can record similar conversations regularly over the course of the school year (for example, once a month). Doing so could give you a good indication of what the children in your classes enjoy and why, and how their views change over time. If, initially, they can only talk about their drawings in their first language, help them to gradually begin formulating their thoughts in the second language by providing key phrases such as 'I enjoy working in a group because I like sharing with my friends.'

Task 24: Getting the children to decide

Get the children in your class to vote for a topic to do in class. For example, in a class in India one of the teachers I worked with asked her class of six-year-olds what they wanted to do, and they voted for reading and writing ghost stories. The children themselves recommended stories to the teacher, and they enthusiastically read them, acted them out, and even wrote their own stories. Even if you work with a rigid curriculum, try to find opportunities to ask the children about learning materials and make an effort to include their choices.

Task 25: Getting the children to act as researchers

You might like to invite your children to work on investigating an aspect of the English classroom together. For example, you may focus on reading. First, get the children together to brainstorm possible questions that they can ask one another. Encourage as many questions as possible and group them according to themes. Then get the children to choose five or six questions (covering two or three themes) and get them to go around and ask at least ten other children these questions. Then get them to write up the responses and present these as graphs, pie charts, or textual summaries. Reflect on the process and think about what they might like to do next for their new investigation.

GLOSSARY

accommodation: One of the processes in Piaget's theory of cognitive development. It is the process of interpreting new knowledge in a way that requires changes made to old knowledge. See also *assimilation*.

acculturation: The process of psychological change that happens as a result of cultures coming into contact. These changes can result in shifts in customs or social habits relating to, for example, food, clothing, and language.

action research: This is the kind of research that teachers undertake in their own classrooms; action research is typically cyclical, consisting of 'plan–intervene–reflect' cycles.

age of arrival (AOA): A commonly used variable in SLA research; it denotes the age at which children first arrive in the new country; often contrasted with length of residence.

analytical learning/learners: Mature learners who are able to analyze and manipulate component parts of language and look at language in an abstract way.

assimilation: One of the processes in Piaget's theory of cognitive development. It is the process of interpreting new knowledge on the basis of existing understanding. See also *accommodation*.

bottom-up processing skills: Language learners often have to build up their understanding of listening or reading texts from constituent parts; for example, recognizing an *-ing* ending tells you that the word you are looking at is a verb, even if you do not know what it means.

chunks: Words and phrases in a text (spoken or written) that belong together, for example 'see you tomorrow'. Learning new language in chunks is easier than learning the constituent parts separately. Using chunks can make speakers' production faster.

class inclusion: The understanding that some objects/sets are also the sub-components of larger objects/sets, such as a table is a sub-set of furniture.

classroom research: Not laboratory research, but the kind of research that happens in real classrooms. This type of research is often conducted by teachers.

cognitive strategies: Learning strategies related to memory and thinking, such as rehearsal or memorization, sometimes referred to as direct strategies. For example, to remember the planets of the solar system, learners write the names down and read them again and again until they remember the names without looking.

conservation: In Piaget's theory, this is a logical thinking ability which means that a child is able to appreciate that a given amount of liquid is not going to change in volume when poured into a differently shaped container.

constructivism: A learning theory that suggests that children/people construct knowledge from their experiences.

content and language integrated learning (CLIL): A popular approach to teaching/learning and syllabus development, where a second or foreign language is taught as most relevant to authentic content.

criterion-referencing assessment: This is a type of assessment where each child's performance is compared or judged against a set of independent criteria, rather than against the performances of others in the group.

cultural adaptation: The process and time it takes for a person to get comfortable and fit into a new cultural environment after relocating.

cumulative repetitive story: A story that contains repetitive and highly predictable language that children can easily remember and join in with; for example, 'Where are you going?' 'To see the queen.' This occurs in the story of Chicken Licken every time the chicken meets another animal.

deep orthography: A language has a deep orthography if the letter and sound correspondence is irregular and it is hard to know how to pronounce something that is written down (see also *shallow orthography*).

diagnostic assessment: An approach to assessment that focuses on identifying individual learner developmental needs.

egocentrism: In Piaget's theory, this is the view that young children are only able to contemplate the world from their own point of view and find it difficult to appreciate other people's perspectives.

enculturation: The process of learning one's own culture. Parents/Carers play a major role in enculturating their children.

English as a foreign language (EFL): English is learned as a school subject in an environment where children do not have many opportunities to use the language outside the classroom; for example, in Japan or Italy.

English as a second language (ESL): English is integrated into the curriculum in an environment where children have many opportunities to use the language outside the classroom, for example children of other nationalities learning English in Australia or the USA.

English for Young Learners (EYL): An abbreviation that is often used to emphasize English courses that are aimed at young learners.

English medium instruction (EMI): A type of school where all subjects are taught in English, even though the larger society does not necessarily use English as the main language and English is not the mother tongue of the students.

executive control: The cognitive skill of shifting attention in one's head by suppressing one item at the expense of another; this is particularly strong in bilinguals.

exploratory talk: The type of talk in groups that is characterized by mutual trust and respect, careful listening, building on each other's ideas, carefully questioning and discussing alternatives, and working towards shared agreements.

exposure: All the language that children hear in and outside the school; for example, listening to the teacher, watching television, listening to radio programmes, listening to children in the playground.

first language: One's mother tongue.

formative assessment: A type of assessment that is more concerned with the process of learning than the outcome of learning.

global learners: Learners who tend to want to understand the main ideas of a task or text rather than giving analytical attention to detail.

higher-order thinking skills (HOTS): More complex thinking skills requiring more cognitive processing, such as creative thinking and problem-solving (see also *lower-order thinking skills*).

holistic learning/learner: Learners who are not yet able to analyze and manipulate language in an abstract way; they learn language by understanding meaningful messages. For example, in a song children will not understand every word but they will have an idea of what they are singing about.

immersion language environment: A language environment where the learner has access to the target language outside the classroom and a real need to use the language; see also ESL.

information-gap task: An interactive activity where two children have different information on cards or pictures. They have to talk and complete the task without showing their information, cards, or pictures to each other; for example, a 'spot the difference' task.

integrated approach: A curriculum where different subjects, such as science, geography, and maths, are integrated with learning a second language. This is often referred to as the cross-curricular approach.

interactional modifications: Alternative language forms used by speakers to achieve understanding or avoid misunderstanding in conversations; for example, 'I said Alsatians, Alsatians are dogs, they look like wolves.'

interdependence: The degree to which members of a group are dependent on each other; in collaborative tasks learners need to pull together and they depend on each other.

kinaesthetic learner: Learners who like to touch and feel things or move their bodies in expressive ways to aid their learning and communication.

learning styles: Learners' preferences with regard to their personalities and perceptual differences; for example, a learner might be predominantly visual.

learning to learn: Fostering growing awareness about the learning process; for example, how to monitor progress, how to plan, how to memorize new information.

logographic: A writing system where each symbol represents a concept rather than a sound.

lower-order thinking skills (LOTS): Thinking skills such as remembering and understanding; they are the foundation of higher-order thinking skills (see *higher-order thinking skills*).

metacognitive strategies/ability: Learning strategies that help learners to plan, monitor, and evaluate their own learning. This is often referred to as the 'metacognitive' cycle.

metalanguage: language for talking about language, for example 'nouns' and 'verbs'.

metalinguistic awareness: Learners' ability to reflect on language and language use, to be able to talk about language (see *metalanguage*).

morphographic: A writing system where the representation of a morpheme is based solely on its meaning.

mother tongue: One's first language.

multiple intelligences: This theory sees intelligence as broken up into different modalities rather than just measured by a single **IQ** test. It is closely associated with the work of Howard Gardner.

multisensory teaching: Teaching that takes into account children's perceptual differences and integrates colours, sound, movements, and touch into as much of everyday practice as possible.

naturalistic learning environment: A language environment where learners have the opportunity to listen to and respond to a great variety of meaningful target language input. (See also *immersion language environment*)

norm-referencing assessment: In this type of assessment, an individual is judged against the average of the group.

operations: In Piaget's theory, this is the process of mentally working something out.

phonographic: A method of teaching reading and writing by pointing out the correspondence between sounds and letters.

portfolio assessment: A type of alternative assessment where learners can select sample work to showcase their best achievements.

regulation/regulate: According to socio-cultural theory (Vygotsky) learners move from other-regulation to self-regulation. This is to do with whether they can take control of aspects of their learning or if they need others to help them to control their learning.

research ethics: Academic research is built on a foundation of trust, and there are basic ethical principles to adhere to, such as protecting research participants' anonymity, privacy, or vulnerability. Ethical principles originate from medical research and they need adjusting for other disciplines such as social research, including language learning/teaching.

scaffolding: An instructional strategy whereby the more knowledgeable partner (often a parent or teacher) offers carefully adjusted support to help the child to carry out a task so that the child can finally take over control of the task.

schematic knowledge: Schema are structures for representing concepts in memory; they are created as a result of experiences with people, objects, and events. Schematic knowledge is the knowledge of these schema in one's memory; these aid students with reading and listening.

second language: Not the mother tongue; a language that is learned after the mother tongue has been established.

self-efficacy: The belief of individuals that they are able to control their own motivation and behaviour to do things.

shallow orthography: A language has a shallow orthography if the letter and sound correspondence is regular and it is easy to know how to pronounce something that is written down (see also *deep orthography*).

social constructivism: A variety of constructivism that emphasizes the collaborative nature of learning.

social/affective strategies: Strategies to do with communicating and relating to each other in a social group, and strategies that help to control emotions and feelings.

socio-economic status (SES): The social standing of a group in society; it is measured by a combination of income, education, and occupation.

storyline: An approach to teaching which relies on partnership between the teacher and the learners. The teacher creates the main line or plot and the learners fill it in with the story. When applied to language teaching, it combines creating imaginary scenarios with practising the four skills in a meaningful way based on real-life type tasks.

summative assessment: A type of assessment that focuses on the end product rather than the process of learning.

top-down processing skills: The process in which language learners rely on their knowledge of the world and their predictions about content when they try to interpret reading and listening texts.

Total Physical Response (TPR): A teaching method developed by James Asher; it relies on the coordination of language and physical movement.

washback effect: This refers to the effect (usually negative) of the exam or test on the way the students are taught.

zone of proximal development (ZPD): An imagined space that stretches between the level of achievement a child can reach on their own and the level achieved with some scaffolding or help offered by an expert, adult, or peer.

REFERENCES

Ahlquist, S. (2012). Storyline: A task-based approach for the young learner classroom. *ELT Journal, 67(1)*, 41–51.

Ahlquist, S., & **Lugossy, R.** (2015). *Stories and storyline.* Hong Kong: Candlin & Mynard ePublishing.

Bandura, A. (1977). *Social learning theory.* Englewood Cliffs, NJ: Prentice Hall.

Barac, R., Bialystok, E., Castro, D. C., & **Sanchez, M.** (2014). The cognitive development of young dual language learners: A critical overview. *Early Childhood Research Quarterly, 29*, 699–714.

Becker, C. (2015). Assessment and portfolios. In J. Bland (Ed.), *Teaching English to young learners: Critical issues in language teaching with 3–12 year olds* (pp. 261–278). London: Bloomsbury.

Bentley, K. (2015). CLIL scenarios with young learners. In J. Bland (Ed.), *Teaching English to young learners: Critical issues in language teaching with 3–12 year olds* (pp. 91–112). London: Bloomsbury.

Berk, L. (2012). *Child development.* Boston, MA: Allyn and Bacon.

Berry, J. W., Phinney, J. S., Sam, D. L., & **Vedder, P.** (2006). Immigrant youth: acculturation, identity and adaptation. *Applied Psychology, 55(3)*, 303–332.

Besser, S., & **Chik, A.** (2014). Narratives of second language identity amongst young English learners in Hong Kong. *ELT Journal, 68(3)*, 299–309.

Bladon, R. (2013). *The Heron and the Hummingbird.* Oxford: Oxford University Press.

Bladon, R. (2015). *The Magpie and the Milk.* Oxford: Oxford University Press.

Bland, J. (2015). Drama with young learners. In J. Bland (Ed.), *Teaching English to young learners: Critical issues in language teaching with 3–12 year olds* (pp. 219–238). London: Bloomsbury.

Bourke, K. (2014). *Oxford discover 5: Student book.* Oxford: Oxford University Press.

Bronfenbenner, U. (1979). *The ecology of human development.* Cambridge, MA: Harvard University Press.

Browne, A. (2007). *Silly Billy.* London: Walker.

Butler, Y. G. (2004). What levels of English proficiency do elementary school teachers need to attain to teach EFL? Case studies from Korea, Taiwan, and Japan. *TESOL Quarterly, 38(2)*, 245–278.

Butler, Y. G., & **Lee, J.** (2010). The effects of self-assessment among young learners of English. *Language Testing, 27(1)*, 5–31.

Butler, Y. G., Someya, Y., & **Fukuhara, E.** (2014). Online games for young learners' foreign language learning. *ELT Journal, 68(3)*, 265–275.

Byram, M. (1997). *Teaching and assessing intercultural communicative competence.* Clevedon: Multilingual Matters.

Cabrera, M. P., & **Martínez, P. B.** (2001). The effects of repetition, comprehension checks, and gestures, on primary school children in an EFL situation. *ELT Journal, 55(3)*, 281–288.

Calabrese, I., & **Rampone, S.** (2015). *Cross-curricular resources for young learners.* Oxford: Oxford University Press.

Chi, M. T. H. (1978). Knowledge structures and memory development. In R. S. Siegler (Ed.), *Children's thinking: What develops?* Hillsdale, NJ: Lawrence Erlbaum.

Chomsky, N. (1965). *Aspects of the theory of syntax.* Cambridge, MA: MIT Press.

Clark, M. (1990). *Fables: Best of Aesop's fables.* London: Walker Books.

Cliff, P. (2010). *YLE tests flyers.* Oxford: Oxford University Press.

Cohen, D. (2002). *How the child's mind develops.* Hove: Routledge.

Coppock, V. (2011). Children as peer researchers: Reflections on a journey of mutual discovery. *Children and Society, 25(6)*, 435–446.

Cory-Wright, K. (2014). *Our world: Student's book 6.* Andover, UK: National Geographic Learning.

Council of Europe (2001). *Common European Framework of Reference for Languages: Learning, teaching, assessment.* Cambridge: Cambridge University Press.

Coyle, D. (1999). Theory and planning for effective classrooms; supporting students in content and language integrated learning contexts; planning for effective classrooms. In J. Masih (Ed.), *Learning through a foreign language: Models, methods and outcomes* (pp. 46–62). London: CILT.

Coyle, D., Phillip, H., & **David, M.** (2010). *CLIL: Content and language integrated learning.* Cambridge: Cambridge University Press.

Coyle, Y., & **Gómez Gracia, R.** (2014). Using songs to enhance L2 vocabulary acquisition in young children. *ELT Journal, 68(3)*, 276–285.

Cummins, J. (2000). *Language, power and pedagogy: Bilingual children in the crossfire.* Clevedon: Multilingual Matters.

Cummins, J. (2009). Transformative multiliteracies pedagogy: School-based strategies to close the achievement gap. *Multiple Voices for Ethnically Diverse Exceptional Learners, 11(2)*, 38–56.

Dalton-Puffer, C., & **Smit, U.** (2007). *Empirical perspectives on CLIL classroom discourse.* Vienna: Peter Lang.

DeKeyser, R. M. (2012). Age effects in second language learning. In S. Gass & A. Mackey (Eds.), *Handbook of second language acquisition* (pp. 442–460). London: Routledge.

Djigunović, J.M. (2015). *Individual differences among young EFL learners: Age-or proficiency-related? A look from the affective learner factors perspective.* In Djigunović, J.M. & Krajnović, M. M. (Eds.), *Early learning and teaching of English: New dynamics of primary English* (pp.10–36). UK: Multilingual Matters

Donaldson, M. (1978). *Children's minds.* London: Fontana Press.

Dörnyei, Z. (2001). *Motivational strategies in the language classroom.* Cambridge: Cambridge University Press.

Edelenbos, P., & **Kubanek-German, A.** (2004). Teacher assessment: The concept of 'diagnostic competence'. *Language Testing, 21(3)*, 259–283.

Ellis, N. C. (2013). Second language acquisition. In G. Trousdale & T. Hoffmann (Eds.), *Oxford Handbook of Construction Grammar* (pp. 365–378). Oxford: Oxford University Press.

Enever, J. (Ed.). (2011). *Early language learning in Europe.* London: British Council.

Foster-Cohen, S. H. (1999). *An introduction to child language development.* London: Longman.

Gardner, H. (2006). *Multiple intelligences: New horizons.* New York: Basic Books.

Gardner, H. (1983). *Frames of mind: The theory of multiple intelligences.* New York: Basic Books.

Garton, S., Copland, F., & **Burns, A.** (2011). *Investigating global practices in teaching English to young learners: ELT research paper.* London: British Council.

Geva, E., & **Wang, M.** (2001). The development of basic reading skills in children: A cross-language perspective. *Annual Review of Applied Linguistics, 21,* 182–204.

Gibbons, P. (2002). *Scaffolding language, scaffolding learning: Teaching second language learners in the mainstream classroom.* Portsmouth, NH: Heinemann.

Gibbons, P. (2006). *Bridging discourses in the ESL classroom: Students, teachers and researchers.* London: Continuum.

Gibbons, P. (2009). *English learners, academic literature and thinking.* Portsmouth, NH: Heinemann.

Guo, Z. (2014). *Young children as intercultural mediators: Mandarin-speaking Chinese families in Britain.* Bristol: Multilingual Matters.

Hasselgren, A. (2005). Assessing the language of young learners. *Language Testing, 22,* 337–354.

Hayes, D. (2014). *Factors influencing success in teaching English in state primary schools.* London: British Council.

Hazari, S. (2013). Equipping young learners with learning to learn strategies by developing their meta-cognitive skills through reflection. (Unpublished MA dissertation). University of Warwick.

Howell, S. M., & **Kester-Dodgson, L.** (2012a). *New treetops: Class book and workbook 2a.* Oxford: Oxford University Press.

Howell, S. M., & **Kester-Dodgson, L.** (2012b). *New treetops: Class book and workbook 3a.* Oxford: Oxford University Press.

Jeon, S. A. S. (2014). The impact of playing commercial online games on young Korean learners' L2 identity. In S. Rich (Ed.), *International perspectives on teaching English to young learners* (pp. 87–103). Basingstoke: Palgrave Macmillan.

Joshua, J. (2015). Evaluating the 'Singing your Way to Learn English' Programme. (Unpublished MA dissertation). University of Warwick.

Kampa, K., & **Vilina, C.** (2014). *Oxford discover: Student book 3.* Oxford: Oxford University Press.

Kellett, M. (2005). *How to develop children as researchers: A step-by-step guide to teaching the research process.* London: Sage.

Kellett, M. (2010). *Rethinking children and research: Attitudes in contemporary society.* London: Continuum.

Kent, J. (1974). *The fat cat.* London: Puffin Books.

Kersten, K., & **Rohde, A.** (2015). Immersion teaching in English with young learners. In J. Bland (Ed.), *Teaching English to young learners: Critical issues in language teaching with 3–12 year olds* (pp. 71–90). London: Bloomsbury.

Kinsella, C., & **Singleton, D.** (2014). Much more than age. *Applied Linguistics Special Issue, 35(4),* 441–462.

Koustaff, L., & **Rivers, S.** (2014). *Oxford discover: Student book 1.* Oxford: Oxford University Press.

Kuchah Kuchah, H., & **Pinter, A.** (2012). 'Was this an interview?' Breaking the power barrier in adult–child interviews in an African context. *Issues in Educational Research, 22(3),* 283–297.

Lenneberg, E. H. (1967). *Biological foundations of language.* New York: Wiley.

Linse, C., & **Gamboa, A.** (2014). Globalization, plurilingualism and young learners in Mexico and beyond. In S. Rich (Ed.), *International perspectives on teaching English to young learners* (pp. 123–138). Basingstoke: Palgrave Macmillan.

Long, M. (1983). Native speaker/non-native speaker conversation and negotiation of comprehensible input. *Applied Linguistics, 4(2),* 126–141.

Mackey, A., Kanganas, A. P., & **Oliver, R.** (2007). Task familiarity and interactional feedback in child ESL classrooms. *TESOL Quarterly, 41(2),* 285–312.

Mercer, N., & **Littleton, K.** (2007). *Dialogue and the development of children's thinking.* London: Routledge.

Mihaljević Djigunović, J. (2016). Individual learner differences and young learners' performances on L2 speaking tests. In M. Nikolov (Ed.), *Trends, issues, and challenges in assessing young language learning* (pp. 243–261). Switzerland: Springer International Publishing.

Modugala, M. (2012). Listening to children's voices as a way to reconstruct textbooks. (Unpublished MA dissertation). University of Warwick.

Mourão, S. (2015). English in pre-primary: The challenges of getting it right. In J. Bland (Ed.), *Teaching English to young learners: Critical issues in language teaching with 3–12 year olds* (pp. 51–69). London: Bloomsbury.

Muñoz, C. (2014). Contrasting effects of starting age and input on the oral performance of foreign language learners. *Applied Linguistics Special Issue, 35(4)*, 463–482.

Murphy, V. (2014). *Second language learning in the early school years: Trends and contexts.* Oxford: Oxford University Press. The first chapter is free to download at: www.oup.com/elt/teacher/sllearly

Oliver, R. (1998). Negotiation of meaning in child interactions. *The Modern Language Journal, 82(3)*, 372–386.

Oxford, R. (2011). Strategies for learning and second or foreign language. *Language Teaching, 44(2)*, 167–180.

P21. (2009). *Learning Environments: A 21st Century Skills Implementation Guide.* Retrieved from: http://www.p21.org/storage/documents/p21-stateimp_learning_environments.pdf

Peimbert, L., & **Monterrubio, M.** (2014). *Bebop band student's book 1.* London: Macmillan.

Papp, S., & **Salamoura, A.** (2009). An exploratory study into linking young learners' examinations to the CEFR. *Cambridge ESOL: Research Notes, 37*, 15–22.

Park, H. (2014). Engagement with English story books in the child's spontaneous play; a case study of a young Korean English learner. (Unpublished MA dissertation). University of Warwick.

Pellerin, M. (2014). Language tasks using touchscreen and mobile technologies: Reconceptualizing task-based CALL for young language learners. *Canadian Journal of Learning and Technology, 40(1)*, 1–23.

Phillips, S. (1993). *Young learners.* Oxford: Oxford University Press.

Phillips, S., Grainger, K., & **Redpath, P.** (2012). *Incredible English: Class book 5, second edition.* Oxford: Oxford University Press.

Piaget, J. (1923). *The language and the thought of the child.* New York: Harcourt Brace and World.

Prasad, G. (2013). Children as co-ethnographers of their plurilingual literacy practices: An exploratory case study. *Language and Literacy, 15(3)*, 4–30.

Puchta, H., & **Williams, M.** (2011). *Teaching young learners to think: ELT activities for young learners aged 6–12.* London: Helbling Languages.

Rixon, S. (1999). Where do words in EYL textbooks come from? In S. Rixon (Ed.), *Young learners of English: Some research perspectives.* Harlow: Pearson Education Ltd.

Rixon, S. (2013). *British Council survey of policy and practice in primary English language teaching worldwide.* London: British Council.

Romaine, S. (1995). *Bilingualism, second edition.* Oxford: Blackwell.

Rowland, C. (2014). *Understanding child language acquisition.* London: Routledge.

Saslow, J., & **Ascher, A.** (2015). *Teen2teen plus: Student and workbook 3.* Oxford: Oxford University Press.

Schneider, W., & **Bjorklund, D.** (1992). Expertise, aptitude and strategic remembering. *Child development, 63,* 461–473.

Schwermer, K., Chang, J., & **Wright, C.** (2013). *Oxford phonics world 5: Letter combinations.* Oxford: Oxford University Press.

Scro, R. (2014). *Our world: Student's book 5.* Andover, UK: National Geographic Learning.

Shipton, P. (2014). *The big storm.* Oxford: Oxford University Press.

Simmons, N. (2014). *Family and friends starter: Class book.* Oxford: Oxford University Press.

Singleton, D., & **Ryan, L.** (2004*). Language acquisition: The age factor, second edition.* Clevedon: Multilingual Matters.

Snow, C. (1986). Conversations with children. In P. Fletcher & M. Garman (Eds.), *Language acquisition: Studies in first language development* (pp. 69–89). Cambridge: Cambridge University Press.

Sowa, E. (2014). Addressing intercultural awareness-raising in the young learner EFL classroom in Poland: Some teacher perspectives. In S. Rich (Ed.), *International perspectives on teaching English to young learners* (pp. 104–122). Basingstoke: Palgrave Macmillan.

Stanley, G. (2013). Integrating technology into secondary English language teaching. In G. Motteram (Ed.), *Innovations in learning technologies for English language teaching* (pp. 43–66). London: British Council.

Swain, M. (2000). The output hypothesis and beyond: Mediating acquisition through collaborative dialogue. In J. P. Lantolf (Ed.), *Sociocultural theory and second language learning.* Oxford: Oxford University Press.

Swain, M., & **Lapkin, S.** (1998). Interaction and second language learning: Two adolescent French immersion students working together. *The Modern Language Journal, 83,* 320–338.

Thomsen, H. (2003). Scaffolding target language use. In D. Little, J. Ridley, & E. Ushioda (Eds.), *Learner autonomy in the foreign language classroom: Teacher, learner, curriculum and assessment* (pp. 29–46). Dublin: Authentik.

Tomasello, M. (2003). *Constructing a language: A usage-based theory of language acquisition.* Cambridge, MA: Harvard University Press.

Tomlinson, B. (2015). Developing principled materials for young learners of English as a foreign language. In J. Bland (Ed.), *Teaching English to young learners: Critical issues in language teaching with 3–12 year olds* (pp. 279–293). London: Bloomsbury.

United Nations. (1989). *The United Nations' convention on the rights of the child.* New York: United Nations.

Ushioda, E. (1996). *The role of motivation.* Dublin: Authentik.

Ushioda, E. (2012). Motivation. In A. Burns & J. Richards (Eds.), *The Cambridge guide to pedagogy and practice in second language teaching* (pp. 77–85). Cambridge: Cambridge University Press.

Valente, D. (2015). Doing Diversity in Programmes for Children and Teenagers. *IATEFL C&TS Publication, 1.*

Vasilopoulou, E. M. (2014). Greek children's views of alternative assessment practices. (Unpublished MA dissertation). University of Warwick.

Vygotsky, L. (1978). *Mind and society: The development of higher mental processes.* Cambridge, MA: Harvard University Press.

Webb, K. (Ed.). (1979). *I like this poem.* Harmondsworth: Penguin.

Wells, G. (1981). *Learning through interaction: The study of language development.* Cambridge: Cambridge University Press.

Wells, G. (1985). *Language, learning and education.* Windsor: NFER-Nelson Publishing Company Ltd.

Wood, D., Bruner, J. S., & **Ross, G.** (1976). The role of tutoring in problem solving. *Journal of Child Psychology and Psychiatry, 17,* 89–100.

Wray, A. (2000). Formulaic sequences in second language teaching: Principle and practice. *Applied Linguistics, 21(4),* 463–490.

Zandian, S. (2013). Participatory activities, research and language classroom practice. In M. Allstrom & A. Pinter (Eds.), *English for young learners forum: Proceedings from the conference in Uppsala, 19 June 2012* (pp. 133–142). Uppsala: Uppsala University.

INDEX

Page numbers annotated with 'g' and 't' refer to glossary entries and tables respectively.